"Richard Falk did it again. A masterly survey and with knowledge and wisdom. *Chaos and Counterre* ticated assessment of what is going on in the MEN. It is a major contribution to the field as well as (Critical) International Relations Theory. Highly recommended."

—FUAT KEYMAN
Director of Istanbul Policy Center, Professor, Sabancı University

"The blogposts collected in this volume showcase both the immediacy of contemporaneous reporting and the reflective, thoughtful analysis that has characterized all of Falk's writing over many decades. His deep knowledge of the region (especially Turkey) gives extraordinary depth and texture to his compelling insights; and the power of his narrative and the excitements—and disappointments—he records impel the narrative forward with intense force."

—LALEH KHALILI
Author, *Time in the Shadows: Confinement in Counterinsurgencies*,
Professor, School of Oriental and African Studies, Univ. of London

"Richard Falk's groundbreaking investigative work on Palestine and Israel is well known. But he has also followed the swift tide of events in the rest of the Middle East with fine attention to the complex questions of international law and morality that they inevitably raise. *Chaos and Counterrevolution* provides crucial analysis, helping readers worldwide to understand what has been happening in many Arab countries, and in Turkey and Iran."

—MARWAN MUASHER
Vice President for Studies, Carnegie Endowment for International Peace

"*Chaos and Counterrevolution: After the Arab Spring* offers a tour de force inside the Middle East region. It presents candid and lucid analyses of interconnected complexities ranging from a lurking colonial past and hegemonic policies, to rising expectations and dashed hopes following the Arab spring. Richard Falk depicts the essence of the struggle between hegemony and emancipation in the region. He tells it as it is: painful but very real."

—EMAD EL-DIN SHAHIN
Editor in Chief, *The Oxford Encyclopedia of Islam and Politics*

About the author

Richard Falk is professor emeritus of international law at Princeton University, the author of over twenty books and a specialist on the role of international law in global politics. The United Nations Human Rights Council appointed Falk as a United Nations special rapporteur on the situation of human rights in Palestine in 2008.

Chaos and Counterrevolution
After the Arab Spring

Richard Falk

Zed Books
LONDON

Chaos and Counterrevolution: After the Arab Spring
was published in 2015 by Zed Books Ltd, The Foundry,
17 Oval Way, London SE11 5RR, UK

www.zedbooks.co.uk

First published in 2015 by Just World Books of Charlottesville, VA, USA.

Just World Books is an imprint of
Just World Publishing, LLC.

www.justworldbooks.com

Typesetting by Diana Ghazzawi for Just World Publishing, LLC.
Cover designed by www.kikamiller.com

A catalogue record for this book is available from the British Library

ISBN 978-1-78360-670-2 hb
ISBN 978-1-78360-669-6 pb

MIX
Paper from
responsible sources
FSC FSC® C013604
www.fsc.org

Printed and bound by CPI Group (UK) Ltd, Croydon, CR0 4YY

For Moulay Hicham El Alaoui and Malika Benabdelali,
in friendship, with admiration and affection

Contents

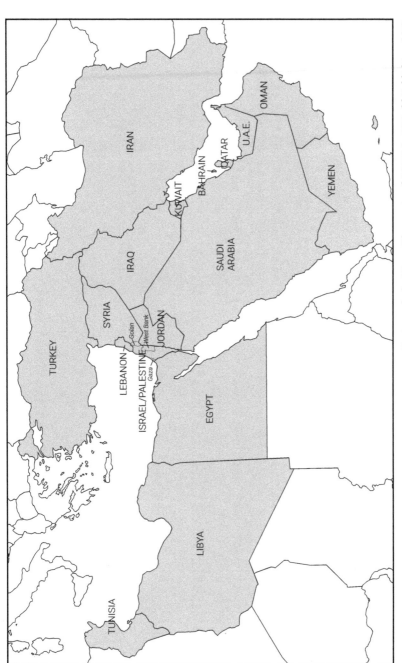

Introduction

Preliminary Observations

Writing in the blogosphere these last several years has been instructive in several ways, but none more so than in the region known in the West as the Middle East but in most of Asia as West Asia. Here, more than in any other part of the world, twenty-first-century geopolitics are being played out, disclosing strong tensions within the region as well as the complex interplay between the region and a global system that exhibits ever-changing blends of hard and soft power. The Middle East also has been an arena of multiple conflicts around the rise of nonstate actors as significant political players, challenging the notion embedded in the UN's structure and international law that sovereign states and *only* states are participants in the world order. The state system fights back by categorizing these upstart political actors as agents of "terrorism," criminalized until the pendulum of diplomacy swings in their direction and enables relevant political actors to negotiate agreements.

For the past twenty years my academic interests in the Middle East have been centered on the Israel–Palestine conflict. With this focus, I have particularly devoted attention to the uphill struggle to achieve a just and sustainable peace for the peoples of Palestine and Israel. This led me to make sharp criticisms of the partisan pro-Israeli policies that dominate the Western approach, including rejecting the American political fiction that peace between the two peoples can only be achieved via direct negotiations presided over by the United States and consisting of a bargaining process that excludes the relevance of international law. I continue to believe that for many years this futile diplomatic framework has allowed Israel to engage in unilateral behavior that undermines the supposed goal of these negotiations: establishing an independent and sovereign Palestine. The Palestinian ordeal remains an open wound that has negative regional ramifications, seriously inhibiting parallel efforts to create peace and stability throughout the Middle East as a whole.

The American grand strategy in the region has generally been to lend U.S. support to repressive and authoritarian governments so long as their leadership remains friendly to the West and avoids identifying itself actively with the Palestinian struggle. If the regime is perceived as hostile or unable to govern its territory, then it can under certain circumstances become a target of a U.S.-led military intervention designed to produce friendly, compliant, and effective leadership. The efforts to get rid of the regimes of Saddam Hussein in Iraq, Muammar Qaddafi in Libya, and Bashar al-Assad in Syria are illustrative of this pattern.

From some perspectives, Washington's policy has been a success. Despite the dispossession of several hundred thousand Arabs from historic Palestine in 1948, today, throughout the entire Arab world, not a single government actively supports the Palestinians' ongoing quest for their entitlements under international law. Only the nongovernmental political entity Hezbollah actively challenges Israel and supports the Palestinian struggle; it pays the political price by being deemed a terrorist organization. The two countries in the region that do seek a resolution that would respect Palestinian rights under international law are, ironically, the two main non-Arab states, Iran and Turkey. Iran's hostility to Israel is partly responsible for Iran's diplomatic isolation and, in recent years, the deterioration of Turkey's relations with Israel has contributed to a dramatic weakening of Ankara's previously good standing with the United States and Europe.

In addition, the West has achieved relative stability in relation to the principal sources of oil and gas in the region. That is, Western governments' pro-Israeli policies have not led to Arab retaliation via oil supplies and prices. Furthermore, Western states have consciously given Israel a military edge over its possible Arab adversaries and even allowed it to acquire, possess, and develop an arsenal of nuclear weapons, while imposing a regime of coercive nonproliferation on other states in the region. Iraq was attacked and occupied under the pretext of avoiding nuclear proliferation; for several years Iran has been subject to threats of military attack, destabilizing covert operations, and severe sanctions in response to allegations that it intends to acquire nuclear weaponry. Many of my posts try to analyze the United States' regressive effort to exert control over the entire Middle East in a strategic partnership with Israel.

In this volume, which covers a period roughly corresponding to the second term of the Obama administration, I have also tried to follow the ebb and flow of Turkey's internal politics, as well as its relation to the region as a whole. Living in Turkey for part of each year has encouraged me to comment on Turkish foreign and domestic policy under the leadership of the Justice and Development Party (AKP) and its charismatic leader, Recep Tayyip Erdoğan.

Turkey, despite some serious human-rights issues, functions as a democratic society. The AKP's performance has resulted in political moderation coupled with steady economic growth at a time when most countries were experiencing recession. Turkey, more than any country in the region, has reached out beyond its borders to expand economic, political, and cultural relations. The Turkish people have consistently endorsed this approach in a series of elections dating back to 2002, much to the acute displeasure of the opposition, which is dominated by the Europeanized and secular Turkish elites had who previously held political and economic power since the founding of the Turkish republic under the aegis of Kemal Atatürk. This intense and frustrated opposition also seems convinced that the AKP is steering Turkey away from secularism and toward an Islamic political future, and claims that foreign-policy moves within the region since the Arab Spring have been endangering Turkish security. I interpret the AKP leadership's policies and behavior far more positively than do its harsh critics, both in relation to its success governing an important sovereign state during a difficult and uncertain time and its role as a creative source of influence within the region and beyond.

I wrote my blog posts addressing the Palestine agenda during the time that I served as Special Rapporteur for Occupied Palestine on behalf of the UN Human Rights Council; they were collected and published by Just World Books last year in a companion volume to this one, bearing the title *Palestine: The Legitimacy of Hope*. For this reason, the present volume gives only peripheral attention to Palestinian developments, while my preoccupations with Turkey are accorded major attention—reflecting my frequent contact with the country and involvement in the political debates about its policies and leaders.

There is an inevitable randomness associated with a selection of blog posts. I can make no credible claim of comprehensive or systematic coverage. In retrospect, I wish especially that I had devoted more attention in the regional context to the important and changing role played by Saudi Arabia; only Saudi Arabia and Turkey are active in spreading their influence beyond the Middle East. For many years the Saudis have poured billions of dollars into disseminating the Wahhabi variant of Islam throughout the Indian subcontinent and Africa, funding madrassas and fueling much of the Islamic radicalism that has been so threatening to the West. Yet it is Turkey, which limits its extraregional diplomacy to expanding trade and investment along with cultural contacts, which has met with the most criticism in the West. If we inquire about this tolerance of the Saudis' international promotion of Wahhabism, as contrasted with the critical posture toward Turkey during the AKP period, three interrelated explanations emerge: oil, Iran, and Israel.

The Saudi monarchy, which presides over both vast oil reserves and the holiest sites of Islam, has behaved in ways that at first glance appear strange and in conflict with its identity as a strict Muslim state. Reflecting its anxious rivalry with Shi'a Iran since the overthrow of the Shah in 1979, Saudi policy in the region has seemed to be adopting a sectarian orientation of support for Sunni initiatives. Yet this sectarian posture, which is in evidence in relation to Iraq and Syria, has clashed in recent years with the Saudis' strong opposition to all forces—Sunni-oriented or not—they see as challenging established patterns of governance through a politics of upheaval, of the sort that occurred in the first phases of the Arab Spring. On closer examination, this unexpected turn away from promoting Sunni-oriented political movements, principally associated with the various branches of the Muslim Brotherhood in the region, is an outgrowth of the overriding priority that the House of Saud accords to its own stability and survival.

This evident priority helps us to understand Saudi Arabia's distress in reaction to the overthrow of the anti-Islamist Mubarak regime in Egypt, as well as its warm support for the mid-2013 military coup that forced the elected president, who was associated with the Muslim Brotherhood, out of office. Saudi concerns about the threats posed by a democratic movement in the region, especially if Islamic in nature, reached a new high point in the summer of 2014 in the form of a startling show of support for Israel, even as Israel carried out a massive, punitive military operation against Hamas in Gaza. This confusing posture eludes easy generalization, but needs to be integrated into any overall depiction of the Middle East in this period of turmoil and preoccupation with Islamic political activities. In this regard, what may be most notable about Saudi Arabia's political behavior is the *secondary* significance it accords to religious identity in its foreign policy, as compared to the House of Saud's *primary* commitment to withstanding all democratizing tendencies in the region. The confusion is heightened by the extremity of its merciless interpretation and application of Islamic strictures internally to quell dissent, suppress women, and deny freedom.

Background Observations

The last several years in the Middle East cannot be adequately understood without some sense of the background of the region in the Cold War period and, even before that, in the aftermath of World War I. As some of my posts discuss, the present legacy of turmoil and oppressive governance is partly attributable to the kind of artificial political communities that were imposed on the region, principally through the colonial ambitions of Britain and France (as expressed in the notorious Sykes-Picot Agreement of 1916). These colonial powers effectively undermined President Woodrow Wilson's resolve to rely on principles of self-determination to demarcate the political communities that would emerge from the collapsed Ottoman Empire after 1918. Beyond European scheming to control the region there was the Balfour Declaration, issued by the British foreign secretary and later endorsed by the League of Nations. This lent the imprimatur of international approval to the Zionist project to establish a Jewish homeland in historic Palestine, a project accountable for decades of lethal friction and much suffering.

When the Berlin Wall fell in 1989, a century of preoccupation with Europe as the global front line of ideological ferment and deadly warfare came to an end. Geopolitical priorities shifted to the Middle East and, to a lesser extent, East Asia. The Arab world, plus Turkey, Iran, and Israel, contained the most explosive forces unleashed in the past fifty years, as well as controlled a large proportion of the world's oil supply and reserves. Oil had become the most vital strategic resource in this period, and its control and pricing was integral to the stability of the world economy and to Western prosperity and security. At this writing, the sharply falling price of oil in recent months has led to further uncertainties in the region and world and, if this continues, will likely somewhat diminish the geopolitical importance of the Middle East although water scarcities are likely to keep a geopolitical spotlight on the region.

The reverberations of the revolution in Iran, which ended the Pahlavi monarchy in 1979, also made the Middle East crucial—and made political Islam a threat to Western hegemony and Israeli security. The revolution allowed a mobilized, unarmed populace to overthrow an established, if corrupt and repressive, monarchy that enjoyed the full backing of the United States, a shocking outcome that took Washington and the region completely by surprise. These events were particularly threatening to the prior center of Islamic governance in the region, Saudi Arabia, with a leadership that based its legitimacy as a dynastic monarchy on its custodial role as the protector of Islam's holiest sacred sites, facilitator of the annual hajj, disseminator of Wahhabism around the world, and possessor of the world's largest oil reserves. For the Iranian monarchy to be overthrown by a religiously oriented political movement suggested that a similar kind of populist movement could find fertile ground in Saudi Arabia. In reaction, Saudi Arabia did its best to avoid such speculation by making the world think that the struggle with Iran was essentially sectarian, pitting against one another the two main Islamic tendencies, Sunni and Shi'a. This response seemed designed to divert attention from Ayatollah Khomeini's threatening contention that monarchic rule of a territorial state was incompatible with fundamental Islamic values, which would render the Saudi Arabian monarchy as illegitimate as the Shah's royal arrangements in Iran had been.

It should be recalled that the Shah had been presiding over a Western-oriented government that was a major intelligence outpost of the United States during the Cold War. Iran had also seemed successfully integrated into neoliberal globalization ever since its democratic predecessor, Mohammad Mossadegh, was overthrown by a 1953 coup aided and encouraged by the CIA. More than thirty-five years after the Iranian Revolution, the West has yet to come to terms with Iran. A split in the Western approach has been emerging, with the Obama administration favoring a carefully negotiated diplomatic accommodation while Tel Aviv pushes hard for an escalating confrontation.

To assess the pervasive turmoil and irreconcilable conflicts in the region, it is vital to understand the degree to which Washington's freedom to maneuver is constrained by Israel's influence on its foreign policy. This was illustrated in early 2015 when House Speaker John Boehner invited Israel's prime minister, Benjamin Netanyahu, to address a joint session of Congress with the declared purpose of refuting Obama's recourse to diplomacy to defuse the threat of a military confrontation with Iran. As I argue in Chapter 6 of this book and have long believed, the most salutary initiative for the Middle East as a whole would be to establish a nuclear-weapons-free zone, coupled with a regional mutual security framework agreement that includes Iran and Israel. If these steps were reinforced by effective geopolitical pressure to accept the Israel–Palestine normalization proposals set forth in 2002 (known as the Arab Peace Initiative), regional prospects for peace and security would be greatly improved. This, in turn, would allow regional leaders to turn their attention and devote their resources to such unmet challenges as massive unemployment, poverty, and climate change. According to scientists and experts, the Middle East, for a variety of reasons, is more vulnerable to the harmful effects of climate change than any other part of the world.[1] This rarely commented-upon threat to the Middle East highlights what may be the central tragedy of the region: the geopolitical paralysis arising from Israel's promotion of turmoil and disunity in the Arab world disempowers regional and global problem-solving mechanisms at a time of growing ecological jeopardy.

The Arab Spring

My experience in the Middle East was very much affected by my role as UN Special Rapporteur from 2008 to 2014. Part of my duties in this position were to arrange official fact-finding missions and present semiannual

---

1. See Tina Isanti, "The New Climate Normal," *BQ*, February 2015, www.bqdoha.com/2015/02/climate-change-in-the-middle-east; Laurence Caramel, "Temperatures to rise by six degrees in Middle East countries," *Guardian*, January 8, 2013, www.theguardian.com/environment/2013/jan/08/middle-east-temperature-rise-climate.

reports to the Human Rights Council and General Assembly. As I attempted to carry out this UN mission in mid-December 2008, Israel denied me entry and expelled me. This had the unintended effect of making me a visitor to the countries neighboring Israel, my best default option to gather the information I needed to evaluate Israel's record of compliance with the Fourth Geneva Convention and international human rights standards as an occupying power of Palestine. Along with my frequent visits to Turkey, this UN experience made me much more aware of and interested in what was taking place in the region. It also gave me some additional firsthand contact with a region about which I had long been concerned as a student and critic of U.S. foreign policy. Ever since the Vietnam War I have had a special interest in Iran; I visited the country during the last stages of its revolution and met with the new leadership of the country.

I mention these biographical items as background for my contact with and great interest in the unfolding of the Arab Spring. In the course of my attempts to visit Gaza by way of Egypt—my only option for entering Palestine after my expulsion—I found myself in Cairo three times after the upheaval that ousted Hosni Mubarak from the presidency. The first of these visits was only few weeks after the dramatic events in Tahrir Square reached their climax on January 25, 2011. My sequential posts on Egypt in Chapter 2 exhibit my impressions over the last three years as to what was happening, what to fear, and what to hope for. Because of my familiarity with somewhat comparable developments in Turkey, it felt natural to compare the trajectories of these two leading states in the Middle East. I had contact with a wide range of Egyptians, but particularly the liberal urban elites of Cairo, who at first welcomed the outcome of the movement but gradually became more wary of its consequences. Many soon moved into the ranks of the opposition after Mohamed Morsi of the Muslim Brotherhood became Egypt's first democratically elected president in mid-2012.

For me, as these posts suggest, Egypt was a microcosm of the movement bearing the hopeful label of Arab Spring. From the outset I was skeptical about this designation, noting that the old governmental establishment remained in control of the Egyptian state. What seemed to make some of this optimism plausible was the apparent consensus that the Egyptian armed forces were ready to preside over a political transition process that would shape the future of the country through parliamentary and presidential elections and a new constitution. These expectations were upheld at first, but when the Muslim Brotherhood unexpectedly emerged as the dominant political force and arguably overplayed its hand, the democratic consensus quickly began to unravel. This first became apparent in the close 2012 presidential election, in which the candidate of the old Mubarak order came within a couple of percentage points of prevailing; it later took hold in the form of an expanding and increasingly alienated opposition that produced a worsening crisis of legitimacy for the Morsi government. This culminated in the July 2013 coup that brought General Abdel-Fattah el-Sisi to power and drove the Muslim Brotherhood from the commanding heights, either to prison or underground. This turnabout in Egypt has been signaled in the past year by the government dismissing the charges leveled against Mubarak shortly after his overthrow and reasserting authoritarian rule, with the full backing of all countries in the region except Qatar and Turkey. More recently, even both of these have moved toward accepting post-Morsi governance in Egypt.

It is important to keep in mind that what took place in 2011 was a clear indication of deep societal dissatisfaction throughout the Arab world with the authoritarian status quo, including its reliance on a neoliberal approach to economic development. At first, it was widely hoped that this dissatisfaction would produce a meaningful package of reforms supporting some measure of democracy, as well as a commitment to uphold human rights and establish a more equitable economic climate. Yet it quickly turned out that the regional scope of the Arab Spring was subject to a variety of national responses. Indeed, the posts collected in this volume address the interplay between an overarching regional narrative and several national variations, interactions further complicated by a variety of extraregional interventions.

The optimistic initial mood was partly a result of the origins of the regional anti-authoritarian movements in Tunisia and Egypt, the two countries in the region governed by leaders who were ready to remove themselves from power rather than initiate a civil war. When popular uprisings emerged in Syria, Libya, Bahrain, and Yemen, those regimes reacted far more aggressively; the implications of the name "Arab Spring" quickly became problematic.

After the Arab Spring

Admittedly, even such a withdrawal of unrealistic prospects can be questioned as endorsing the enthusiasm of the initial events in early 2011. As I suggest in this volume, especially in posts interpreting developments in Egypt, there was never a firm basis for such a hopeful outlook, except possibly in Tunisia, where it all started. I recalled the similar prematurity of affixing the label "Prague Spring" to events in 1968 Czechoslovakia that were viewed at the time as a successful challenge to Soviet-style repression. As subsequent events soon showed, Moscow was not prepared to live with the outcome of a democratic movement; the old order was crudely restored to control. As I suggest in Chapter 6, on Iran, transformative politics are unrealistic and unrealizable until the former establishment is effectively destroyed and a new bureaucracy and armed forces are put in its place. Iran did this after 1979, for better and worse, and its overthrow of the established order has survived the test of time. Egypt did not do this and has slipped back into an authoritarian mold that is more repressive and brutal than the old Mubarak regime.

Elsewhere in the region, the first signs of upheaval did not prompt acquiescence but rather invigorated the structures of repression—or prompted cosmetic gestures of reform. Two different strands of response occurred, neither with positive results for democratic values or the wellbeing of the citizenry. As Chapter 4, on Syria, illustrates, the Damascus government opted from the beginning to fight back rather than give ground. It did so in a brutal manner that led the opposition to opt for insurrection and civil war rather than surrender; although this produced support and sympathy from other political actors within and without the region, it did not restore order. It led to a reign of death, devastation, and displacement that has inflicted severe suffering on the Syrian people and continues to place a question mark next to the future of the country. The Syrian tragedy has been complicated and intensified by the emergence of the Islamic State in Iraq and Syria (ISIS),[2] a radical Islamic movement that emerged in part as resistance to the American occupation of Iraq after 2003. Its nature is not fully clear, but its political vision questions the legitimacy of the sovereign states that resulted from colonialist diplomacy after World War I. ISIS proclaimed a caliphate as the basis of governance for the territories in Syria and Iraq under its control in 2014.

A variant on the Syrian experience of civil war occurred in Libya, where Muammar Qaddafi, a wily dictator long despised by the West, reacted with genocidal rhetoric and tactics to an uprising challenging his rule. Because Libya has lots of oil and many European connections, NATO intervened in March 2011, with the partial blessing of the UN Security Council. The UN granted a limited mandate in response to urgent calls for intervention, based on a humanitarian emergency facing the civilian population of Benghazi. However, the actual military operation NATO carried out sought from its beginning to shift the internal balance of forces in Libya and achieve regime change. Qaddafi was summarily executed by antigovernment militants and a new leadership friendly to the West was handed the reins of government, though it lacked much of a political base in the country. Libya was awash with weaponry; local militias, long suppressed, emerged to challenge the control, capacity, and legitimacy of the leadership in Tripoli. The result so far has been

---

2. It is also known as the Islamic State in Iraq and the Levant (ISIL). The Arabic name is *al-Dawla al-Islamiya fi Iraq wa al-Sham*, with *al-Sham* translating as either "the Levant" or "Syria." It is also called Da'ish or DAESH for its Arabic initials. See Faisal Irshad, "Isis, Isil or Da'ish? What to Call Militants in Iraq," BBC News, June 24, 2014, www.bbc.com/news/world-middle-east-27994277.

chaos and bewilderment, a pattern that has also brought much violence and uncertainty to Yemen.

Elsewhere in the Arab world, after some gestures of reformist response in countries such as Morocco, Jordan, Bahrain, and Saudi Arabia, the old patterns of authoritarian normalcy have for the present been restored. The situation at the end of 2014 exhibited counterrevolution, chaos, and authoritarianism. The only vestiges of the spirit of 2011 that gave rise to the Arab Spring can be found in Tunisia. Yet even in this small country the democratic transition, although far more robust than elsewhere in the region, seems in some ways to be a throwback to the Ben Ali leadership's authoritarian outlook, though it was achieved far more consensually than in Egypt.

What Next?

The posts collected here make no real effort to project the future for the region or its various political actors. What is evident from what I have written is the rise of nonstate actors during the period after 2011. It is evident that Hezbollah, the al-Nusra Front, and ISIS are major players in the main continuing struggles in Syria and Iraq. Also evident is the degree to which the states in the region seem unable to accept a pluralist ethos as the essential ground of democratic governance. Only Turkey and Tunisia are experimenting with a secular framework for political activity that affirms the legitimacy of diversity and works to accommodate religious freedom with religiously neutral government. Although Turkey has a far more solid foundation for such pluralism, further sustained by impressive leadership and successful economic achievement, its stability continues to be threatened by deep cleavages involving class, region, and views as to religious and political freedom. I have, especially in posts dealing with Egypt, Turkey, and Iran, tried to depict these various terrains of struggle; the sections devoted to Syria and Libya are preoccupied with refuting those who favor military intervention. My position in these posts, undoubtedly influenced by my decade of opposition to the U.S. role in Vietnam, is to consider intervention almost always a symptom of the problem rather than a preferred course of action.

What I hope becomes clear throughout this volume is that the excitement associated with the initial upheavals of 2011 was genuine and deserved affirmation, despite being accompanied by unrealistic and romanticized expectations. The dark happenings that followed have eclipsed most of these hopes, at least temporarily, but seem not to be the end of the story. The heady days of the Arab Spring provided an interlude of empowerment for the long-repressed peoples of the region. Whether this experience produced a new subjectivity, one that will be wiser in the future about relating its means employed to the ends sought, remains to be seen. Such learning about sustaining mass empowerment seems directly connected to the revival of hopes for political dignity and economic equity in the Arab world.

Richard Falk
March 2015

1

Regional Perspectives

The general introduction is oriented around regional developments during the period covered by the blog posts in this section, and those broader issues will not be again addressed here. The themes emphasized can be briefly identified. They include a reminder of the unpredictability that exists throughout the region, and gives rise to a series of 'black swans,' that is, transformative events that are unanticipated until they happen, and then are laboriously explained by "the experts." The complexity of the region has become apparent in recent years. More than other parts of the world the Greater Middle East (Arab world + Iran + Turkey + North Africa) is crosscut by a series of transnational conflicts and ideological passions that are additionally complicated as a result of their linkages to extraregional global patterns of intervention and rivalry.

Attention is also given to the Arab Spring as a regional phenomenon, and as an expression of distinctive challenges to the established order in each of the countries in the Greater Middle East. As we now know, the democratic promise unleashed by the extraordinary developments in early 2011 generated a phase two that mingled promises of democratic reform with authoritarian pushback, producing a variety of coopting and counterrevolutionary reactions that have caused the further hardening of authoritarian regimes, instances of persisting civil strife, and some cosmetic reforms.

Among the situational factors that has proved so significant has been various types of political polarization, perhaps most starkly observed in Egypt, but also evident in Turkey, Tunisia, and elsewhere. Several of the posts published here try to comprehend the specific contours and toxic effects of polarization, and how it diminishes prospects for democratization and respect for human rights. From the outset of the Arab Spring, reinforced by my several visits in recent years to the Middle East, I became more and more aware of the intensity of polarization, and its effect of delegitimizing opposing views whether it takes the form of majoritarian democracy that is contemptuous of the outlook of the opposition or the form of a discontented citizenry that withdraws legitimacy from the political leadership, whether or not it has been elected.

In addition to polarization are problems of sectarianism within Islam, the tensions that exist between Sunni and Shi'a Islam, as politicized through the patronage of their principal rival proponents in Riyadh and Tehran. There are intensifying interactions between political polarization, sectarianism, and dynastic anxieties about grassroots political Islam, best exhibited by extreme hostility toward the various country branches of the Muslim Brotherhood. The United States played the sectarian card during its decade of occupation of Iraq with disastrous results, and then belatedly has tried to urge the Shi'a leadership in Baghdad to be more inclusive.

Finally, the emergence of dreaded forms of political extremism are examined as consequences of external intervention and occupation, most especially the ramifications of the U.S.-led 2003 invasion and occupation of Iraq and the ongoing civil war raging in Syria since 2011. The challenges posed by these outbreaks of extremism prompt yet another cycle of extraregional intervention justified on counter-terrorist and humanitarian grounds, being addressed militarily with no willingness to explore diplomatic paths to regional stability. The U.S. government is particularly responsible for this dysfunctional reliance on military intervention implemented mainly by way of air strikes. The picture of the Greater Middle East that emerges from these posts is not encouraging, but as is stressed, the turbulence in the region is likely to cause unexpected eruptions in the years ahead that might bring more positive tendencies to the surface in more durable forms than what emerged in 2011. What lies ahead is obscure, but likely to alter dramatically our present expectations for political developments in the region and how these relate to world politics.

The posts in this section exhibit my early concerns as to whether the upheavals in the region, especially Egypt and Tunisia, could attain their democratizing goals, given the fact that only the rulers and immediate entourage were removed from power. The entrenched bureaucracy remained the core of the governing regime whether they approved of the upheaval or not. Furthermore, trusting the armed forces to manage a transition to a more democratic governing process seemed naïve, given their privileged role and material interest in stabilizing the former authoritarian regime.

Can Humanitarian Intervention Ever Be Humanitarian?

August 4, 2011[1]

Not since the debate about the Kosovo war of 1999 has there been such widespread discussion of humanitarian intervention, including the semantics of coupling "humanitarian" with the word "intervention." At one extreme of this debate about language stands Gareth Evans, former foreign minister of Australia and a staunch advocate of displacing the discourse on "humanitarian intervention" by relying on the concept of "responsibility to protect" (R2P). Evans was, in fact, co-chair of the International Commission on Intervention and State Sovereignty, which came up with the idea of R2P a decade ago. This approach to intervention was skillfully marketed to the international community, including the United Nations. Evans writes that they made the conceptual case for R2P "by changing the focus from the 'right' to 'responsibility,' and from 'intervene' to 'protect,' by making clear that there needed to be as much attention paid to prevention as to reaction and non-coercive measures, and by emphasizing that military coercion—which needed to be mandated by the UN Security Council—was an absolute last resort in civilian protection cases."[2]

Insisting that the coercive actions in the Ivory Coast and Libya show the benefits of this approach, as contrasted with the supposed failures in the 1990s to take action in Rwanda, Bosnia, and Kosovo, Evans feels so vindicated by recent events as to plead that we "please lay 'humanitarian intervention' language to rest once and for all." This raises three questions: Should we? Will we? And does it really matter? My answer to the first two is "no," and to the third, "not much." My basic problem with the R2P approach is that it downplays the role of geopolitics in the diplomacy of decisions both to intervene and not to intervene. By hiding this fundamental element in the decision process behind a screen of moralizing language, talking of R2P rather than humanitarian intervention invites misunderstanding as well as encouraging imperial ambitions.

At the other semantic extreme is Michael Walzer, who, writing in *Foreign Affairs*, insists that the idea of humanitarianism has become a central feature of world politics in the early twenty-first century. He starts his article with some hyperbolic language to this effect: "Humanitarianism is probably

1. http://richardfalk.wordpress.com/2011/08/04/can-humanitarian-intervention-ever-be-humanitarian/.

2. Gareth Evans, "Humanitarian Intervention Is Only Justified When..." *Global Brief* (Summer 2011), 60.

the most important 'ism' in the world today, given the collapse of communism, the discrediting of neoliberalism, and general distrust of large-scale
ideologies."[3] I find this sentiment so exaggerated as to defy reasoned discussion; one wonders how such an incredible sentence escaped the scrutiny
of the eagle-eyed editors of *Foreign Affairs*. Walzer appears to be suggesting
that humanitarianism now eclipses realism and nationalism as an influential
global force in the world of ideas and statecraft, which is not only farfetched
and wrong but especially surprising considering that Walzer is, without question, one of the world's most respected and influential thinkers on the ethical dimensions of relations among sovereign states. His overall effort in the
article is to demonstrate that this humanitarian impulse is a matter of duty
for governments and should not be treated as a species of charity. This is a
potentially valuable distinction that becomes clear when he comes to discuss
humanitarian intervention without even mentioning the R2P approach, presumably because it obscures rather than illuminates the underlying issues of
choice.

Walzer looks behind the semantics of intervention to appraise the
responses to situations where populations are genuinely at risk. He faults the
UN Security Council as having a dismal record due to its failures "to rescue
those in need of rescuing," giving Rwanda and Bosnia as examples. Walzer
goes on to conclude that the "UN Security Council rarely acts effectively in
crises, not only because of the veto power of its leading members but also
because its members do not have a strong sense of responsibility for global
security, for the survival of minority peoples, for public health and environmental safety, or for general well-being. They pursue their own national interests while the world burns."[4] This passage sounds to me like an old-fashioned
reaffirmation, after all, of realism and nationalism and is far more descrip-
tively credible than Walzer's assertion that humanitarianism is the recently
emergent dominant ideology.

Coming to specifics, Walzer understandably turns his attention to
Libya as having generated a new debate about humanitarian intervention.
He summarily dismisses leftist suspicions about Western recourse to hard-
power solutions to international conflict situations, but also acknowledges
that this NATO intervention does not seem to be succeeding in making
good on its initial humanitarian claim. Nevertheless, he gives the interveners a surprising clean bill of health as far as their intentions are concerned:
"Their motives were and are humanitarian, but not sufficiently shaped by

---

3. Michael Walzer, "On Humanitarianism," *Foreign Affairs* 90(4): 69–80.
4. Ibid., 75.

considerations of prudence and justice."[5] Walzer is alive to the complexity of international political life, which makes him skeptical about endorsing generalized solutions to such general problems as what to do about a menaced civilian population. Instead he advocates a situational approach to gross civilian vulnerability. He argues that any state can serve as a humanitarian agent, even without necessarily receiving permission from the international community for a use of nondefensive force. In Walzer's words, "[t] here is no established procedure that will tell us the proper name of the agent." He gives approval to several non-Western examples of humanitarian intervention: Vietnam in 1978 against the Khmer Rouge in Cambodia; India in 1971 against Pakistan in what was then East Pakistan and is now Bangladesh; and Tanzania in 1979 against the bloody tyranny of Idi Amin in Uganda. These uses of force are endorsed as serving humanitarian ends even though they failed to receive any mandate to act from the Security Council and even though in each instance, despite rescuing a vulnerable population, the predominant motivation to intervene seemed clearly nonhumanitarian in character. In contrast, Walzer pushing to the outer limit his central thesis as to the rise of humanitarian diplomacy, writes, "In these circumstances, decisions about intervention and aid will often have to be made unilaterally.... The governing principle is, Whoever can, should"[6]— which is the second extraordinary statement made in his article.

Such a volitional framework governing interventionary initiatives negates, without even an explanatory comment, the essential effort of contemporary international law to prohibit *all* international uses of force that are neither instances of self-defense (as defined by the UN Charter in Article 51) nor authorized by the UN Security Council. In this respect, Walzer seems to be endorsing a kind of ethical anarchism as the best available means for achieving global justice in these situations. At this point he veers back to his confidence in the purity of geopolitical motives by contending that "what drives" these uses of force "is not only humanitarian benevolence but also a strong sense of what justice requires."[7] This is written as if imperial ambitions, even if packaged as "grand strategy," should not be a concern. What about the protection of vulnerable states that are victimized by geopolitical maneuvers associated with resources, markets, and congenial ideology? It might be well to recall that it was a notorious tactic of Hitler's expansionist foreign policy to intervene, or threaten to do so, for the sake of protecting German minorities allegedly being abused in neighboring countries.

---

5. Ibid., 77.

6. Ibid., 79.

7. Ibid.

Returning to a comparison of perspectives, Evans sets forth a series of guidelines that he believes will make it more likely that uses of force in these interventionary settings will respect international law while at the same time recognizing sensitivities in the postcolonial world about giving approval to military encroachments upon sovereign space, which are invariably of a North/South character if acted upon by the United Nations (that is, the North as agent of intervention, the South as the site where force is used). His five criteria, which are law-oriented and deferential to the authority vested in the Security Council, are: (1) the seriousness of the risk; (2) the purposeful and discriminate use of force to end a threat of harm; (3) force as a last resort; (4) the proportionality of the military means authorized with respect to the humanitarian goals of the mission; (5) the likely benefit of the contemplated use of force to those being protected. While Walzer seems willing to live with unilateralism, Evans seeks a consensual foundation for such uses of force, so he insists that the final mandate for an R2P operation must be shaped within this five-part framework and based on formal Security Council authorization. Walzer argues—more opportunistically and geopolitically naively—that states should be empowered to act even without proper authorization if they have the will and means to do so. His examples of humanitarian interventions by non-Western states (Vietnam, India, Tanzania) were all neighbors of the target state and were at the time contested to varying degrees due to the play of geopolitical forces, not as a reflection of different levels of humanitarian urgency. In this regard, the strongest humanitarian argument was undoubtedly present in support of the Vietnam intervention in Cambodia to stop a massive genocide, but this was also the most controversial, as it contravened the American policy of placating China to increase pressure on the Soviet Union. Acting under the umbrella of R2P is most likely to generate intense controversy when the United States acts with or without European backing (Iraq, Afghanistan, Kosovo, Libya), especially if the humanitarian claim seems marginal or functions as a cloak hiding strategic and imperial goals. Only in the Libyan debate did R2P figure prominently; it seems to have led several members of the Security Council, including China and Russia, to abstain rather than vote against the resolution that gave NATO the green light to commence its military campaign.

In this sense Evans's claims need to be taken seriously: not because they represent a step forward, but rather because they weaken the overall effort of the UN and international law to minimize war and military options in international political life.

What makes these discussions serious is their bearing on life-and-death issues for vulnerable peoples and their supposed benefactors. On the one side, Noam Chomsky is right to worry about "military humanism," which he depicts as cleverly disguising the grand strategies of hegemonic political actors as global public-works projects. In effect, humanitarianism is the pathetic fig leaf selected to hide the emperor's nudity. Chomsky points to "double standards" as proof positive that, whatever the explanation given for a particular intervention by the United States or NATO, the claimed humanitarian motivation is window dressing, not the primary consideration. He treats Western silence about decades of brutal Turkish suppression of the Kurdish movement for human rights as an illuminating example of geopolitical blinkering whenever it seems inconvenient to take action on behalf of a victimized minority. In my view, the most extreme instance of double standards involves the failure of the UN System or "a coalition of the willing" to take any action to protect a Palestinian population that has endured an oppressive occupation for more than forty-four years, despite the direct responsibility of the UN and colonialists for the Palestinians' ordeal.

On the other side of this debate among progressives is Mary Kaldor, who worries that without the intervention option, dreadful atrocities would take place with even greater frequency. She supported intervention to protect the endangered Albanian population of Kosovo, fearing that, otherwise, the genocidal horrors of Bosnia would likely have been repeated, including even the grisly massacre of Srebrenica. At the same time, Kaldor was not indifferent to the risks of abuse by the great powers and tried, in the manner of Gareth Evans, to condition her endorsement of intervention with a framework of guidelines that (if followed) would apply the restraints of international humanitarian law and minimize exploitative opportunities for intervening powers. This framework was embodied in the report of the Independent International Commission on Kosovo, of which Kaldor was an influential member. That report also took account of the inability of the interveners to win UN Security Council approval (in this instance, because of the expectation of Russian and Chinese vetoes). The report took the position that, in situations of imminent humanitarian catastrophe, it would be *legitimate* to intervene if the capabilities were available to exercise effective proportionate force, although *unlawful* given the UN Charter's prohibition on all nondefensive claims to use force. It is, of course, not generally desirable to create exceptions to restraints that enjoy the status of fundamental rules of international law, but it can seem even more discrediting for the role of law in world affairs to be paralyzed in humanitarian emergencies by rigid rules and procedures that produce inaction and expose vulnerable peoples to genocide or severe crimes against humanity.

There is no right and wrong in such a debate. Both orientations are in touch with relevant realities; there is no principled way to choose between such contradictory concerns beyond assessing the risks, costs, and likely effects of intervention or inaction in each instance. Judgment here is necessarily operating in a domain of radical uncertainty: that is, nobody knows! This raises the crucial question of what to do when nobody knows. It is this unavoidable responsibility for a decision when the consequences are great and available knowledge is of only limited help that points to the difficulties of the human condition, even putting to one side the distorting effects of greed, ambition, civilizational bias, and the maneuvers of geopolitics. The late, great French philosophical presence, Jacques Derrida, explored this dilemma in many discourses that related freedom to responsibility, with some collateral damage to Enlightenment confidence in the role of reason in human affairs. For Derrida, making such decisions is an unavoidable ordeal that is embedded in what it means to be human, combining helplessness with urgency.

I would suggest two lines of response. First, there are degrees of uncertainty, which makes some decisions more prudent and principled, although it is inevitably difficult to envision outcomes given "the fog of war." In this regard, everything is guesswork when it comes to composing a balance sheet of horrors. Still, it seems plausible to insist that Rwanda in 1994 was a lost opportunity to spare many lives that were taken in a genocidal onslaught, a claim strengthened now and later by the preexisting presence of a UN peace-keeping force in the country and the informed judgment of the UN commander on the ground as well as many observers. General Roméo Dallaire, who commanded the UN Assistance Mission for Rwanda, indicated at the start of the crisis that five thousand additional troops, plus a protective UN mandate to act, could have prevented most of the killings, estimated to total more than eight hundred thousand.[8] From the perspective of prudence, military intervention on behalf of minorities trapped in major states is almost always an unattractive option, although nonmilitary support and censure initiatives may have positive effects in some instances. Intervention is unattractive because the costs are high, the target state has major capabilities, the scale of an effective intervention would exceed the political will to protect a threatened minority, and, most important, there is a high risk of starting a general war.

The Libyan intervention in 2011 was labeled falsely and the mission authorized was light years away from NATO's operational goals. In effect, this amounted to a disguised form of an unlawful use of force, coupled with a dereliction of duty on the part of the UN Security Council to close the gap between its mandate and the actual operation. Besides, those being protected (or, more accurately, helped) in a struggle for control of the country were a shadowy organization thrown together on the spot, lacking in cohesion, and

---

8. See also Linda Melvern, *Conspiracy to Murder: The Rwandan Genocide* (London: Verso, 1994).

almost from the outset taking recourse to violence in a manner that violated the spirit and character of the inspiring Arab Spring popular movements in neighboring Tunisia and Egypt. At the same time, there was a humanitarian challenge: the dictatorial leader, Colonel Muammar Qaddafi, was delivering bloody rants and the civilian population was under siege in Benghazi, definitely in a situation of imminent risk. Under these circumstances, a carefully delineated protective move under UN auspices could have been justified, but it would have depended on placing NATO troops in situations of potential danger. The kind of air campaign that has been waged by inflating and exceeding the actual UN mandate depicted in Security Council Resolution 1973 has been discrediting for UN peacekeeping and authority purposes. It has been ineffectual in stopping the violence in Libya and is likely responsible for its spread. So far the intervention has resulted in not a single NATO casualty (while causing a rather large number of Libyan civilian deaths). Whether the stalemate will produce a negotiated compromise remains uncertain, but the shape and execution of the intervention suggest the inadequacy of allowing governments to make decisions and policies relating to humanitarian catastrophes either on the basis of their own calculus or through reliance on a UN framework that is susceptible to major geopolitical manipulation.

There is a preferable, although imperfect, alternative proposal that has been around for several years: establish a UN Emergency Peace Service (UNEPS) capable of being activated through the joint authority of the Secretary-General and a supermajority of two-thirds of the Security Council membership in reaction to either a humanitarian catastrophe arising from political policies or conflict or a natural disaster that exceeds the response capabilities of the national government. The UNEPS should ideally be funded by imposing some kind of small global tax on the sale of luxury goods, international travel, currency transactions in financial markets, or some combination of these. If this proves impractical, then voluntary contributions by nonpermanent Security Council members would be acceptable. The whole idea would be to break the present links, to the extent possible, between "humanitarian interventions" and geopolitics. The only means to do this would be through creating a maximally independent international agency that would engender confidence in its good faith through its prudent tactics and effective operations. Unlike such delegated interventions as the Gulf War of 1991, the Kosovo War of 1999, and the Libyan War of 2011, the UNEPS would rely on tactics geared toward minimizing risks to a threatened population and would operate under the mandating authorities' strict supervision while carrying out intervention or relief missions. Its capabilities would be constructed from the ground up, with separate recruitment, training, doctrine, and command structures.

This seems like such a sensible innovation for the benefit of humanity that it may seem puzzling why it has never gained significant political support from UN members—but it should not be puzzling. For decades global reformers have been advocating a UN tax, often called a "Tobin Tax" after James Tobin, the Nobel economist who first floated such a proposal. They have also advocated the kind of UNEPS recommended above: for instance, it was carefully outlined in a proposal developed by Robert Johansen, a prominent political scientist who has for years been associated with the Kroc Institute of International Peace Studies at the University of Notre Dame, in collaboration with other scholars.[9] Such a practical solution to this daunting challenge is not on the table because it would weaken geopolitical actors' leverage over the resolution of conflict situations. Reverting to the earlier discussion of Walzer, it is precisely because humanitarianism is marginal to the conduct of world politics that the UNEPS proposal seems utopian. In relation to Evans, geopolitical forces can accommodate his framework, which is probably well intended but provides intervening states with a rationalization for their desired uses of force without significantly interfering with their discretion to intervene or not. As the Libyan debate and decision confirm, geopolitics remains in control despite recourse to framing action through the lens of R2P. More principled and effective action in the future will require a great deal of pressure from global civil society in collaboration with middle powers—the sort of coalition that led to the surprising establishment of the International Criminal Court in 2002 over the opposition of such international stalwarts as the United States, China, Russia, and India.

Global Revolution after Tahrir Square
November 9, 2011[10]

The history-making global Occupy movement, with a presence in more than nine hundred cities, would not have happened in form or substance without the revolutionary awakening of the world's youth. That awakening resulted from riveting events that culminated in the triumphal achievement of driving Hosni Mubarak from the pinnacle of Egyptian state power. We need also to acknowledge that the courage exhibited by those gathered at Tahrir Square

---

9. Robert C. Johansen, ed., *A United Nations Emergency Peace Service to Prevent Genocide and Crimes against Humanity* (New York: World Federalist Movement Institute for Global Policy, 2006), www.responsibilitytoprotect.org/files/UNEPS_PUBLICATION.pdf.

10. http://richardfalk.wordpress.com/2011/11/09/global-revolution-after-tahrir-square/.

might not have been exhibited to the world if not for the earlier charismatic martyrdom by self-immolation of an unlicensed street vendor of vegetables, Mohamed Bouazizi, in the interior Tunisian city of Sidi Bouzid on December 17, 2010. Perhaps the eruptions would have stopped at the Tunisian border were it not for Egyptians' readiness to erupt after the death of Khaled Said (a young activist not previously widely known) in Alexandria on June 6, 2010. This brutal police murder ignited Egyptians' moral passion, which was expressed and disseminated widely through a Facebook campaign called "We are all Khaled Said." We also must not overlook the mobilizing and social networking talents of digitally minded, younger urban Egyptians, without whom the movement might never have taken off in the first place, or the later encouragement provided by TV portrayals of encounters between gangs of Mubarak hooligans and the demonstrators.

History is always overdetermined when transformative events are analyzed in the aftermath of their occurrence. So it is, and will be, with Tahrir Square, which has quickly become a shorthand to signify the hopes, fears, and methodology of the twenty-first century's first revolutionary moment, conceived narrowly as an Egyptian happening or more broadly as the inspirational foundation of a revolutionary impulse that has expanded into a phenomenon of genuinely global scope. What is beyond doubt is that the world Occupy movement proudly and credibly claims an affinity with Tahrir Square, although not without celebrating each movement's important particularities. It is reasonable to believe that these movements would not have occurred or would have taken a different form without the overall inspiration provided by the several dramas encompassed beneath the banner of the Arab Spring, and not only by Tahrir Square understood in isolation from its regional setting.

I want to stress the unique North/South character of this inspiration as the core of its originality, as well as its relation to a broader realignment of the political firmament that is slowly taking account of the collapse of the Eurocentric imperial order that began more than half a century ago with the collapse of British rule in India. This decolonizing process still has a long way to go, as recent military operations in Libya, threats to Iran, and Israel's daily colonialist defiance of international law remind us. The interventionary currents of transnational political violence continue to flow only in one direction: North-South. After World War II, the United States militarily replaced the European colonial powers as the principal global custodian of Western interests. This anachronistic West-centrism continues to dominate most international institutions and is especially evident in the UN Security Council, in which the Euro-American alliance possesses a veto power it uses to block many efforts to promote global justice and to prevent such emergent political actors as India, Brazil, and Turkey from playing a role commensurate with their stature and influence.

What is exciting, then, about the resonance of Tahrir Square is that the youth of the North looked southward and found inspiration for their incipient struggle for revolutionary renewal of the world economic and social order, as well as for equity in their immediate circumstances. This isn't only because of its priority in time of the Egyptian events but because, for the first time, activists in the North relied on the South to develop its conception of how to practice democratic politics outside of governmental structures, a political learning process evident at the various Occupy sites. The ethos of revolution in Tahrir Square and elsewhere in the region, with the partial exception of Libya, was nonviolent, youth-dominated, populist, leaderless, and without program, demanding drastic change of a democratizing character. On its surface such a revolutionary orientation seems extremely fragile, subject to fragmentation and dissolution once the negatively unifying hated ruler is induced to leave the stage of state power, and—if the challenge from below turns out to be more durable—possibly vulnerable to a violent counterrevolutionary restoration of the old regime. The irony of ironies associated with the Arab Spring is that only in Libya does the old order seem gone forever, and there the uprising was tainted in its infancy by its dependence on thousands of NATO air strikes and a leadership that seemed mainly contrived to please the West. In Egypt a few months ago, though, in the still-exalted aftermath of what the January 25th Movement achieved, there was a self-aware and wide chasm between those optimists who spoke in the language of "revolution" and more cautious observers who claimed only to have been part of an "uprising." At this moment, these latter, more pessimistic interpretations seem more in line with an Egyptian process that can be best described as "regime stabilization," at least for now.

What will happen with the Occupy movement is of course radically uncertain at present. Is it a bubble that will burst as soon as the first cold wave hits the major cities of the North? Or will it endure long enough to worry the protectors of the established order who will unleash state violence, as always, in the name of "law and order"? Are we witnessing the birth pangs of "global democracy" or something else that has yet to be disclosed or lacks a name? We must wait and hope, and maybe pray, above all acting as best we can in solidarity, keeping our gaze fixed on horizons of desire. What is feasible will not do!

The Polarization of Immature Democracies
June 28, 2013

Prelude

To begin with, I know of no truly mature political democracy—although, to be sure, some rest on more stable political bases than others. Most importantly, some forces of opposition despair of ever succeeding through democratic procedures, while others pin their hopes on the next election or the one after that. Some democracies have greater economic stability than others, can boast of higher growth rates, or possess a larger private sector and bigger middle class with more to lose. Some states are more vulnerable to foreign interference than others; some have formidable foreign enemies that seek regime change or something worse.

Perhaps more victimized than most modern societies, Germany, devastated after World War I, was caught in the midst of recovering from a humiliating military defeat by vindictive victors, and the resulting economic depression featured high unemployment and runaway inflation. Its pathetic enactment of liberal democracy could neither find credible solutions nor adopt principled positions. It should not be surprising that an extreme form of political polarization emerged in response, producing disastrous results not only for Germany but for Europe and the world: communism versus fascism. Battles raged between these antagonists in the streets of German cities and the Nazis emerged triumphant, even at the ballot box, helped by the complicity of cartelized big business and the ethos of the Bavarian elites, hostile to any hint of democratic politics. The rest is history.

Today there exist an assortment of deeply worrisome encounters between political extremes brought on by a range of conditioning circumstances. As a first approximation I will mention three disturbing instances, each distinctive, yet each afflicted by destructive polarized politics: the United States, Turkey, and Egypt.

Infernal Polarization and the Creative Dialectic

Before offering some comments on the three cases, it seems helpful to clarify what I mean by "polarization." There are several features, all of which vary with context, including the grievances, goals, outlook, and unity of the opposition as well as the response of those in control of the government, the economy, and sometimes the military. However, there are also certain shared characteristics that encourage generalizations:

    On discourse: In a polarized polity, the opposition seldom reasons and never listens, while those governing rarely hear what critics say and almost never engage in serious self-scrutiny. Both sides see reasonableness more often as a lack of conviction and principle than as an expression of respect and inclusiveness: moderation is out, polemics are in.

On governance: Both sides are generally inhibited from offering compromises and accommodations for fear of seeming weak and thereby alienating their base of support.

On tactics: The opposition seeks instability, dissatisfaction, and, if possible, a climate of opinion that demands change either by constitutional means or by a populist uprising that makes the country ungovernable; the government, in contrast, obtains law and order by whatever means are at its disposal, often provoking worse opposition by employing excessive force.

There is also an emergent form of polarization that may be more likely to produce positive results and seems often to be hiding behind the curtain of its infernal other. It is a youth-oriented rejection of all traditional forms of political rivalry: parties, programs, politicians. "A pox on both your houses!" This kind of creative dialectic takes many forms depending on heritage, context, and cultural sensibilities.

In its most radical forms, a creative dialectic moves with a bottom-up momentum, sometimes substituting humor, sensuality, and satire for polemics, valuing all forms of inclusion, welcoming the participation of LGBTQ activists, celebrating the joy of living, and committing to governing from below. A rather restrained form of such a creative dialectic can easily be confused with "infernal polarization." Such a dialectic flourished in Tahrir Square during those remarkable eighteen days in January 2011, reflected in the spirit of the 99% that brightened the skies above Wall Street in New York, St. Paul's Cathedral in London, and many other cities for some hopeful months later that same year. It just recently manifested again during the early days of the Gezi Park protests in Istanbul and the Brazilian risings. A benevolent future for democratic societies depends on nourishing these forces of mainly youth and malcontents, who have "invented" their version of a creative dialectic while not partaking of the largely negative energies of infernal polarization that are pushing many societies to the risky precipices of implosion.

Why infernal? The legitimating premise of a democratic society is some form of consent by the governed, normally by the political verdicts delivered at periodic, fair, and free elections. In extreme instances of infernal polarization, the opposition seeks to change the rules of the political game by forcing the elected leaders to surrender their power or face chaos or a military takeover. It may be democracy to end autocracy (as with Mubarak) or it make take aim at democracy (as with Morsi); ultimately, this is the politics of the Reichstag fire (1933), the military takeover in Algeria after the Islamists' 1991 electoral triumph, and the unfulfilled fantasies of extreme Kemalists in Turkey.

An abusive or highly incompetent and corrupt majority invites radical forms of dissent, so it is not fair to place all the blame on the opposition. It all depends. An autocratic option for the governing majority is to cancel elections, invite a military to take over, and throw in the towel of democratic legitimacy. In effect, polarization becomes infernal because it inclines both government and opposition to adopt extreme positions, usually for contradictory reasons. Either the majority becomes oppressive and greedy or the minority becomes desperate, despairing of gaining control over the levers of governance by fair play. Of course, in racist Rhodesia or apartheid South Africa it was the abusive minority that held the majority in chains, yet had the temerity to claim lawful and legitimate governance. At minimum, infernal polarization jeopardizes and impairs the quality of democracy; its persistence is likely to impose a death sentence on what can be called the "realm of decent politics."

Comparisons

The mildest instance of infernal polarization is currently evident in the United States—although it may be the most consequential, given America's global projection of hard power and its world leadership role. Increasingly, the domestic political atmosphere is beset by a polarizing opposition that rejects reason in its preoccupation with inducing the elected leadership to fail and thus disappoint the electorate, even if the result is overall decline for the society (especially its poorest half). The Tea Party mentality of opposition to the Obama presidency is mainly expressed by way of polarizing rhetoric and irresponsible congressional behavior, but its worldview is extremist and regards right-wing advocates of antidemocratic and even violent tactics with a scary sympathy. In the background is the post-9/11 governmental effort to monitor the behavior of the entire citizenry, regarding each person—citizen or not—as a potential terrorist and a potential target for assassination. On one side of the divide is a rejection of compassionate governance and an unconditional libertarian distrust of government, while on the other side is the expectation that citizens will forfeit their freedoms to the Orwellian security claims of a government engaged in perpetual war against its enemies, who could be hiding in the bushes anywhere in the world, including within U.S. borders—or even deep in the bowels of its most secretive bureaucratic domains.

How else to interpret the vindictive fury, the cries of "treason!" even by supposedly liberal politicians and media stalwarts against such public-spirited whistleblowers as Chelsea Manning and Edward Snowden? To tell the secrets of government is not a matter of breaching security but a massive acknowledgment of cruelty and criminality. The messenger must be mercilessly destroyed, so as to frighten potential future messengers, and the message shredded and forgotten. Whether such a pattern of governance and opposition is to remain relatively "mild" is a matter for debate, but so far the framework of constitutional government has been superficially maintained; neither an appeal to nor any threat of a military coup seems imminent.

Less containable within the boundaries of constitutional government is the virus of infernal polarization that has been afflicting Turkey for the past eleven years, ever since the AK Party (Adalet ve Kalkınma Partisi, or AKP) gained a plurality in the 2002 elections. The traditional Kemalist opposition, long the governing majority, in particular has seen its grip on power slip away in this young century as the AKP has won successively more impressive electoral victories. At base there is a polarization that is sometimes confusingly characterized as an opposition between traditional and modern values. There is an important dimension of rivalry and distrust that pits the religiously observant against the secularly permissive, but the real tension is between different visions of modernity *expressed* as secularism versus religion. The AKP is all for modern business and science and has turned many keys of power over to the private sector, although its main leaders are privately devout, avoid alcohol and gambling, pray daily, and marry women who cover their heads. There are also class and regional tensions: the AKP is seen as a slightly disguised movement of political Islam, while the secular opposition and its political parties represent the social and nationalist elites associated with the life and leadership of Mustafa Kemal Atatürk, who above all envisioned a modern future for the country that would depend on mimicking European lifestyles and church/state relations.

These Europeanized elites were never really willing to cede power to their AKP rivals. They counted on a military intervention to end the political nightmare, validated by judicial activism from a high court dominated by Kemalist holdovers who shared the sense that the AKP posed a dire threat to the Turkish republic as established by Atatürk. When the opposition's anti-democratic plans failed to materialize it grew increasingly frustrated and bitter, beginning to see itself as a permanently beleaguered opposition with little hope of regaining control. On the other side, as the AKP and its charismatic leader, Recep Tayyip Erdoğan, rode ever-higher waves of success, they became contemptuous of their opposition and seemed to pose an autocratic threat given concrete form via Erdoğan's "presidential project."

Simultaneously, many urban youth in Turkey yearned for a permissive social milieu and a redeeming purpose for their lives, and deeply resented Erdoğan's tendency to express his constraining personal lifestyle preferences as if they should become the law of the land. It was this combination of factors that suddenly erupted in reaction to the plans to transform Gezi Park into a shopping center. What was evident, along with the anti-Erdoğan animus, was a clash between the old style of party politics, as the negation of the AKP, and this new style, which refrained from articulating its vision but appeared to seek substantive and participatory democracy that not only included and responded to all elements in society, even the most marginal, but also seemed intent on reinventing the modalities of opposition and governance. There is confusion in Turkey partly because this new youth politics of revolution is intertwined with the old party politics, whose practitioners want to enjoy the fruits of power, prestige, and influence. It is encouraging and appropriate for this innovative current of Turkish politics to be holding nightly forums to discover what it is they believe and desire and how to go about attaining it.

This political and cultural thrust of the Turkish protests needs to be understood against a background of economic stability and fantastic progress as assessed by standard economic indicators. Somehow, despite the inequality of benefits associated with this spurt of growth and the presence of a large impoverished underclass, the AKP has so far maintained the support of the poor and disenfranchised. The agenda of social and economic rights was not entirely absent from the Turkish demonstrations, but it was certainly not salient. In contrast, the Brazilian protests, also coming after a decade of progress and left-of-center political leaders, found their unity in these social-justice issues, especially in rallying against the perception of corruption at the top and distorted priorities, such as building expensive sports stadiums for international events while the Brazilian poor languished. Unlike Turkey's, Brazil's political scene is not polarized, at least for now; there is no comparable antipathy toward (or enthusiasm for) Dilma Rousseff as exists toward Erdoğan, though its opposition, because more motivated by material demands, may be more sustained.

Egypt is by far the most precarious of these three instances of infernal polarization, especially at the moment. For months it has become evident that Mohamed Morsi's incompetent and beleaguered elected government faces an irreconcilable opposition that will only be satisfied by Morsi's resignation and early presidential elections. As this process slides toward its dreaded moment of truth on June 30 (a year to the day after Morsi was sworn in as president), both sides have promised a show of populist force in the streets of Cairo and elsewhere in the country. Morsi has become, for the opposition, the new Mubarak. The latter provided the unifying element in those remarkable days of January 2011; unlike Mubarak, however, Morsi has legions of Muslim supporters rallying to his side beneath the banner of "No to violence, yes to legitimacy." The formerly anti-Mubarak secular/ Copt opposition is now allied with the Mubarak remnant, as well as those who once hoped for change but now just want normalcy, especially with respect to the economy.

As Esam al-Amin has brilliantly analyzed,[11] the outcome for Egypt is uncertain but extremely dangerous. The country is in the midst of stagger-ing unemployment—especially among the young, it is near 50 percent—with poverty, stagnant development, a failing tourist sector, and dwindling cur-rency reserves, and is also engaged in a potentially dangerous conflict with Ethiopia over the damming of the upper Nile, whose waters are indispensable to Egypt's subsistence as a nation. In other words, the political confrontation on June 30 takes place against a backdrop of economic and foreign policy crisis; it will not be resolved in the street, because both sides seem to have formidable backing. The only way to avoid such a dismal and demoralizing unraveling would seem to be either the opposition suddenly moderating its demands or the military re-entering the governing process, thereby canceling the extraordinary achievement of Tahrir Square—which would be a regres-sion of unimaginably demoralizing proportions.

I recall my visit to Cairo weeks after the overthrow of Mubarak, when great excitement about and support for an inclusive democratic process existed in most circles, although some suspicions were also voiced. At that time, the sec-ular forces seemed confident that they could control Egypt's political future. The sentiment expressed in Cairo was that the Muslim Brotherhood (MB) should by all means be encouraged to participate in elections and was likely to win support at the 30 percent level. It was further conjectured that this would be fine, but that if support rose to 40 percent the country would be in trouble. When the initial parliamentary elections disclosed far stronger Muslim support than anticipated, including over 20 percent for Salafist par-ties far more socially conservative and politically constraining than the MB, it was clear that the future was not what the anti-Mubarak secular liberals expected or wanted.

With the passage of time, especially since Morsi managed to win the presidency in a close vote, this implacable opposition hardened to the point of outright defiance. No matter what kind of peace offerings Morsi made, the opposition was not interested. The composition of this opposition is also a restored blend of Mubarak *fulools* (holdovers from the old regime),

---

11 Esam al-Amin, "Egypt's Fateful Day," *Counterpunch*, June 26, 2013,
    www.counterpunch.org/2013/06/26/egypts-fateful-day.

disenchanted secular liberals, and a reenergized revolutionary youth, quite a political brew. This would seem an expedient coalition, likely to survive only so long as the Brotherhood runs the country. If the Egyptian situation is not bad enough, a variety of foreign governments would like to push the political process in one direction or another, including the Gulf giants Saudi Arabia and Qatar and, of course, the United States and Israel. For different reasons, it would seem that all these foreign meddlers, if the situation further deteriorates, will side with the opposition, which certainly has feeble democratic credentials and is suspected, like the Kemalist opposition in Turkey, of favoring a takeover by the repoliticized Egyptian military.

A Concluding Observation

Infernal polarization is unlikely to give rise to efficient and humane forms of democratization unless transformed from within by a creative dialectic that seeks to transcend traditional political encounters. As the future unfolds, it will become clearer whether this positive scenario has sufficient traction to end polarization and offer something new by way of democratic governance. At present, there are few reasons to be hopeful about these prospects for the United States, Turkey, and Egypt. In some respects, Turkey offers the most hope of the three cases: its governing leadership has achieved much that is beneficial for the society, and the polarized opposition seems capable of exerting strong reformist pressures that yet fall short of threatening to capsize the ship of state.

Certain Forms of Polarization Doom Democracy

August 5, 2013[12]

Doubting Democracy

We are living in a time when tensions within societies seem far more disruptive and inhumane than the rivalries between sovereign states that fueled international wars in the past. More provocatively, we may be living in a historical moment when democracy, as the government of choice, gives rise to horrifying spectacles of violence and abuse. These difficulties with the practice of democracy are indirectly, and with a heavy dose of irony, legitimizing moderate forms of authoritarian government. After years of assuming that democracy was "the least bad form of government" for all national settings, there are ample reasons to raise doubts. I make such an admission reluctantly.

---

12. http://richardfalk.wordpress.com/2013/08/05/polarization-doomed-egyptian-democracy.

There is no doubt that authoritarian forms of rule generally constrain everyone's freedom, especially that of the politically inclined. Beyond this, there is a kind of stagnant cultural atmosphere that often accompanies autocracy—but not always. Consider Elizabethan England, with Shakespeare and his cohort of literary giants. There have been critical moments of crisis when society's most respected thinkers blamed democracy for the political failings of the time. In ancient Greece, the cradle of Western democracy, Plato, Aristotle, and Thucydides came to prefer nondemocratic forms of government, fearful of the politics of the mob that led Athens into imprudent and costly foreign adventures.

Only twenty years ago the collapse of the Soviet Union was being hailed throughout the West as an ideological triumph of liberal democracy over autocratic socialism. Prospects for world peace during the 1990s were directly linked to the spread of democracy, while such other reformist projects as strengthening the UN or respecting international law were put aside. European and American universities were much taken with the theory and practice of "democratic peace," documenting and exploring its central claim that democracies never go to war against one another. If such a thesis is upheld, it has significant policy implications. It would follow, for example, that if more and more countries become "democratic" the zone of peaceful international relations is enlarged. This encouraging byproduct of democracy for sovereign states was reinforced by the experience of the European Union, which, while nurturing democracy, established a culture of peace in what had for centuries been the world's worst war zone.

In the post–9/11 period the Bush presidency embraced "democracy promotion" as a major component of a neoconservative U.S. foreign policy in the Middle East. Skepticism of such an endorsement of democracy was widespread, especially in the aftermath of the 2003 invasion of Iraq. The U.S. government's self-appointed role as the agent of democratization in the region drew harsh criticism. Basing democracy promotion on military intervention completely discredited the American approach. Beyond this, foreign leaders and world public opinion rejected Washington's arrogant insistence that it provided the world with the best political model of legitimate government.

Despite this pushback, there remained an almost universal acceptance of the desirability of democracy as the wave of the future. Of course, there were profound disagreements when it came to the practice and limits of democracy and some support in the region for monarchies as sources of stability and unity. Democracies uphold their reputations by protecting citizens from state abuse and empowering the people to confer authority on the national government, particularly by way of political parties, elections, and rights of expression and assembly. Recently, the idea has reemerged that the citizenry enjoys an ultimate right to hold a government accountable: if the government misplays its hand too badly, it can be removed from power even before a new cycle of elections, without relying on formal impeachment procedures. What makes this populist veto so disturbing in recent experience is its tendency to enter into coalitions with the most regressive elements of the governmental bureaucracy, especially the armed forces, police, and intelligence bureaucracies. Such coalitions are on their surface odd, bringing together the spontaneous rising of the people with the most coercive elements of state power.

The Arab Upheavals

The great movements of revolt in the Arab world in 2011 were justly celebrated as exhibiting an unexpected surge of brave, anti-authoritarian populist politics that achieved relatively bloodless triumphs in Tunisia and Egypt and shook the foundations of authoritarian rule throughout the region. Democracy seemed to be on the march in a region most Western experts had written off as incapable of any form of governance that was not authoritarian. They interpreted Arab political culture through an Orientalist lens that presupposed political passivity and elite corruption, backed up, as necessary, by a militarized state.

It is sad that only two years later a gloomy political atmosphere is creating severe doubts about the workability of democracy, not only in the Arab world but more widely. What has emerged is the realization that deep cleavages in the political culture give rise to crises of legitimacy and governability that can be managed, if at all, only by the application of brute force. These conflicts are destroying the prospects of effective and humane government in a series of countries throughout the world.

The dramatic and bloody atrocities in Egypt since the July 3 military takeover have brought these realities to the forefront of global political consciousness. But Egypt is not alone in experiencing toxic fallout from crises of polarization. Daily sectarian violence between Sunnis and Shi'a in Iraq make it evident that, after an anguishing decade of occupation, the American crusade to liberate the country from dictatorship has failed. Instead of a fledgling democracy, the United States has left behind a legacy of chaos, the threat of civil war, and a growing belief that only a new authoritarianism can bring stability to the country. Turkey, too, is enduring the destabilizing impact of polarization, which has persisted in the face of eleven years of extraordinary AKP success at strengthening the political institutions, weakening the military, improving the economy, and greatly enhancing the international standing of the country. Polarization should not be treated as just a Middle Eastern problem. The United States, too, is increasingly afflicted by a polarizing struggle between its two main political parties that has made democratic government that humanely serves the citizenry or the national public good a thing of the past. Of course, this robust de-democratizing trend in America owes much to the monetizing machinations of Wall Street and the spinning of 9/11.

The nature of polarization is diverse and complex, reflecting its context. It can be socially constructed around the split between religion and secularism, as in Egypt or Turkey; in relation to divisions internal to a religion, as in Iraq; or as between classes, ethnicities, or political parties. Historically, each case of polarization has its own defining set of circumstances, often highlighting minority fears of discrimination and marginalization, class warfare, ethnic and religious rivalry (e.g., Kurdish self-determination).

Egypt and Turkey

The circumstances of polarization in Egypt and Turkey, although vastly different, share the experience of Islam-oriented political forces emerging from the shadows after years of marginalization and, in Egypt's case, brutal suppression. In both countries the armed forces had long played an important role in keeping the state under the control of secular elites that served Western strategic and neoliberal economic interests. Up to now, despite periodic trials and tribulations, Turkey seems to have solved the riddle of modernity much more persuasively than Egypt.

In both countries, electoral politics mandated radical power shifts unacceptable to displaced secular elites. Opposition forces in the two countries, after enjoying decades of power and influence, suddenly saw themselves displaced by *democratic* means, with no credible prospect of regaining political dominance through success in elections, having ceded power and influence to those who had previously been subjugated and exploited. Those displaced were unwilling to accept their diminished role, including this lowered status in relation to societal forces whose values they regarded as antimodern and threatening to their lifestyles. They complained bitterly, organized feverishly, and mobilized energetically to cancel the verdict of the political majority by whatever means possible. To many, though not all, recourse to extrademocratic means to regain power, wealth, and influence seemed the only viable political option, but it had to be framed as a "democratic" outcry of the citizenry against the state. Of course, the state has its own share of responsibility for the traumas of polarization. It overreacts, acts on worst case scenarios, adopts paranoid styles of addressing opposition grievances, and contributes to a downward spiral of distrust and animosity. The media, either to accentuate the drama of conflict or because it is partisan, often heightens tensions, creating a fatalist atmosphere of "no return" for which the only possible solution is "us or them"—that is, the mentality of war.

The Politics of Polarization

The opposition waits for some mistake by the governing leadership to launch its campaign of escalating demands. Polarization intensifies. The opposition is unwilling to treat the verdicts of free elections as the final word on the entitlement to govern. At first, it exhibits such unwillingness through extreme alienation. Later on, as opportunities for opposition arise, this unwillingness is translated into political action and, if it gathers enough momentum, the desired crises of legitimacy and governability bring the country to the brink of collapse. Much depends on material conditions. If the economy is doing reasonably well, calmer heads usually prevail, which may help explain why the impact of severe polarization has been so much greater in Egypt than Turkey. Morsi has succumbed to the challenge while Erdoğan has survived. Reverse the economic conditions and the political outcomes might also be reversed.

The Egyptian experience also reflects the extraordinary sequence of recent happenings. The Tahrir Square upheavals of January 25 came after thirty years of Mubarak rule. Mubarak's removal created a political vacuum that the armed forces quickly filled, accompanied by the promise that a transition to democracy was the consensus goal binding all Egyptians, and that once this goal was reached the generals would retire from the political scene. The popular sentiment then favored an inclusive democracy, which in 2011 was a coded way of saying that the Muslim Brotherhood should compete for power in the political process. There were anxieties about this in the anti-Mubarak ranks; the Brotherhood was sensitive to these secular and Coptic concerns, even pledging that it had no intention of competing for the presidency of Egypt. All seemed well and good, with popular expectations wrongly assuming that the next president of Egypt would be a familiar secular figure, a renegade or opportunistic *fulool*. In the spring of 2011 the expectations were that Amr Moussa (former secretary-general of the Arab League) would be elected president and that the Muslim Brotherhood would be a strong, but minority, force in the Egyptian parliament. As the parliament would draft a new constitution for the country, this was likely to be the first show of strength between the two major poles of Egyptian political opinion.

Several unforeseen developments made this image of Egypt's political future unrealizable. Above all, the Muslim Brotherhood was far more successful in the parliamentary elections than anyone had anticipated. These results stoked the fears of the secularists and Copts, especially given the previously unappreciated political strength of several Salafist parties. Religiously oriented political parties won more than 70 percent of the contested seats, creating control over the constitution-making process. This situation was further stressed when the Brotherhood withdrew its pledge not to seek control of the government by fielding a candidate for the presidency. The whole transition process after January 2011 was presided over by administrative entities answerable to the Supreme Council of the Armed Forces (SCAF). Several popular candidates were disqualified, and a two-stage presidential election was organized in 2012 in which Mohamed Morsi narrowly defeated Ahmed Shafik, the former prime minister who epitomized Mubarak's persisting influence. In a sense, Egyptian people's electoral options involved none of the front-rank Egyptian revolutionary forces responsible for Mubarak's overthrow or the ideals that animated those who filled Tahrir Square in the revolutionary days of January 2011. The Brotherhood supported the anti-Mubarak movement only belatedly, when its victory was in sight, and was not ideologically inclined to support inclusive democratization; Shafik never supported the upheaval and did not even pretend to be a democrat, promising instead to restore law and order and economic normalcy.

During the single year of Morsi's presidency, the politics of extreme polarization took center stage. It is widely agreed that Morsi was neither experienced nor adept as a political leader in what would have been a very challenging situation even if polarization had not aggravated the situation. The Egyptian people anxiously expected the new leader to restore economic normalcy rapidly after the recent prolonged disorder and decline. He was a disappointment, even to many of those who had voted for him, in all of these regards.

It was also expected that Morsi would immediately signal a strong commitment to social justice and to addressing the plight of Egyptian unemployed youth and subsistence masses, but no such promise was forthcoming. In fairness, it seemed doubtful that any president could have satisfied the majority of Egyptians. The challenges were too formidable, the citizenry too impatient, and the old Mubarak bureaucracy remained strategically placed and determined to resist the tidal wave of change to the extent that their positions allowed. Mubarak and some close advisors had fallen, but the judiciary, the armed forces, and the Ministry of the Interior were *fulool* strongholds. In effect, the old secularized elites were still powerful, unaccountable, and capable of obstructing the elected government reflecting the political will of the Egyptian majority. Morsi was elected president, but he inherited a mission impossible.

The Authoritarian Temptation

What was surprising, and disturbing, was the degree to which the protest movement so quickly and submissively linked the future of Egypt to the good faith and prudent judgment of the armed forces. All it received in exchange was the forcible removal of Morsi, the renewal of a suppressive approach to the Brotherhood, and some rather worthless reassurances about the short-term nature of military rule. General Abdel-Fattah el-Sisi from the start made it clear that he was in charge, although he designated an interim president, Adly Mansour, the recent chief judge of the Supreme Constitutional Court and a longtime Mubarak careerist. Mansour's new prime minister has selected a new cabinet, supposedly consisting of technocrats, who will serve until a new government is elected. Already, several members of this civilian gloss on a military takeover of the governing process in Egypt have registered complaints about the excessive force being used against pro-Morsi demonstrations.

Better Mubarakism than Morsiism was the underlying sentiment relied upon to fan the flames of discontent throughout the country, climaxing with the petition campaign organized by Tamarod that led to the June 30 demonstrations of millions, underpinned by an ultimatum from the armed forces that led to Morsi's detention and arrest and the rise to political dominance of el-Sisi, an ominous figure who has led a military coup that talks of compromise and inclusive democracy while acting to criminalize the Muslim Brotherhood and its leadership, using lethal violence against those who peacefully refuse to fall into line.

I am not suggesting that such a return to authoritarianism in this form is better for Egypt than the democracy established by Morsi or favored by such secular liberals as Mohamed ElBaradei. Unfortunately, to be effective, this challenge, directed at a freely elected democracy by a massive popular mobilization, required an alliance with the coercive elements composing the deep state. Such a dependent relationship involved a Faustian bargain: getting rid of the hated Morsi presidency, but doing so with an eyes-closed acceptance of state terror. This included large-scale shootings of unarmed pro-Morsi demonstrators and a set of double standards dramatized by el-Sisi's call to the anti-Morsi forces to give him a mandate to crush the Brotherhood by coming into the streets aggressively and massively. Egypt is well along a path that leads to demonic autocratic rule—and that is will be needed to keep the suppressed Brotherhood from preventing the reestablishment of order. El-Sisi's coup will be written off as a failure if substantial street challenges and bloody incidents continue, which would surely interfere with restoring the kind of economic stability Egypt desperately needs in coming months if it is to escape the dire destiny of being a "failed state." The legitimating test for the el-Sisi coup is "order," not "democracy," so the authoritarian ethos prevails—yet if this means a continuing series of atrocities, it will surely lead to yet another crisis of governability for the country.

The controversial side of my argument is that Egypt lacks the political preconditions for establishing democracy; in such circumstances, a premature attempt to democratize the political life of the country will lead not only to disappointment but to political regression. At this stage, Egypt will be fortunate if it can return to the relatively stable authoritarianism of the Mubarak dictatorship. Because of changed expectations and the Morsi leadership's unlawful displacement, it has now become respectable for the Tamarod, self-appointed guardians of the Tahrir Square revolution, to talk of "cleansing" the Muslim Brotherhood. It is sad to take note of the noxious odors of fascism and genocide contaminating the political atmosphere in Egypt.

The very different experience in Iraq, too, suggests that ill-advised moves to install democracy can unleash polarization in a destructive form. Despite his crimes, Saddam Hussein's authoritarian rule kept polarization in check. The attempted transition to democracy produced sectarian polarization in such drastic forms that it will either lead to an even more oppressive new authoritarianism or a civil war in which the victor rules with an iron hand.

In the postcolonial world it is up to the people of each country to shape their own destiny; outsiders should rarely interfere, however terrible the civil strife. I hope the peoples of the Middle East will learn from these polarization experiences to be wary of entrusting the future of their countries to the vagaries of majoritarian democracy, but also to resist moves by politically displaced minorities to plot their return to power by relying on antidemocratic tactics, coalitions with the military, and the complicity of the deep state. There is no single template. Turkey, although threatened by polarization, has been able to contain its most dire threats to political democracy. Egypt has not been so lucky. For simplistic comparison, Turkey has had the benefits of a largely evolutionary process that allows for a democratic political culture to take hold at the societal and governmental levels. Egypt, in contrast, has experienced abrupt changes in a setting of widespread economic distress and a form of polarization that denied all legitimacy to the antagonist, making the armed forces into a friend of the opposition because it was the enemy of their enemy. If this be democracy, then authoritarianism may not be the worst of all possible worlds in every circumstance.

Two Forms of Lethal Polarization

November 17, 2013[13]

It can be tempting to suggest that political life in both Turkey and Egypt is being victimized by a similar deepening of polarization between Islamic and secular orientations. To some extent this is true, but it is also misleading. Turkey continues to be victimized by such a polarization, especially during the eleven years the AKP has governed the country, and arguably more so in the latest period. In Egypt, "polarization" hardly describes the far more lethal form its political cleavage has taken. It has become an overt struggle for the control of the political destiny of the country being waged between the Egyptian armed forces and the Muslim Brotherhood, the two organized political forces capable of projecting their influence throughout the entire country, including rural areas. This bitter struggle in Egypt engages religious orientations on both sides; even the military leadership and upper echelons of the armed forces are observant Muslims, in some cases extremely devout adherents of Salafi belief and practice.

In effect, at this point, there is not a distinctly secular side that can be associated with post-coup Egyptian leadership under the caretaker aegis of the armed forces, although clearly most of the liberal, secular urban elite and many of the left activists sided with the military's moves, at least initially. Recent reports suggest more and more defections, although the price for making such a change of heart public can be high. For General el-Sisi the essence of the conflict seems to be between what is irresponsibly alleged to be a "terrorist" opposition—which has been broadened somewhat to extend beyond the Muslim Brotherhood to whomever dares question the tactics or intentions of the new leadership—and political forces supposedly committed to a democratic future for the country on the other. If the core of the opposition can be effectively portrayed as terrorists in this post–9/11 world, then criminalizing their activities and organization and neglecting their rights will seem prudent, even a necessary ingredient of national security, to many.

The Egyptian state-controlled media, along with the mainstream media in the West, has so far allowed the Egyptian post-coup leadership to get away, literally, with murder! Governments have also indirectly endorsed this sort of distorted presentation of the conflict, which has, somewhat surprisingly, achieved strong backing throughout the Arab world, with a few notable exceptions. Among the grossest distortions are the unchallenged depiction of the Muslim Brotherhood as purveyors of violence, given that the organization renounced violence after 1978 and has generally maintained such a

---

13. http://richardfalk.wordpress.com/2013/11/17/two-forms-of-lethal-polarization.

posture despite decades of suppression and provocation by Mubarak's government, and more recently by the forces arrayed against it. It should also be appreciated that Morsi's clear counsel to his followers from the time of the coup was to insist on the legitimacy of the elected government and to resist the claims of the post-coup leadership, but to do so nonviolently.

It is important to understand that neither the Egyptian nor Turkish experience of polarization has been a symmetrical process. In each instance, the side that is fairly beaten by democratic procedures, especially elections, refuses to accept the implications of political defeat. Rather than form a responsible opposition with an alternative political program, such an embittered opposition has taken recourse to extraconstitutional means to regain power and strives to justify such extremist advocacy and initiatives by demonizing its adversary, especially the leader. In contrast, the side that enjoys democratic legitimacy relies on its right to govern, and sometimes on its performance, to justify retaining governing authority. There is no doubt that Morsi was in a radically different position than Erdoğan after his narrow electoral victory in 2012—with an economy on a downward slippery slope, a public with high expectations of a post-Mubarak change for the better, and a complete lack of governing experience.

This phenomenon of polarization is becoming more widespread, an expression of growing alienation within societies as a response to disappointment with traditional political parties and leaders. As dissatisfaction and frustration with prevailing forms of governance grow in many countries, opposition movements become ever more embittered and tend to blame the elected leader with venomous rhetoric. Often such excessive attacks provoke a government response that further discredits the leader in the eyes of the opposition, widening the gap between those governing and those in the opposition. If the angered opposition senses it cannot win at the ballot box, it will be tempted to mobilize a populist politics in the street—and sometimes it manages to enlist those parts of government bureaucracy (often the judiciary and security forces) aligned, openly or secretly, with efforts to create crises of legitimacy and governance.

From such a combustible mix come explosive possibilities on both sides, ranging from coups to authoritarian abandonment of democratic procedures. Each side produces a self-serving narrative of national survival that shifts the blame entirely to its political enemy. There is no effort at dialogue, which is essential for the political health of a democratic society beset by serious challenges and policy disagreements. This does not mean the two sides are equally persuasive, but it does suggest that few informed and judicious voices can be heard above the noise of the fray.

Outsiders also complicate the scene, whether they favor the government or the opposition. Each unique national situation must be taken into account. There are many variables, including history, culture, geography, stage of development, economic performance, levels of unemployment and poverty, quality of governance, role of violence, respect for human rights and the rule of law, and degrees of corruption. Yet, at the same time, there are patterns and transnational similarities that make certain regional generalizations illuminating.

Comparing Turkey and Egypt suggests this broader regional, indeed global, pattern of polarization that is undermining political discourse in more and more countries. The Turkish political scene is still very much shaped by the lingering, socially constructed, and politically maintained legacy of Kemal Atatürk and his radical modernization project, which sought a total eclipse of Turkey's Ottoman past. This endeavor, although highly influential, never completely succeeded in creating a post-Islamic normative order, although it did manage to produce a highly secularized and Europeanized upper middle class in the main cities in western Turkey that clings fiercely and rather sadly, with its own unacknowledged religious intensity, to the outmoded Kemalist legacy as the only usable past.

In Atatürk's defense as a historical figure, it should be remembered that the challenges facing Turkey after World War I were primarily to create a strong unified state out of the ruins of the Ottoman Empire while withstanding the European imperial ambitions rampant elsewhere in the region. Turkey's defeat of colonial ambitions was spectacular, but it led to a dysfunctional form of hypernationalism that had three prominent features: an attempted erasure of minority identities, a discriminatory insistence on confining religious values and practices to private space/beliefs that particularly victimized Turkish women, and a deferential mimicry of Europe (especially France) in its construction of a secular polity.

Each of these undertakings, over time, generated strong forms of resistance that could never be fully overcome. Minority identities were not extinguished, especially for the large and diverse Kurdish minority; Islamic political orientations did not disappear and kept seeking limited acceptance in public space; and the European model never won the allegiance of the Turkish masses. What did occur in Turkey until the end of the twentieth century was political domination by secular elites relying on the mantle of Kemalist legitimacy, with power bases in the main cities and total control of the bureaucratic structures of Turkish governance, including a crucial alliance between the civilian secular leadership and the armed forces. As a left challenge of a Marxist character emerged after World War II, secular control was sustained by a series of military coups to make sure that capitalist ideology was not frontally challenged. The Cold War pushed Turkey to adopt an anticommunist foreign policy of a distinctly Western direction. It was made responsible for the vital southern flank of NATO, and seemed to follow Washington's geopolitical line without dissent.

What happened after the Cold War ended was a growing populist rejection of the societal structures of Kemalist Turkey without yet daring to make any direct and explicit challenge to the legacy. Kemalism was merely circumvented and adapted to a new set of conditions and social priorities without ever being confronted. The AKP's ascent in the 2002 elections, a result reinforced by larger victories in 2007 and 2011, achieved a sea change in the tone and substance of state/society relations in Turkey. It came about in stages and may yet be reversed when new elections are held in 2015. There was Kemalist resistance from the outset: fears that Turkey was on its way to becoming a "second Iran." When such fears failed to materialize or to erode pro-AKP support, there occurred a variety of coup plots that never came to fruition, largely because the neoliberal economy was flourishing, the AKP was cautious and pragmatic in its early years of leadership, the secularist "deep state" remained a brake on governance by the elected leaders, and the West, especially the United States, was eager to show the Islamic world that it could have a positive relationship with a government that did not hide the devout Muslim convictions of its principal leaders.

The dynamics of polarization are such that when the opposition's electoral prospects are perceived to diminish, the opposition, especially if it formerly controlled the state, grows angry and impatient with the workings of constitutional democracy and explores other ways to regain control of the state, opting for populist forms of protest and democratic accountability that it had earlier ruthlessly suppressed.

In the Turkish case, opposition tactics along these lines were surprisingly unsuccessful in the first decade of the twenty-first century, although a number of unstable contingencies contributed to the avoidance of a coup. Such frustration over a decade, even accompanied by impressive economic growth statistics and diplomatic prominence, did not lead the old Kemalist forces to acquiesce to the new political order. Instead, they only enraged the opposition. These intensified frustrations, which brought anti-AKP resentment to a fever pitch, were directed especially at the charismatic, populist, impulsive, and provocative prime minister, Recep Tayyip Erdoğan, a man who evokes the strongest passions of love and hate. Erdoğan shows why democracy is at risk from above and below in Turkey. The government has ample grounds to feel threatened by the tactics, extremism, invective, and hostility of the opposition, which does not even bother to hide its contempt for democratic procedures. In turn, the leadership, especially given

Erdoğan's brand of highly unpredictable emotional politics, strays from democratic procedures itself, partly as an understandable defensive reflex. It has grounds to view the opposition as illegitimate, including its most vituperative media critics, which can easily slide into the embrace of a kind of defensive authoritarianism.

Egypt's descent into the vortex of hyperpolarization has certain resemblances to the Turkish experience, but also significant differences other than the relationship of contending forces to the poles of religion and secularism. In effect, secularism isn't really a pole in Egypt but at most one of the constituencies anti-Morsi forces mobilized in the pre-coup period. Many secularists might not even have realized that by opposing the Muslim Brotherhood they were opting for the restoration of a brutal regime like Mubarak's, which seemed to have alienated virtually the whole of the country during the excitement of the January 25 movement in 2011. At that time, the armed forces were seen as standing aside while the Egyptian masses cast off a cruel and corrupt dictatorship that had reduced them to subjugation and collective misery. In retrospect, this was an optical illusion: the armed forces seemed willing to let Mubarak go to avoid having his possibly reformist son become the next leader but was not at all ready to transform the governing process of the country—despite the overwhelming mandate to do just that. It now seems clear that the Egyptian military would struggle against any political developments that threatened control of its budget, regulated its business activities, or restricted its discretion to manage the security policies of the Egyptian state (in collaboration with internal police and intelligence forces).

Against this background, including the structural problems Mubarak's neoliberal approach to development generated, the Muslim Brotherhood would have been wise to abide by its initial public pledge to not field a candidate for the presidency and to limit its electoral ambitions. Possibly, sensing its popularity as a transitory opportunity in a fluid situation and maybe deceptively encouraged by the SCAF, the MB thought it was entitled to compete for leadership to the full extent of its popularity. Its years of community organizing and welfare services paid off in parliamentary results far in excess of what had been predicted. It seemed to be a mandate to lead the country, but there also seemed to be a series of insurmountable challenges that were unlikely to be met, whoever gained controlled of the government.

When it became clear that the MB was stronger than expected and would not limit its goals, much of the liberal anti-Mubarak opposition panicked. The prospect of living under a MB government induced many Egyptians to swing back to the Mubarak side, leading Ahmed Shafik, a *fulool* mainstay, to win almost 50 percent of the vote in the June 2012 runoff election. It was a defeat, but considering the near-zero support for the old established order in the heady days of Tahrir Square, this result suggested a dramatic reversal of political mood, at least in the urban centers of Egypt. Shafik's near-victory should have been interpreted as a signal that counterrevolutionary tremors would soon begin to shake the foundations of political stability in Egypt. Polarization took multiple forms in the ensuing months, with Morsi faltering as a leader, partly for failures of his own making, and the opposition stridently insisting that things were out of control, worse than the worst times under Mubarak. There was also evidence that, to mobilize the populace, the opposition had orchestrated fuel shortages and food price hikes, eroding Morsi's image as someone who could lead post-Mubarak Egypt into better times. The outcome, perhaps exaggerated in the media, was a huge mobilization of anti-Morsi forces that produced the largest public demonstrations in Egyptian history and set the stage for the July 3 takeover. July 3 gave the armed forces a blank check to do whatever they wanted to do, including, if necessary, eliminating the MB (a third of the populace) from the political scene. What followed was a series of massacres and abuses of state power on a scale that would have shocked the conscience of humanity if it had been reported to the world in an honest and responsible fashion. Instead, what appear to be a series of thinly disguised crimes against humanity of a severe character were swept under the rug of world public opinion; the new regime received financial and diplomatic support and many diverse wishes for success.

When a polarized opposition resorts to unlawful means to regain or seize power, the nature of the regional and global response can be critical to its success or failure. There were strong geopolitical incentives for welcoming the Egyptian coup—and thus not complaining too much about its bloody aftermath. There are less clear reasons to favor the defeat of the AKP government in Turkey, especially given its role in NATO and the world economy, as well as the absence of a responsible and credible opposition, yet there are regional and global actors who would greet the fall of the AKP with smiles of satisfaction.

In these instances, polarization amounts to a deadly virus that attacks the body politic in countries with weak constitutional traditions, especially if they are beset by economic disappointment and significant regional and global hostility due to ideological and political tensions. So far, Turkey's immune system has been strong enough to neutralize the virus, while Egypt, having virtually no protection against it, has succumbed. If there is hope for a brighter Egyptian future, it will become evident in the months ahead, as the Egyptian body politic seeks belatedly to destroy the virus threatening its quality of life. For Turkey, the future remains clouded in comparable uncertainty; it may be that polarized alienation, combined with the mistakes associated with too long a tenure in office, will yet lead to the democratic downfall of Erdoğan and the AKP.

2

Egypt

I had the opportunity to visit Egypt shortly after the dramatic Tahrir Square uprising in early 2011 that caused the downfall of the authoritarian leader, Hosni Mubarak, who had ruled Egypt for thirty years. I visited twice more, at eight-month intervals, during 2012. It was evident, as I talked with a wide range of Egyptians from many sectors of society, that an economic and political downward spiral was taking place before my eyes. This process was accelerating, leading the lofty expectations, hopes, and dreams so prevalent in the period immediately following the overthrow of Mubarak to disappear. What remained was a toxic atmosphere of enmity, distrust, tension, and confrontation.

Above all, it became evident that the unexpected electoral and popular strength of the Muslim Brotherhood (MB) was unwelcome among large segments of Egyptian public opinion, especially in Cairo. This reaction was reinforced by the morning-after realization among the poor and urban business and tourist sectors that, despite their original excitement about the uprising, it was not bringing about any material benefits. Instead, most Egyptians faced a deteriorating standard of living. The economy was stagnating, the old oligarchs were still in control, and tourists were staying away from the country because of its perceived unrest. These tendencies seemed further strengthened by the opposition and by the intense concerns of the Gulf monarchies and Israel about the prospect that popular elections would produce an Islamoriented government. Bottom-up politics, especially those with an Islamic edge, are anathema to the Gulf monarchs, who fear that any formation of political Islam in the greater Middle East whose strength rests on popular support and a democratic mandate could threaten the stability of their top-down, Islam-oriented structure of governance and privilege.

This national and regional dynamic culminated in the victory of Mohamed Morsi, the default candidate of the Muslim Brotherhood, in a runoff election for the Egyptian presidency in June of 2012. The armed forces reluctantly certified the outcome after tense days of suspense. What set off alarm bells in my head at the time was the closeness of the vote (51.7 percent to 48.3 percent), considering that Morsi's runoff opponent was Ahmed Shafik, an overt product of the Mubarak era whose campaign promised to restore the old order, openly rejecting the vision of a new Egypt that had animated the spirit of Tahrir Square. It was evident that apprehension about a Brotherhood presidency had persuaded many supporters of the overthrow of Mubarak to vote for Shafik as the lesser evil.

As the posts in this section increasingly reflect, I believe that Morsi was given a mission impossible. His success as a leader depended on a cooperative public, an obedient judiciary, and a supportive international political environment. None of these conditions existed. At the same time, I expected Morsi and the Brotherhood to respond more skillfully to this admittedly difficult situation, moving cautiously on such agenda items as drafting a constitution or implementing Islam-oriented social policies and doing a better job of coopting the more liberal elements in the opposition. I also hoped that this elected leadership would create more public understanding of the difficulties of the transition period, including Washington's ambivalence and Tel Aviv's outright hostility. I was suspicious about what to expect from the armed forces, but I shared the common Egyptian perception that the armed forces and the Brotherhood had worked out a bargain of mutual forbearance. This seems to have been true in the early months of the Morsi presidency, but as public unhappiness with the political and economic status quo grew month by month in 2012 and became a strong national movement in the beginning of 2013, the leadership of the Egyptian armed forces clearly began to side with the street demonstrations against the government.

During my last visit to Cairo, in early December 2012, the handwriting was clearly written on the wall. Morsi's rule was increasingly challenged by more and more organized opposition forces, bolstered by strong support from the Coptic minority. In retrospect, it was a tragic error for the MB to withdraw its original pledge in 2011 not to compete for some of the seats in the Egyptian Parliament or put forward a candidate for the presidency. If it had held back, allowing someone from the old Cairo secular establishment to lead the country during the transition period, it would almost certainly have avoided the bloody counterrevolutionary campaign designed to criminalize its leaders and destroy its organized presence. The crackdown started in mid-2013 and continues to the present, spreading beyond the Brotherhood to all social forces that dare to challenge the Sisi leadership in any way.

Of course, it is always somewhat problematic to assess tactics after the fact, especially as other considerations likely influenced the MB to seek as much political power as the Egyptian public would confer via the five competitive elections in 2011 and 2012, including the fear that its organizational strength and grassroots popularity would not last. It was understandable to believe that after enduring decades of repression, this was the Brotherhood's moment and if it was allowed to pass, another chance to govern might never return. Its leaders might have sincerely felt that passivity at such a moment, when the people supported their political aspirations and outlook, would have been interpreted by many as a betrayal of public sentiment damaging to their reputation.

What remains obscure and highly contested is the nature of the MB as a political actor: whether it was as moderate and accommodationist as it claimed or as extremist as its critics contend; whether its heavy-handed, exclusionary, and sectarian style of governance produced the coup that brought General Abdel-Fattah el-Sisi to power, or if this merely provided a pretext for a power play. Several features of the situation are not in doubt:

- That the MB was politically inexperienced and could not fulfill the expectations of those who supported Mubarak's overthrow, especially those who hoped for improvements in their material situation and a quick revival of the Egyptian economy.
- That the Gulf monarchies, especially Saudi Arabia and the United Arab Emirates (UAE), were deeply threatened by the popularity of the MB; that the liberal, anti-Mubarak secular forces that had originally supported the overthrow had seriously underestimated the MB's level of populist strength and, when it became evident, switched sides and were joined by the leadership of the Egyptian armed forces, Copts, the mainstream media, and most of the business community.
- That this anti-Morsi coalition acted to create a crisis of legitimacy in the months leading up to the July 3, 2013, coup, including manipulating fuel and food prices and supplies to convince the Egyptian public that the Morsi government was leading the country to collapse.
- That the 2011 upheaval had left the Mubarak bureaucracy in place, including the judiciary and intelligence service, which meant that the Egyptian public sector remained overwhelmingly committed to restoring secular authoritarian governance and hence to obstructing Morsi's attempt to govern.

After the Sisi coup, the Gulf monarchies immediately bestowed large infusions of cash upon the new leadership, and the fuel and food shortages immediately disappeared. It seems there was a genuine populist turn toward the armed forces as the failures of MB governance had generated widespread disillusionment. In this atmosphere there emerged a broadly shared sense among Egyptians that they must choose between a military authoritarian order and an Islamically administered, repressive chaos. In effect, it seemed that the only choices were rule by the military or by the MB. The folk wisdom of the Arab world came to the surface during this anti-Morsi movement in the form of a widely quoted proverb: "The people prefer a hundred years of tyranny to a single year of chaos." It seems also that most of the region was willing to support the new Sisi leadership for strategic reasons, as was the United States, despite Sisi's ruthless moves against the constitutional order, mass atrocities against Brotherhood followers and leaders, and punitive moves against political activists who took to the streets to oppose this restoration of authoritarianism. Part of fuel for the anti-Morsi bonfire came from the stalled economy, for which the MB was held responsible, although it is doubtful whether any leadership could have done much better.

The Egyptian experience epitomizes the difficulties of achieving a smooth transition from authoritarian forms of government to inclusive constitutional democracy, as accentuated by an economic situation stressed by mass unemployment, corruption, and severe inequalities. The intense polarization in Egypt, which was reinforced by the anxieties of a vulnerable and influential Coptic minority, suggests two complementary conclusions: that the MB and Islam-oriented political parties enjoyed sufficient grassroots support to win the first series of free elections decisively and that, at the same time, such an outcome proved unacceptable to those Egyptians who feared and loathed the prospect of a religiously oriented leadership, perhaps more so because it enjoyed electoral approval. Egypt became a battleground between secularism and political Islam in which democracy was the loser. If this overall interpretation is generally accurate, it raises doubts as to whether democratization is a viable option not only for Egypt but for many countries in the region. Only Turkey and Tunisia seem so far to be navigating the precarious path of combining political stability, credible economic performance, and some endorsement of Islamic values (within an avowed secular and pluralist constitutional framework) with a functioning, although blemished, democratic system of government.

The Egyptian developments are now being assessed in light of the emergence of ISIS as the primary threat to regional order and Western interests and values. In such a context, so long as the government in Cairo can maintain domestic order, few questions will be asked about encroachments on human rights and abandonment of democratizing progress. ISIS also has fanned the flames of Islamophobia in the West more than any development since the 9/11 attacks in 2001, giving rise to dangerous contentions that the West is at war with Islam which, if not counteracted, could become self-fulfilling.

At the time of high hopes in 2011, many argued that what had taken place was irreversible, that the long-oppressed Arab masses had broken the chains of fear once and for all, and that "a new subjectivity" was coming into being among the people of the greater Middle East. It is too soon to tell whether this was wishful thinking. It may overlook the degree to which the purveyors of authoritarianism have also learned from their failures and, given the chance, can instill politically paralyzing fear through even greater reliance on state terror. The West took several centuries to establish reasonably reliable institutions of accountable government during periods of normalcy, though the slow process included several terrible regressions. The European uprising of 1848 has been compared to the Arab Spring, and its counterrevolutionary sequels seem to parallel what has happened in Egypt in recent years. Yet this was not the end of the story; democracies did, in the end, emerge in Europe, although slowly.

The achievements of democratic governance in Europe and North America continue to be periodically tarnished during times of economic and political crisis, as reactions to the 9/11 attacks in the United States illustrate. These secular democracies also proved vulnerable to the rise of fascism, showing that their institutions were catastrophically reversible given certain severe domestic challenges. Each historical situation is unique, so we must wait and see whether there will be further reactions to the Egyptian currently disappointing rollback of the Arab Spring. What we can say is that Egypt, more than any other country in the Arab world, is a political weathervane whose behavior is regionally influential beyond its borders, for better and for worse.

Egypt's Transformative Moment: Revolution, Counterrevolution, or Reform

February 4, 2011[1]

Since the fall of the Berlin Wall in 1989, four transformative events have reshaped the global setting in enduring ways. When the Soviet empire collapsed two years later, the way was opened for the triumphalist pursuit of the American imperial project. The United States seized the opportunity for geopolitical expansion, proclaiming its self-anointed global leadership as "the sole surviving superpower." This first rupture in the character of world order produced a decade of ascendant neoliberal globalization in which state power was temporarily and partially eclipsed by the oligarchs of Davos who met annually to shape global policy under the banner of the World Economic Forum. The U.S. government became the well-subsidized sheriff of predatory globalization while bankers and corporate executives set the policy agenda. Although it is not often stated, the 1990s provided the first evidence of the rise of nonstate actors and the decline of state-centric geopolitics.

The second rupture came with the 9/11 attacks. The impact of the attacks transferred the locus of policymaking authority back to the United States as state actor, under the rubrics of "the war on terror," "global security," and "the long war." This counterterrorist response to 9/11 produced arguments for preemptive warfare (the "Bush Doctrine"). This militarist foreign policy was put into practice in March 2003, when the United States initiated a "shock and awe" war against Iraq despite the refusal of the UN Security Council to back its plans. This second rupture turned the entire world into a potential battlefield, with the United States launching a variety of overt and covert military and paramilitary operations without appropriate authorization from the UN or deference to international law. Aside from this disruption of the liberal international order, the continuing pattern of securitizing responses to 9/11 involves disregard for the sovereign rights of states in the global South. Many states in Europe and the Middle East have also been complicit in violating basic human rights, including torture and "extreme rendition" of terrorism suspects and providing "black sites" where persons deemed hostile to the United States are detained, interrogated, and tortured. The neoconservative ideologues who rose to power during the Bush presidency seized upon 9/11 to enact their pre-attack grand strategy of "regime change" in the Middle East, starting with Iraq, which they portrayed as "low-hanging fruit" that would

---

1. https://richardfalk.wordpress.com/2011/02/04/
   egypt's-transformative-moment-revolution-counterrevolution-or-reform.

have multiple benefits once picked: military bases, lower energy prices, oil supplies, regional hegemony, promoting Israeli regional goals.

The third rupture involves the continuing, deep worldwide economic recession that started in 2008 and has produced a widespread rise in unemployment, declining living standards, and rising costs for basic necessities, especially food and fuel. These developments have illustrated the inequities, abuses, and deficiencies of neoliberal globalization but have not led to regulations designed to even out the gains from economic growth, avoid market abuses, or even guard against periodic market collapses. This deepening crisis of world capitalism is not currently being addressed; alternative visions, even the revival of a Keynesian approach, have little political backing. This crisis has also exposed the European Union's vulnerability, given varying national capabilities to deal with these challenges. All of these economic concerns are complicated and intensified by the advent of human-induced global warming and its dramatically uneven impacts.

A fourth rupture in global governance is associated with the unresolved turmoil in the Middle East and North Africa. The mass popular uprisings that started in Tunisia have provided the spark that set off fires elsewhere in the region, especially Egypt. These extraordinary challenges to the established order have vividly inscribed on the global political consciousness the courage and determination of ordinary people living in these Arab countries, especially youth, who have been enduring for their entire lives intolerable conditions of material deprivation, despair, alienation, elite corruption, and merciless oppression. The outcomes of these movements are not yet knowable and will not be for months, if not years, to come. It is crucial for supporters on the scene and around the world not to become complacent; it is certain that those with entrenched interests in the old oppressive and exploitative order are seeking to restore former conditions to the extent possible, or at least salvage what they can. In this regard, it would be a naïve mistake to think that transformative and emancipatory results can come from eliminating a single hated figure such as Ben Ali in Tunisia or Mubarak in Egypt, even if including their immediate entourage. Sustainable significant change requires a new political structure as well as a new process that ensures free and fair elections and adequate opportunities for popular participation. Real democracy must be substantive as well as procedural, bringing human security to the people, including providing for basic needs, decent work, and police who protect rather than harass. Otherwise, the changes wrought merely defer the revolutionary moment to a later day, and an ordeal of mass suffering will resume until that time comes.

To simplify, what remains unresolved is the fundamental nature of the outcome of these confrontations between the aroused populace of the region and state power, with its autocratic and neoliberal orientations. Will this outcome be transformative, bringing into being authentic democracy based on human rights and an economic order that puts the needs of people ahead of the ambitions of capital? If it is, then it will be appropriate to speak of the Egyptian Revolution, the Tunisian Revolution, and maybe others in the region and elsewhere to come, just as it was appropriate to describe the Iranian outcome in 1979 as the Iranian Revolution. From this perspective a revolutionary result may not necessarily be a benevolent outcome, beyond ridding the society of the old order. In Iran a newly oppressive regime resting on a different ideological foundation emerged (which was itself challenged after the 2009 elections by a popular movement calling itself the Green Revolution). So far this use of the word "revolution" expresses hopes for the Arab world rather than realities.

What has actually taken place in Iran, and what seemed to flow from the onslaught unleashed by the Chinese state in Tiananmen Square in 1989, was "counterrevolution"—that is, the restoration and reinforcement of the old order and the systematic repression of those identified as participants in the challenge. Actually, such words can be misleading. What most followers of the Green Revolution seemed to seek in Iran was reform, not revolution: that is, changes in personnel and policies and protection of human rights, not to the structure or constitution of the Islamic Republic.

It is unclear whether the movement in Egypt is at present sufficiently unified or reflective to have a coherent vision of its goals beyond getting rid of Mubarak. The state's response, besides trying to crush the uprising and banish media coverage, is to offer, at most, promises of reform: fairer and freer elections, respect for human rights. It is rather obscure about what this means and even more so about what will happen in the course of an "orderly transition" under the auspices of temporary leaders closely tied to the old regime, many of whom possess close links with Washington. Will a cosmetic agenda of reform hide the actuality of a politics of counterrevolution? Or will revolutionary expectations overwhelm the pacifying efforts of the "reformers"? Might there be a genuine mandate of reform, supported by elites and bureaucrats, enacting sufficiently ambitious changes in the direction of democracy and social justice to satisfy the public? Of course there is no assurance—or likelihood—that the outcomes will be the same or even similar in the various countries undergoing these dynamics of change. Some will see "revolution" where "reform" has taken place, and few will acknowledge the extent to which "counterrevolution" can break even modest promises of reform.

At stake, as it has not been since the collapse of the colonial order in the Middle East and North Africa, is the unfolding and shaping of self-determination in the entire Arab world, and possibly beyond.

How these dynamics will affect the broader regional agenda is not apparent at this stage, but there is every reason to suppose that the Israel–Palestine conflict will never be quite the same. It is also uncertain how such important regional actors as Turkey or Iran will deploy their influence (or not). And, of course, the behavior of the elephant not formally in the room, that is, the United States, is likely to be a crucial element in the mix for some time to come, for better or worse.

The Toxic Residue of Revolution: Protecting Interests, Disregarding Rights
February 8, 2011[2]

There has been no talk from either Washington or Tel Aviv, the governments with most to lose as the Egyptian Revolution unfolds, of military intervention—at least not overtly. Such restraint expresses geopolitical sanity more than postcolonial morality, but still it enables some measure of change to take place that unsettles the established political order at least temporarily. Yet by means seen and unseen, external actors are seeking to shape and limit the outcome of this extraordinary uprising of the Egyptian people, especially the United States, with its distinct blend of presumed imperial and paternal prerogatives. The most defining feature of this American-led diplomacy-from-without is the seeming propriety of *managing* the turmoil so that the regime survives and the demonstrators return to what is perversely being called "normalcy." I find it most astonishing that President Obama so openly claims the authority to instruct the Mubarak regime about how to respond to the revolutionary uprising. I am not surprised at the effort and would be surprised by its absence; I am only surprised by the lack of any sign of imperial shyness in a world order supposedly built around self-determination, national sovereignty, and democracy. Almost as surprising is Mubarak's public insistence that such interference in the guise of guidance is irrelevant to his leadership, even if behind closed doors he listens submissively and acts accordingly. The geopolitical theater performance of master and servant

---

2. http://richardfalk.wordpress.com/2011/02/08/
   the-toxic-residue-of-colonialism-protecting-interests-disregarding-rights.

suggests the persistence of a colonial mentality on the part of both colonizers and national collaborators.

The only genuinely postcolonial message would be one of deference: "Stand aside, and applaud." The great transformative struggles of the last century involved a series of challenges throughout the global South to get rid of the European colonial empires. But political independence did not bring an end to less direct, but still insidious, methods of control designed to protect economic and strategic interests. Such a geopolitical dynamic meant relying on political leaders who would sacrifice the well-being of their own people to serve the wishes of their unacknowledged former colonial masters or their Western successors (the United States having largely displaced France and the United Kingdom in the Middle East after the Suez Crisis of 1956). These postcolonial servants of the West are well-paid autocrats vested with virtual ownership rights to the indigenous wealth of their country, provided they remain receptive to foreign capital. In this regard the Mubarak regime was (and remains) a poster child of postcolonial success. Western liberal eyes have long been accustomed not to notice the internal patterns of abuse integral to this foreign policy success. If occasionally they are noticed by some intrepid journalist, he or she is then ignored or, if necessary, discredited as some sort of "leftist." If this fails to deflect criticism, the liberals point out, usually with a condescending smile, that torture and the like come with the Arab cultural territory, a reality to which savvy outsiders adapted without any discomfort. Actually, in this instance such practices were quite convenient, Egypt being one of the interrogation sites for the insidious practice of "extreme rendition," in which the CIA transports terror suspects to accommodating foreign countries that willingly provide torture tools and facilities. Is this what President Obama means by a "human rights presidency"? The irony should not be overlooked that his special envoy to the Mubarak government in the crisis was none other than Frank Wisner, an American with a most notable CIA lineage.

This kind of postcolonial state serves American regional interests (oil, Israel, containing Islam, avoiding unwanted nuclear proliferation) in exchange for vesting power, privilege, and wealth in a tiny, corrupt national elite that sacrifices the well-being and dignity of the national populace in the process. Such a structure in the postcolonial era, where national sovereignty and human rights infuse the popular consciousness, can only be maintained by erecting high barriers of fear, reinforced by state terror, that are designed to intimidate the populace from pursuing their goals and values. When these barriers are breached, as recently in Tunisia and Egypt, then the fragility of the oppressive regime is glaringly apparent. The dictator either runs for the nearest exit, as did Tunisia's Ben Ali, or is dumped by his entourage and foreign friends so that the revolutionary challenge can be tricked into a premature accommodation. This latter process seems to represent the latest maneuvers of the palace elite in Cairo and their backers in the White House. Only time will tell whether the furies of counterrevolution will win the day, possibly by gunfire and whip, possibly through mollifying gestures of reform that become unfulfillable if the old regime is not totally reconstructed—because corruption and gross disparities of wealth amid mass impoverishment can only be sustained, post-Tahrir Square, through reimposing oppressive rule. Without oppression it will not be able to withstand very long demands for rights, for social and economic justice, and, in due course, for solidarity with the Palestinian struggle.

Here is the crux of the ethical irony. Washington respects the logic of self-determination so long as it converges with American grand strategy, and is oblivious to the will of the people whenever it sees such expression as a threat to the neoliberal overlords of the globalized world economy or the strategic alignments so dear to State Department and Pentagon planners. As a result the United States tries to bob and weave, celebrating the advent of democracy in Egypt and complaining about the violence and torture of the tottering regime while doing what it can to manage the process from outside—which means preventing genuine change, much less a democratic transformation of the Egyptian state. Anointing the CIA's main contact person, Mubarak loyalist Omar Suleiman, to preside over the transition process on behalf of Egypt seems a thinly disguised plan to throw Mubarak to the crowd while stabilizing the regime he presided over for more than thirty years. I would have expected more subtlety on the part of the geopolitical managers, but perhaps its absence is one more sign of the imperial myopia that so often accompanies the decline of great empires.

It is notable that most protesters, when asked why they risk death and violence in the Egyptian streets, respond with variations on "We want our rights" or "We want freedom and dignity." Of course joblessness, poverty, food insecurity, and anger at the corruption, abuses, and dynastic pretensions of the Mubarak regime offer an understandable infrastructure of rage that undoubtedly fuels the revolutionary fires, but it is rights and dignity that seem to float to the surface of this awakened political consciousness. These ideas, which are to a large extent nurtured in the hothouse of Western liberal consciousness and then innocently exported as a sign of goodwill, much like "nationalism" a century earlier, might originally be intended only as public relations, but over time such ideas gave rise to the dreams of the oppressed and victimized and, when the unexpected historical moment finally arrives, burst into flames. I remember talking a decade or so ago to Indonesian radicals in Jakarta, who spoke of the extent to which their initial involvement in anticolonial struggle had been stimulated by what they had learned from their Dutch colonial teachers about the rise of nationalism as a political ideology in the West.

Ideas may be disseminated with conservative intent, but if they are later appropriated on behalf of the struggles of oppressed peoples, they are reborn and serve as the underpinnings of a new emancipatory politics. Nothing better illustrates this Hegelian journey than the idea of "self-determination," initially proclaimed by Woodrow Wilson after World War I. Wilson sought above all to maintain order, believed in satisfying the aims of foreign investors and corporations, and had no complaints about the European colonial empires. For him, self-determination was merely a convenient means to arrange the permanent breakup of the Ottoman Empire into a series of ethnic states. Little did Wilson imagine, despite warnings from his secretary of state, that self-determination could serve other gods and become a powerful mobilizing tool to overthrow colonial rule. In our time the idea of human rights has followed a similarly winding path: sometimes no more than propaganda to taunt enemies during the Cold War, sometimes a convenient hedge against imperial identity, and sometimes the foundation of revolutionary zeal, as seems to be the case in the struggles for rights and dignity taking place throughout the Arab world.

It is impossible to predict how this future will play out. There are too many forces at play in circumstances of radical uncertainty. In Egypt, for instance, it is widely believed that the army holds most of the cards and that where it finally decides to put its weight will determine the outcome. But is such conventional wisdom not just one more sign that hard-power realism dominates our imagination, and that historical agency belongs in the end to the generals and their weapons and not to the people in the streets? Of course, the army could be merely trying to go with the flow, siding with the winner once the outcome seems clear. Is there any reason to rely on the wisdom, judgment, and goodwill of armies, not just in Egypt, where the commanders owe their positions to Mubarak, but throughout the world? In Iran the army did stand aside and a revolutionary process transformed the Shah's edifice of corrupt and brutal governance; the people momentarily prevailed, only to have their extraordinary, nonviolent victory snatched away in a subsequent counterrevolutionary move that substituted theocracy for democracy. There are few instances of revolutionary victory; in those few instances, it is rarer still to carry forward the revolutionary mission without disruption. The challenge is to sustain the revolution in the face of almost inevitable counterrevolutionary projects, some launched by those who were part of the earlier movement against the old order but are now determined to hijack the victory for their own ends. The complexities of the revolutionary moment require utmost vigilance on the part of those who view emancipation, justice, and democracy as their animating ideals, because there will be enemies who seek to seize power at the expense of humane politics. One of the most impressive features of the Egyptian Revolution up to this point has been the massed demonstrators' extraordinary ethos of nonviolence and solidarity, even in the face of repeated, bloody provocations by the regime's *baltagiyya* (paid government thugs). We can only hope against hope that the provocations will cease and that counterrevolutionary tides will subside, sensing the futility of assaulting history or imploding at long last.

What Is Winning?
The Next Phase for the Revolutionary Uprisings

February 24, 2011[3]

Early in the Tunisian and Egyptian uprisings it seemed that the demonstrators understood winning to mean getting rid of the hated leaders Ben Ali and Mubarak. But as the process deepened it became clear that they demanded and expected more, and that this had to do with restoring the material and spiritual dignity of life in all its aspects.

"Winning" is likely to mean different things in the various countries currently in turmoil. But at the very least winning has so far meant challenging the oppressive established order by determined and incredibly brave nonviolence. This victory over long reigns of fear-induced pacification is itself a great transformative moment in twenty-first-century history, no matter what happens in the months ahead.

As Chandra Muzaffar, the widely respected Malaysian scholar of religion and justice, compelling argues, replacing the old order by electoral democracy, while impressive given the dictatorial rule of the past, will not be nearly enough to vindicate the sacrifices of the protestors. It is significantly better than the worst-case scenarios of "Mubarakism without Mubarak," which would change the faces and names of the rulers but leave the oppressive and exploitative regimes essentially intact. This would definitely be a pyrrhic victory, given the hopes and demands that motivated the courageous demonstrators to withstand without weapons the clubs, rubber bullets, live ammunition, and overall brutality, without knowing what the

---

3. http://richardfalk.wordpress.com/2011/02/24/
what-is-winning-the-next-phase-for-the-revolutionary-uprisings.

soldiers in the streets would do when the beleaguered old guard ordered them to open fire.

What is needed, beyond constitutional democracy, is good and equitable governance: this includes, above all, people-oriented economic policies, an end to corruption, and the protection of human rights, especially economic and social rights. Such an indispensable agenda recognizes that many of the demonstrators were motivated by their totally alienating entrapment in a jobless future combined with the daily struggle to obtain the bare necessities of a tolerable life.

Present here are questions of domestic political will and of the government's capability to redirect productive resources and distributive policies. How much political space is available to alter the impositions of neoliberal globalization, which are responsible for reinforcing, if not inducing, the world economy's grossly inequitable and corrupting effects, resulting in regimes of domestic privilege and deprivation? Not far in the background is an extended global recession that may deepen in coming months due to alarming increases in commodity prices, especially food. According to the UN Food and Agriculture Organization, the world Food Price Index reached a record high in December 2010, a level exceeded by another 3 percent rise in January of this year. Lester Brown, a leading expert on food and the environment, wrote a few days ago that "the world is now one poor harvest away from chaos in world grain markets."[4]

With political turmoil threatening world energy supplies, oil prices are also surging, which could further endanger the uneven, fragile economic recovery in the United States and Europe. Global warming adds a further troubling feature to this deteriorating situation, with droughts, floods, fires, and storms making it difficult to maintain crop yields, much less increase food production to meet the increasing demands of the world's growing population.

These realities will greatly complicate the already formidable difficulties facing new leaders throughout the Arab world who urgently seek to create job opportunities and provide affordable food supplies. This challenge is intensified by the masses' expectations of improved living circumstances: if the autocratic prior regime was responsible for the mass impoverishment of the many and the scandalously excessive enrichment of the few, is it not reasonable to suppose that more democratic successor governments should establish, without much delay, greatly improved living conditions? How can it be claimed that the heroic uprising was worthwhile if ordinary citizens' quality of life does not start improving dramatically almost immediately?

---

4. *International Herald Tribune*, February 23, 2011.

An understandably impatient public may not give new leaders the time they need, given these conditions, to make adjustments that will begin to satisfy these long-denied hopes and needs. Perhaps the public will be patient if there are clear signs that the leaders are trying their hardest, even if actual progress is slow. We need also to be aware that in the polarized conditions that exist in the region, opposition forces are determined to prevent those in office from gaining credibility with the citizenry by improving economic conditions.

Even if the public is patient beyond reason and understands better than can be prudently expected the difficulties of achieving economic justice during a period of transition to a new framework of governance, there may be still little or no capacity to fulfill such expectations due to worsening global conditions. It is quite possible that, if the worst food or energy scenarios unfold, famines and food riots could occur, casting dark shadows of despair across the memories of the historic victories that made the initial phases of each national uprising such a glowing testament to the human spirit, which seemed miraculously undaunted by decades of oppression and abuse.

It needs also to be kept in mind that the demonstrators' slogans have highlighted a thirst for freedom and rights. Even though there is little experience of democratic practice throughout the region, new governing institutions will likely make a serious attempt to distinguish themselves from their hated forebears and allow for all forms of oppositional activity, including freedom of expression, assembly, and party formation. Unlike the problems associated with creating jobs and providing for material needs, establishing the atmosphere of a free society is within the physical capacities of a new leadership if it has the political will to assume the unfamiliar risks associated with democratic practices. We must wait and see how each new leadership handles these normative challenges of transition and to what extent these are intensified by counterrevolutionary efforts to maintain or restore the old structures and privileges. These efforts are likely to be aided and abetted by a range of covert collaborative undertakings joining external actors with those internal forces threatened by impending political change.

If this overview was not discouraging enough, there is one further consideration. As soon as the unifying purpose of getting rid of the old leadership is eroded, if not altogether lost, fissures are certain to emerge within the former opposition movement. There will be fundamental differences between radical and liberal approaches to transition, especially whether to respect the property rights and social hierarchies associated with the old regime or to seek to correct the injustices and irregularities of the past directly. (Some critics of Nelson Mandela's approach to reconciliation and transition in South Africa believe that his acceptance of the social and economic dimensions of the repudiated apartheid structure have resulted in a widely felt sense of revolutionary disappointment, if not betrayal, in South Africa.)

There will also be tactical and strategic differences about how to deal with the world economy, especially with respect to creating stability and attractive conditions for foreign investment. Here tensions emerge between safeguarding labor rights and making investors feel that their operations will remain profitable in the new political environment.

Throughout the Arab world, in addition, there are deep cleavages relating to the proper role of religion and religious values in the public order of a national society and, more concretely, how to relate Islam to the governing process and to the regulation of social, cultural, and educational activities.

This recitation of difficulties is not meant to detract attention from or in any way diminish the glorious achievements of the revolutionary uprisings, but to point to the unfinished business that must be addressed if revolutionary aspirations are to avoid disillusionment. So often, revolutionary gains are blunted or even lost shortly after the old oppressors have been dragged from the stage of history. If ever there exists the need for vigilance, it is at these times when the old order is dying and the new order is struggling to be born. As Gramsci warned long ago, this period of in-between-ness is vulnerable to a wide range of predatory tendencies. It is a time when unscrupulous elements can repress anew even while waving a revolutionary banner and shouting slogans about defending the revolution against its enemies. Another difficulty here is that the enemies may well be real as well as darkly imagined. How many past revolutions have been lost due to the machinations of their supposed guardians?

Let us fervently hope that the mysteries of the digital age will somehow summon the creative energy to manage the transition to sustainable and substantive democracy as brilliantly as the revolutionary uprisings.

When Is an NGO Not an NGO?
Twists and Turns in the Cairo Sky

February 14, 2012[5]

A confusing controversy between the United States and Egypt has raised tensions between the two countries to a level that has not existed for decades. It results from moves by the temporary military government in Cairo to prosecute forty-three foreigners, including nineteen Americans, for unlawfully carrying on the work of unlicensed public-interest organizations that improperly, according to Egyptian law, depend for their budgets on foreign funding. The American press has made much of the fact that one of the Americans charged happens to be Sam LaHood, son of the present U.S. secretary of transportation, adopting a tone that seems to imply that one connected by blood to an important government official deserves immunity from prosecution.

Washington has responded with high-minded and high-profile expressions of consternation, including Hillary Clinton warning that Egypt's annual $1.5 billion aid package (of which $1.3 billion goes to the military) is in jeopardy unless the case is dropped and the organizations are allowed to carry on with their work of promoting democracy in Egypt. Congress may yet refuse to authorize the release of these funds unless the State Department is willing to certify that Egypt is progressing toward greater democratization. President Obama has indicated his intention to continue aid at past levels, given Egypt's importance in relation to U.S. interests in the Middle East, but as in so many other instances, he may give way if the pressure mounts. The outcome is not yet clear; an ultra-nationalistic Congress may yet thwart Obama's seemingly sensible response to what should have been treated as a tempest in a teapot but, for reasons to be discussed, has instead become a cause *célèbre*.

The Americans charged are on the payroll of three organizations: the International Republican Institute (IRI), the Democratic National Institute (DNI), and Freedom House. The first two organizations get all of their funding from the U.S. government. They were originally founded in 1983 after Ronald Reagan urged the British parliament to help build the democratic infrastructure of newly independent countries in the non-Western world, a Cold War countermeasure to the continuing appeal of Marxist ideologies. From the moment of their founding, IRI and DNI were lavishly funded by annual multimillion-dollar grants from Congress, either directly or by way of

---

5. http://richardfalk.wordpress.com/2012/02/14/
   when-is-an-ngo-not-an-ngo-twists-and-turns-beneath-the-cairo-skies.

such governmental entities as the U.S. Agency for International Development (USAID) and the National Endowment for Democracy (NED). The IRI and DNI claim to be nonpartisan, yet both are explicitly affiliated with the two dominant U.S. political parties, with boards, staffs, and consultants drawn overwhelmingly from former government workers and officials associated with these parties. The ideological and governmental character of the two organizations is epitomized by the nature of their leadership. Madeline Albright, Secretary of State during the Clinton presidency, is chair of the DNI board, while former Republican presidential candidate and current senator John McCain holds the same position in the IRI. Freedom House depends on the NED for more than 80 percent of its funding and is similarly rooted in American party politics, and earned a reputation based on its pro-West Cold War partisanship. It was founded in 1941 as a bipartisan initiative by two stalwarts of their respective political parties, Wendell Willkie and Eleanor Roosevelt.

Against this background, Washington's protests and the media assessments seem willfully misleading. Since when does Washington become so agitated on behalf of NGOs under attack in a foreign country? Even mainstream eyebrows should have been raised sky-high when Martin Dempsey, currently chairman of the Joint Chiefs of Staff, was reported to have interceded with his military counterparts on behalf of these Americans while visiting Cairo. When was the last time you can recall an American military commander interceding on behalf of a *genuine* NGO? To paraphrase Bob Dylan, "The answer, my friends, is never." Even the most naïve among us should be asking what is *really* going on here.

The NGOs' spokespeople are treating the allegations as a simple case of interference with the activities of apolitical, benevolent NGOs innocently engaged in helping Egyptians receive needed training and guidance with respect to democratic practices, especially those relating to elections and the rule of law. Substantively, such claims seem more or less true at present, at least here in Egypt. Sometimes the media even refer to these entities as "civil society institutions," which reflects at best a woeful state of unknowing or, worse, deliberate deception. Whatever one thinks of these actors, it is simply false to conceive of them as "nongovernmental" or as emanations of civil society. A more accurate descriptor would be "informal governmental organizations" (IGOs).

It is hardly surprising that a more honest label is avoided, as its use would call attention to the problematic character of the undertakings: namely, disguised intrusions by a foreign government into the internal politics of a foreign country with fragile domestic institutions, by way of behavior that poses, at the very least, a potential threat to that country's political independence.

With such an altered interpretation, the controversy assumes a different character. It becomes quite understandable why an Egyptian government seeking to move beyond its authoritarian past (coupled with geopolitical dependency) would feel the need to tame Washington's Trojan horses. It would seem sensible and prudent for Egypt to insist that such organizations, especially those associated with the U.S. government, be registered and properly licensed in Egypt as a minimum precondition for operating in the country, especially on matters as sensitive as elections, political parties, and shaping the legal system. Surely the United States, despite its long, uninterrupted, stable record of constitutional governance, would not even consider allowing such "assistance" from abroad. Such an offer from, say, Sweden, would be immediately rebuffed and rudely dismissed as an insult to the sovereignty of the United States.

Washington's shrieks of wounded innocence, as if Cairo had no grounds whatsoever for concern, are either the memory lapses of a senile bureaucracy or totally disingenuous. It is well documented that IRI and DNI have actively promoted the destabilization of foreign governments deemed hostile to what was then the American foreign policy agenda: Reagan made no secret of his commitment to supporting political movements dedicated to overthrowing left-leaning governments in Latin America and Asia. For instance, IRI distributed funds to anti-regime forces to get rid of the Aristide government in Haiti, part of a dynamic that led to the 2004 coup, which brought reactionary political forces to power that seemed far more congenial to Washington's ideas of "good governance" at the time.[6] IRI was also openly self-congratulatory about its role in strengthening "center and center-right" political parties in Poland several years ago, which amounts to a virtual confession of interference with the dynamics of Polish self-determination.[7]

Against such a background, several conclusions follow: first, these individuals are not working for genuine NGOs or civil society institutions but on behalf of informal government organizations, or IGOs; second, the specific organizations being targeted in Egypt, especially the DNI and IRI are overtly ideological in their makeup, funding base, and orientation; and third, non-Western governments have compelling reasons to regulate or exclude such political actors given the long American record

---

6. Walt Bogdanich and Jenny Nordberg, "Mixed U.S. Signals Helped Tilt Haiti Toward Chaos," *New York Times*, January 29, 2006, www.nytimes.com/2006/01/29/international/americas/29haiti.html.

7. International Republican Institute, "IRI in Poland," 2001, archived via Wayback Machine, http://web.archive.org/web/20051015103000/http://www.iri.org/countries.asp?id=8369274321.

of interventionary diplomacy. Thus the Washington posture of outrage seems entirely inappropriate once the actions of the Egyptian government are contextually interpreted.

Yet the full story is not so simple or one-sided. It needs to be remembered that the Egyptian governing process, in the year since the uprising, has been controlled by the Supreme Council of the Armed Forces (SCAF), widely believed to be responsible for a wave of repressive violence associated with its fears that some democratic demands threaten its position and interests. Severe abuses of civilians have been convincingly attributed to it. The military is also responsible for a series of harsh moves against bloggers and others who criticize military rule. The Egyptian government is itself seemingly disingenuous, using the licensing and funding technicalities of the NGOs as a pretext for a wholesale crackdown on dissent and human rights to discipline and intimidate a resurgent civil society and a radical opposition movement that remain committed to realizing the democratic promise of the Arab Spring.

There is another strange piece of the puzzle. The United States worked in close harmony with the Egyptian military during the Mubarak period. Why would it not welcome this apparent slide toward "Mubarakism without Mubarak"? Was this not America's preferred outcome all along, being the only outcome that would not rock the Israeli boat or otherwise disturb American interests in the region? Washington has not disclosed its motives at this time for this seemingly pro-democracy approach, but there are grounds for thinking it may be reacting to the electoral success of the Muslim Brotherhood and the Salafist Nour Party and these parties' apparent collaboration with the SCAF in planning Egypt's immediate political future. In such a setting, it seems plausible that sharpening state/society tensions in Egypt by siding with the democratic opposition would keep alive the possibility of a secular governing process that would be less threatening to U.S. and Israeli interests, as well as inducing Egypt itself to adopt a cautious approach to democratic reform. Maybe there are different explanations more hidden from view, but what seems clear is that both governments are fencing in the dark—that is, mounting arguments and counterarguments that obscure rather than reveal their true motivations.

In the end, Egypt, along with other countries, is likely to be far better off if it prohibits American IGOs from operating freely within its national territorial space, especially if their supposed mandate is to promote democracy as defined and funded by Washington. This is not to say that Egyptians would not be far better off if the SCAF allowed civilian rule to emerge in the country and respected human rights and democratic values. Both sides are relying on smokescreens that hide what is at stake in this seemingly trivia controversy: weighty matters of governance and democracy that could determine whether the remarkable glories of the Arab Spring give way to a dreary Egyptian autumn—or even winter.

Egypt between a Rock and a Hard Place
December 10, 2012[8]

I have visited Cairo three times in the last twenty months, the first a few weeks after the departure of Hosni Mubarak in 2011, the second in February 2012 when the revolutionary process was treading water, and this third one over the past ten days. The prevailing mood and expectations have drastically changed between these visits: fears, hopes, and perceptions have altered over time, and are likely to continue to do so.

The Overthrow of Mubarak

During my first visit, shortly after the extraordinary exploits in Tahrir Square, there was a spirit of stunned amazement that made it seem as though the Arab Spring was a genuine historical phenomenon of epic proportions and that Egypt had become the core site of a new post-Marxist radical politics that relied on militant nonviolence and a radical ethos of transformation, but avoided ideology and hard-power tactics. Gandhi and Gene Sharp were invoked as inspirational influences, not Lenin, Mao, or Castro. The uprising was being widely celebrated as a remarkable expression of democratic populism, especially the empowerment of youth and women, with social networking via the Internet accorded a special prominence during the popular mobilization process. The sentiment was summarized in different ways: "The impossible happened." "I never expected to experience this rising up of the people of Egypt." "We have our country back." "I have never been so proud to be an Egyptian." It was an upheaval with transformative potential, magnified and catalyzed by the Tunisian rising immediately prior, which exhibited what seemed to be an innovative form of largely nonviolent radical politics that almost miraculously wrote the script on the set of its unfolding, while occupying Tahrir Square along with other, less media-exposed Egyptian arenas of protest and opposition. (It also, not so incidentally, inspired the Occupy movements that spread around the world in the following months, with Occupy Wall Street as the appropriate epicenter.) It was treated as an amazing instance of "spontaneous empowerment" at the time, although more knowledgeable observers and participants tended to stress a cumulative process with distinct roots in

8. http://richardfalk.wordpress.com/2012/12/10/egypt-between-a-rock-and-a-hard-place.

reactions to prior abuses by the Mubarak police apparatus and in important labor protest strikes.

Of course, even during the afterglow, deep concerns lay just below the surface. Especially, young Egyptian activists whom I met in Cairo issued cautions about the lasting significance of what had taken place and skepticism as to whether the deeper challenges of poverty and class inequality could be effectively addressed without a more ambitious political process that challenged and dismantled the institutional infrastructure of the old regime. Many expressed doubts about whether it was enough to be rid of Mubarak and gave a range of opinions about what still needed to be done if Egypt was to find a path to sustainable and equitable social, economic, and political progress. This outlook was reinforced by the understanding that if forward momentum of this sort was not achieved post-Mubarak, the likely sequel would be regression. There was also widespread skepticism as to whether Egypt could solve the problems of democratic transition while also addressing the inequities and failures of its inherited neoliberal economy with related practices of crony capitalism. Such a challenge could only be met through a new economic order that was far more responsive to the needs of the Egyptian people and less hospitable to capitalist-style investment, a process that would certainly undermine investor confidence at least in the short run, within and without Egypt.

Egyptian friends expressed other concerns to me as well, including worries about what the United States—and Israel—might be doing or plotting behind the scenes to embolden the armed forces to move in counterrevolutionary directions and reverse an emancipatory process that might threaten the regional status quo. They were anxious that these outside forces, which had exerted such a strong influence on Egypt's former configurations of state power, would not give up their leverage without trying to restore the substance, if not the form, of the old, reliable order. It did seem at the time that democratizing forces in the country were almost certain to become hostile to the geopolitical arrangements Washington and Tel Aviv favored, and that these external forces' likely machinations threatened Egypt's political self-determination. At this stage, there was broad agreement that American support was one of the props of the discarded Mubarak leadership and that Egyptian democracy depended on curbing Washington's future influence.

There was also debate in early 2011 about three elements of the domestic political scene: whether the armed forces would facilitate or obstruct the establishment of a constitutional democracy in the country; how to permit the MB to participate in political life while avoiding allowing it to dominate the democratizing process; and who would carry the presidential torch across the finish line.

With respect to the MB, there was uncertainty and controversy as to the orientation of its leadership; some suggested intergenerational conflict between the traditionally conservative older generation and a more modern and moderate younger generation. There was also disagreement as to whether its Islamic orientation was insignificant, because its real goals were to promote private business interests and gain access to the commanding heights of governmental authority. The MB's support was estimated by intellectuals in Cairo at the time as somewhere between 25 and 30 percent; there was almost no mention at this stage of the Salafis as a political force to be reckoned with, and the liberal secular consensus was that it was fine for the MB to take part in the political process as long as its strength did not exceed those estimates; if it did, Egypt would be in deep trouble of a not clearly specified nature: a political process dominated by the MB, even if it came about democratically, was unacceptable for Egypt's urban elites. But such a prospect was widely dismissed as so unlikely as not to be worth discussing. Even before the elections revealed the MB's grassroots strength, there were some prophetic fears that majoritarian democracy was not a legitimate outcome for Egypt. In a way, the MB seemed at first to acquiesce in this understanding, signaling its agreement by pledging not to compete for the presidency, presumably to avoid threatening the ecumenical unity so powerfully displayed at Tahrir Square a few weeks earlier.

The balance of opinion I encountered in late February 2011 seemed to feel that an active role for the armed forces was necessary for any successful transition to constitutional democracy. The alternative was assumed to be a descent into societal chaos, followed by economic collapse. On the role of the armed forces in the upheaval, there were differing assessments, with some thinking that the military leadership had been eager to avoid a Mubarak dynasty and thus initially allowed, even welcomed, the popular rising to let the movement rid the country of the Mubarak factor rather than stage a coup on its own. Yet the military was certainly not willing to loosen its grip on the reins of power and privilege, including its major stake in the private-sector economy, and thus favored a rapid return to normalcy. The surviving military leadership remained tied to an authoritarian style of politics, which in effect meant business as usual from the perspective of Tahrir activists. Others in Egyptian civilian society were more hopeful, believing that the upper echelons of the military, while not revolutionary, shared the reformist goals of the uprising, favored constitutional reforms, and sought to withdraw as quickly as possible from the political arena, limiting its role to facilitating order during a transition to a law-based political democracy.

There were opposite worries, as well, in the afterglow of the Tahrir Square victories: above all, a sense among those who understood politics in a conventional Western liberal manner that this exciting movement lacked leadership, cohesion, program, and vision. As such, it would not be able to meet the challenges of the next phases—managing the practical procedures of governance or competing effectively in electoral arenas for a major role in policymaking circles. This innovative political revolutionary process had the short-term effect of allowing the battle for the future of the country to be waged by two essentially antidemocratic forces with hierarchical structures that were at odds with the disorganized unity of Tahrir Square: the MB and assorted remnants of the old order against an unholy alliance between the Mubarak beneficiaries, the old bureaucracy that had not been deconstructed, big business interests, economic sectors such as tourism and small shopkeepers, and Copts deeply worried about moves toward Islamism. This eventuality culminated in the presidential runoff between Mohamed Morsi and Ahmed Shafik, which is best understood as an electoral confrontation between the MB and a coalition of anti-MB forces.

Many who had flooded the streets a year earlier never cohered sufficiently to envision the "next steps," and seemed either to retreat from political arenas altogether or leave those who were more traditionally organized to compete for power. On a more radical side were those who were outside the mainstream of the earlier uprising, but remained engaged, believing that the movement could only reach its necessary transformative goals if it persisted in a populist mode that kept the poor masses fully mobilized. Among such activists there existed a shared conviction that the revolutionary process urgently needed to be deepened or else the system would quickly slip back to its old ways. This radical element, while affirming the originality of the Tahrir style and outcomes, rejected all efforts to achieve revolutionary goals by means of party politics and elections, including traditional leftist approaches. At the same time, without endorsing a blueprint for transformation, radicals identified their preferred movement with the realization of a just and independent future for the country. This Egyptian radicalism remained committed to Tahrir politics based on maintaining popular unity across the typical divisions of class, religion, and ethnicity, without advocating its own program or leader; it affirmed the continuing need for confrontational tactics. They accepted chaos as the price that must be paid if the movement was to grow into a genuine revolution and not degenerate into either a counterrevolution or a species of liberal reform that would leave the majority of Egyptians in as miserable a shape as during the Mubarak era. In the end this radical vision was based on beliefs in local empowerment and emancipation, the creativity of people, a robust labor movement, and a bottom-up view of political reconstruction, rejecting both MB and liberal secular views of top-down and state-centric political order. This radicalism drew its inspiration from a sense that a new kind of transformative politics had been revealed in Tahrir Square, but that it was a flowering that would wilt if not nurtured by an uncompromising insistence that the well-being and dignity of the Egyptian masses was the core challenge, and could not be achieved by elections, parties, and winning control of the national government.

As for the impending electoral process, there was an emphasis on speculation about the presidency. Who? When? Among Cairo liberals, there was a widespread sense that Amr Moussa would prevail, but even they did not fully trust him to advance democratic values. Moussa had jumped ship from the Mubarak regime early enough to have mainstream credibility and was thought to be on good terms with the military. He was moderate in relation to the MB and widely known inside and outside Egypt, having served as both foreign minister and secretary-general of the Arab League. There was also some enthusiasm for the candidacy of Mohamed ElBaradei, former head of the International Atomic Energy Agency and Nobel Peace Prize laureate. ElBaradei had clean hands, having been outspoken in rejecting the Mubarak past and appearing alongside activists in the square. At the same time, he lacked a national political base, was not an effective speaker or experienced politician, and was perceived as an outsider who had lived too long in foreign countries. More radical voices were dismissive of this preoccupation with the election, believing that their kind of politics would need to learn how to govern without central institutions. They held an inchoate vision of the need for a "new politics" and a distinct lack of confidence, even interest, in the vagaries of "old politics" (parties, elections, centralized bureaucratic institutions, governmental leadership); in effect, they sought a "human security regime" that had never been established anywhere, ever. At the time, such dedication was at once moving and troublesome, an embrace of what Derrida called "democracy to come" with a kind of trust that the modalities of enactment would be discovered in the process of struggle.

Treading Water

A year later in early 2012 these divisions had persisted and hardened; anxieties seemed far more intense, and the aura of excitement that followed the victory of the January 25 movement had definitely receded. There was, first of all, a new sense of impatience, especially among those who needed economic normalcy to sustain their livelihoods. I met tourist guides at the pyramids and storekeepers in Cairo who expressed disappointment about the results of the upheaval, acknowledging that while they had originally been glad to see the end of the Mubarak regime, they had fared personally better back then, and nothing good for them had emerged since the departure of Mubarak. They seemed ready to support whatever leadership could restore stability.

On a different level of perception, the MB's far-greater-than-expected strength in the intervening parliamentary elections, the abandonment of its pledge not to field a presidential candidate, and the surprisingly strong showing of the Salafis changed the electoral landscape considerably. It was evident that folks in Cairo were out of touch with the grassroots sentiments of a conservative society imbued with an Islamic identity. Liberal critics, discounting this assessment, explained the MB's dominance as misleading, representing an underestimation of its organizational strength. The Salafi emergence was similarly discounted as being mainly a product of a massive infusion of Qatari and Saudi funds, but also a consequence of the fact that in the past Salafi groups had shunned conventional party politics. All in all, there were widespread and growing worries about the Islamization of Egyptian political life, with threats to civic freedoms, constitutional democracy, the labor movement, and the economic status quo.

The biggest development was the SCAF's undertaking the task of establishing order in Egypt and assuring a measure of continuity with the past. Although the SCAF leadership insisted that it was only managing the transition, its autocratic style, the recurrence of state violence and torture, and its reluctance to hold Mubarak operatives accountable for past crimes intensified suspicions that its ambition was to control the political future of the country. The SCAF also seemed to constrain democratic choice and exhibit its ideological bias by disqualifying several presidential candidates on highly technical grounds.

The process had gone so far that ElBaradei withdrew as a candidate, and Moussa no longer seemed a favorite to win. Among the negative scenarios being discussed was the idea that the MB and the SCAF had struck a deal that had doomed the country to an unacceptable political future.

Late November, Early December 2012

Of course, lots had happened since my last visit to Egypt. The presidential race had run its course in two rounds. The runoff was between Mohammed Morsi of the MB and Ahmed Shafik, a former Air Force commanding general and outspoken advocate of a "law and order" presidency, representing the two leading Egyptian institutions with the least in common with the spirit of Tahrir Square. The SCAF seemed to hesitate before finally declaring Morsi the winner in a closely contested final vote. Even then it appeared determined to constrain presidential power, but Morsi struck back, retiring the top generals and effectively asserting presidential authority. Morsi also moved to entrust the drafting of the constitution to a parliamentary commission dominated by Islamists, now subject to a national referendum scheduled for December 15th. Then came Morsi's November 22nd bombshell, claiming presidential authority to issue decrees that could not be judicially reviewed. In response to mounting protests he has substantially rescinded this decree, although he has asserted sweeping powers to control future demonstrations and protect the polling process for the constitutional referendum. As matters now stand, the opposition is not pacified and repudiates the drafting process and the substance of several provisions that give the text an Islamic slant, as well as its failure to affirm the equality of women, labor rights, and the Universal Declaration of Human Rights and other international human-rights treaties. They object to its endorsement of Sharia law as the basis of state/society relations and its deference to the antidemocratic demands of the armed forces (including a nonreviewable defense budget, the right to try civilians in military courts, and protection of the military's vested interests in the economy).

So far there have been almost daily clashes, some deadly, in Tahrir Square and throughout Cairo and other cities. There are several lines of response to these developments. The dominant one applauds the return to the streets to renew the struggle for democracy and economic equity, based on the claim that the MB has an undisclosed plan to impose an authoritarian form of Sharia on Egypt through a backroom alliance with the armed forces and neoliberal business and finance interests. The opposition claims to be fighting for an inclusive and pluralistic form of democratic political order that recognizes as stakeholders in constitution-making the several distinct communities that together make up Egyptian society, including seculars, Copts, and liberals. Another, a more radical assessment is that the fundamental issue involves the utter bankruptcy of conventional state-centered politics, coupled with the complaint that "nothing has changed, absolutely nothing." What seems to be happening, expressed in the fighting and the mass protests, is a new subjectivity associated with local empowerment in specific communities and societal sectors, especially women and labor. It is striking that pictures of the confrontation give prominence to women as a major presence among the opposition forces, while visual representations of the ranks of MB militants seem to be all male.

A Few Tentative Conclusions

In the end, several issues have come to the surface of Egyptian political debate in this unfolding drama.

First, a deep division as to the nature of political legitimacy in the Egyptian context, with Islamists resting their claims on the will of the majority (what eighteenth-century Americans derided as the "tyranny of the majority") while the opposition insists on stakeholder democracy that protects distinct constituencies who fear each other and a Sharia Egypt. In this light, both sides seem uncompromising and rest their encounter on contradictory views of democratic legitimacy.

Second, a new fear that the rise of the MB is allowing the forces of Islam to hijack the Egyptian Revolution in a manner that recalls Iran in 1979; in effect, the conviction that it is unacceptable to have Egypt governed by the MB no matter what the electoral outcome. This is accentuated by accusations that the MB has made deals with the armed forces and neoliberal stakeholders, the two most resented features of the Mubarak past. In this regard, no compromise is possible so long as Morsi remains president. This rejectionist position is expressed in the announced boycott of the December 15 referendum, which is being interpreted as a recognition that the referendum was certain to be approved by the Egyptian electorate. In this respect, the opposition is staking its future on populist resistance rather than democratic procedures, although a less extreme reading would stress Morsi's refusal to delay the referendum as demanded. The opposition believes that Egyptians have lost their fear of state power and learned to say "no" and that, while repression may turn to harsh measures, it will not be able to achieve legitimacy or even stability.

Finally, a few are brave enough while living in Egypt to be sharply critical of and disturbed by this polarization (among others, Esam Al-Amin and Emad Shahin), insisting that common ground exists among the contending forces and must be found to avoid national disaster. They claim that Morsi is far more sensitive to pluralist claims than the opposition contends, although he has panicked and made serious "mistakes" that have alarmed opposition elements. In practical terms, they say, the draft constitution is not as flawed as claimed and the Morsi leadership has indicated a willingness to accommodate amendments in the likely event that the referendum passes. Similarly, they argue, the opposition has overreacted and rejected the democratic mandate of the electoral process, which risks pushing the country into a civil war.

Extreme Polarization and Genocidal Politics
August 24, 2013[9]

In these morbid days, there are some home truths worth reflecting upon.

What Happened after Tahrir Square?

In retrospect, the "January 25 Revolution" in Egypt is a "revolution" that never was, now superseded by a "counterrevolution" that was never possible. Why? Dislodging the Mubarak dynasty in 2011 did not even achieve "regime change," much less initiate a transformative political process. There was no revolution to counter. Even more modest hopes for political reform and humane governance were doomed from the start, or at least when Ahmed Shafik, the overtly *fulool* candidate of the discredited Mubarak regime, gained almost half of the vote in the presidential election runoff against Mohamed Morsi in June 2012.

What, then, was Tahrir Square? Part project (getting rid of Mubarak and sons), part fantasy (hoping that the carnivalesque unity of the moment would evolve into a process of democratic state-building), part delusional experiment (believing that the established order of Mubarak elites and their secular opponents would be willing to rebuild a more legitimate political and economic order, even if it meant transferring significant power and status to the Muslim Brotherhood). The 2011 turn to "democracy" in Egypt always contained a partially hidden condition: the MB was welcome to participate in an electoral process so long as it did not receive a majoritarian mandate. It was widely expected that Amr Moussa would be elected president by a strong majority.

Essentially, the fly in the Egyptian democratic ointment was the unsuspected grassroots popularity and nationwide organization strength of Islam, specifically the Muslim Brotherhood, which won decisive control of the political process in a sequence of five elections. Whether reasonably or not, this revelation of Islamic democratic strength frightened the anti-Mubarak liberals into a de facto alliance with the *fulool*, sealing the fate of the Morsi government. Since the legitimating procedures of the elections had repudiated the old order, even in its post-Mubarak liberal, reconstituted self, the anti-MB opposition had to find an alternative strategy. They did: generate crises of governability and legitimacy via a massive populist mobilization and insist that the democracy of the street take precedence over the democracy of the ballot box.

---

9. http://richardfalk.wordpress.com/2013/08/24/1295.

The armed forces were the joker in this political deck. The military leadership seemed at first to go along with the Tahrir Square flow, but strove to maintain the flexibility it would need to control the transition to whatever would come next, anointing itself as the guarantor of order and the indispensable alternative to chaos. Anti-Morsi forces suspected it had made a backroom deal with the MB; it should be recalled that General Abdel-Fattah el-Sisi, besides leading the armed forces, served as minister of defense in the Morsi cabinet up until the day of the coup. As the anti-Morsi momentum gathered, the military took over the movement, either enacting its preferred scenario all along or changing horses in the middle of the race so as to be riding on the winner. In June 2013 the military could credibly claim a popular mandate to restore order and economic stability. The bloody destruction of the MB as a rival source of economic and political power implemented this mandate far more brutally and comprehensively than anticipated.

Think of it: the group that had prevailed in a series of free elections throughout the nation in 2011 and 2012 was scapegoated, transformed overnight into a band of "terrorists" who must be crushed for the sake of peace and security. When the word "terrorist" is deployed to designate the enemies of the state, it signals that the rule of the gun will replace the rule of law. It paves the way for the state to adopt exterminist and genocidal tactics, and what has followed, however shocking, should not have occasioned surprise. In General el-Sisi's carefully chosen words: "Citizens invited the armed forces to deal with terrorism, which was a message to the world and the foreign media, who denied millions of Egyptians their free will and their true desire to change." Decoded, the general is saying that the anti-Morsi "democratic" masses called not only for a new leadership in Egypt but for the destruction of the MB, now being depicted as "terrorists" (despite the absence of terror).

Obviously, there is no place for such terrorists in the new order of post-Morsi Egypt. In the period following the fall of Mubarak, it should be recalled that the MB was widely regarded as a moderate, nonviolent political movement, overtly Islamic in the practices of its members but respectful of political pluralism. In contrast, it is now portrayed by the coup-makers and supporters as the embodiment of exclusivist and fundamentalist Islam led by bloodthirsty extremists, a makeover aided and abetted by a staunchly secular and very influential mainstream media as well as by the maneuvers of the Mubarak deep state, never dislodged after the fall of the ruler.

ElBaradei's disappointing participation in the coup and interim government, followed by his courageous resignation, reflects the ambivalence of true liberals and their confusion: making nice with the military for the sake of regaining political control and economic privilege, yet not wanting too much innocent blood to be spilled in the process. Note that most of the anti-Mubarak "liberals" are opportunistic at the core; despite all that has happened, they still refuse to break with the Sisi government. They have made their choice in a situation seemingly defined as "us versus them," having learned the lesson that constitutional democracy does not work in their favor. Given this intensification of polarization, there seems to be no space left for those few who retain liberal values and reject extremist political tactics, even on their side of the divide. ElBaradei has demonstrated that he is one of those rare principled liberal secularists who refuse to be complicit in crimes against humanity, and for this surge of conscience he has been savagely attacked as a traitor for displaying such a public change of heart, implicitly a moral challenge to those of his general background who continue to cling to el-Sisi's fraying coattails.

Was the Muslim Brotherhood Responsible?

Could the MB have handled things differently and avoided the July 3 scenario? Yes, possibly, if it had kept its pledge to participate as a minority force in the new Egyptian political order, taking self-denying precautions not to dominate the parliament or seek the presidency. In other words, it is likely that if the MB had bided its time and allowed a liberal secular candidate to take initial control of the government and, in all probability, fail, its overall position today might be quite strong. This assessment presupposes that whoever was chosen to be the first post-Mubarak leader would not be able to satisfy the expectations of the Egyptian public with respect to economic recovery and social justice and would be rejected "democratically," most likely by an electoral process. It is doubtful that the severe social-justice problems in the country could be addressed without a break with the neoliberal world economic system; no secularist on the Egyptian horizon was prepared to mount such a challenge. It is quite probable that if such a challenge had been mounted, the army and the MB would have stepped in to abort such moves. It should be remembered that the left criticized the MB from the outset for its acceptance of the neoliberal consensus.

It was reported (how reliably is unknown) that in February 2012, that is, prior to the initial thirteen-candidate presidential election in May, the SCAF and MB had both told Nabil Elaraby, a globally known and respected liberal secularist and at the time secretary-general of the Arab League, that he would have their backing if he ran for the Egyptian presidency. This support would have assured an electoral victory, but Elaraby prudently declined the offer—if indeed this story was accurate.

The MB's gross imprudence in breaking its pledge of noncompetition for the presidency is only now becoming fully apparent. Having waited more than eighty years for a chance to control the destiny of the country, the MB would have been wise to wait a few more to see how things were developing, especially given the societal and bureaucratic forces likely to be arrayed against it if it took center stage. Of course, such a retrospective appraisal always can be made to sound prescient and is unlikely to be instructive.

Some have argued that the Morsi leadership's multiple failures were the proximate cause of the el-Sisi coup. In other words, the MB's fatal mistake was not its unwillingness to stay in the political background and bide its time, but its inability to follow up on its electoral success when occupying the governmental foreground. This argument reasons that had Morsi been more inclusive, more capable in negotiating international loans and attracting foreign investment, more inspirational in promoting a vision of Egypt's future, less heavy-handed in dealing with oppositional activists and secularists, more sensitive to Coptic worries, more competent in stimulating an economic recovery, more reassuring to the Gulf monarchies, and more patient about promoting an Islamic agenda, things might have turned out differently. True, even an efficient and sensitive Morsi government would likely have lost some of its popularity due to the difficulties any leadership would have faced during this period, but it would not have been overthrown, nor would its political base have then been criminalized and crushed by a bloody campaign of merciless state terror.

It is impossible to assess the plausibility of this line of thinking, but I have my extreme doubts. It is notable that, with few exceptions, those who claimed to be most outraged by the strong-arm tactics and incompetence attributed to the Morsi government have averted their eyes from—and even mandated—the far bloodier tactics of the el-Sisi regime, shouting such banal slogans as "the army and the people are one hand."

After the Coup: A Genocidal Mentality?

Although much is unknown, we can discern a toxic pattern in the behavior of the post-coup state: the sequence of four massacres when softer alternatives were readily available to restore order, the moves to criminalize the MB (detaining Morsi, arresting MB leaders, and calling on the public to authorize, via demonstrations, this strategy of oppression against the MB and its supporters), and recourse to the language of "terrorism" to demonize demonstrators peacefully seeking to uphold constitutional rights and demand a return to constitutional government. Such behavior confirms the coup leaders' extreme alienation. In effect, it was more than a coup, less than a counterrevolution (as the old governmental order had remained in place within the Egyptian deep state). If polarization poisoned the well of democratic legitimacy, then its accelerated momentum led to the emergence of a genocidal climate of opinion in Egypt, and the old *fulool* bureaucracy played its assigned part.

In such an atmosphere it is almost to be expected that many of the coup supporters among the Egyptians masses find nothing wrong with the tactics of the security forces since July 3, 2013. They endorse these tactics with an enthusiastic call for el-Sisi to become the next president and view MB followers as outside the pale of humanity, deserving no mercy and entitled to no rights. In this murderous atmosphere, anything goes.

I suppose, in this evolving Egyptian mêlée, we can learn about the way the state-centric world operates by noting which governments are silent, which are approving and supportive, and which ridiculously continue to call on both sides to show "maximum restraint." We still live in a world where hard-power strategic calculations in the inner councils of government almost always outweigh soft-power affirmations associated with democracy, human rights, and nonviolence. It is not a pretty picture, whether one questions the crude pragmatism of such Muslim stalwarts as Saudi Arabia and the Organization of the Islamic Conference or the equivocations of such liberal advocates of human rights and democracy as the United States, the European Union, and even the UN secretary-general.

These Egyptian developments also raise awkward questions about whether there are outer limits to the politics of self-determination, which has authenticated many national movements against European colonialism and oppressive rule. Egypt is in the throes of what might be described as a process of satanic self-determination, and there is no prospect that humanitarian intervention could restore constitutional normalcy even if genuine empathetic motivations were present, which they are not. Which among the governments of the region or the world would have the temerity to seek an application of the Responsibility to Protect (R2P) norm to protect the MB?[10] In 2011 leading NATO countries relied upon R2P in the UN Security Council to obscure their primary mission, which was to destroy Qaddafi's regime in Libya. At this stage, R2P is not an emergent principle of international law, as advocates claim, but an operative principle of geopolitical convenience that becomes relevant when it serves the political and economic interests of the West.

The ethos of human solidarity means that none of us who are dedicated to human rights, to the accountability of leaders for crimes against humanity, and to the quest for humane governance should abandon Egypt in this tragic

10. See Emad Shahin, "Egyptians Pay for Democracy in Blood," *The Conversation*, August 15, 2013, http://theconversation.com/egyptians-pay-for-democracy-in-blood-17085.

hour of need. At the same time, we need to admit that there is no politics of human solidarity capable of backing up a protective ethos even in the face of genocidal tremors. Our responsibilities as "citizen pilgrims" extend beyond lamenting the failures of world order to serve the wellbeing of the Egyptian people. At the least, we need to raise our voices, engage fully in witnessing, and support whatever soft-power nonviolent initiatives can be mobilized on an emergency basis.

Acute Islamophobia in Egypt

August 25, 2013[11]

The Orwellian features of the military takeover in Egypt have received attention, although the use of language to evade unwanted truth continues because incentives to do so persist. For this reason, Washington has remained unwilling to call what happened in Egypt on July 3 a coup, despite its unmistakable character. The nature of Egypt's coup becomes more and more evident daily. It is now clear that not only is the takeover properly described as a coup, but it has turned out to be a particularly bloody coup, now being reinforced by a total lockdown of opposition forces and democratic options, including even dissenting opinions.

It is true that the disgraced members of el-Sisi's façade of civilian leadership, its so-called "interim government," continue to tell a compliant media in Cairo about their intentions to restore democracy, revert to the rule of law, end the state of emergency, and carry the spirit of Tahrir Square forward. They even have the audacity to invoke their allegiance to the overthrow of Mubarak as "our glorious revolution," shamelessly making such a claim at the very moment when their own movement is extinguishing the earlier quest for a just society with its newly empowered and ruthless police and security establishment. The latest reports from Egypt suggest an atmosphere in which state terror prevails without accountability and with a writ so large as to reach even those anti-Morsi civil-society activists who were in the street on June 30 but now have the temerity to question Mubarak's release from prison. Of all the Orwellian ironies, nothing establishes the hypocrisy of the new Egyptian leadership more than their public reassurances of fidelity to the January 25 Revolution while they arrange the release and push for the vindication of Hosni Mubarak!

---

11. http://richardfalk.wordpress.com/2013/08/25/
the-spreading-wings-of-islamophobia-in-egypt.

Less noticed, but at least as insidious, is resurgent Islamophobia of the el-Sisi junta, which runs the country with an unconcealed iron fist. Revealingly, the Western media seem to avert their eyes when reporting on the suppression of the Muslim Brotherhood and its supporters. Now, according to the most recent reports, nonreligious strike leaders and independent journalists are being killed or criminalized if they offer even the mildest criticisms of the harsh oppression that prevails in Egypt. The justifications offered are that they are engaged in "Islamic" politics.[12] "Islamist" is increasingly being used as a synonym for "terrorist," and neither is seen as entitled to the protection of law nor even treatment as a human being. It is hard to grasp this kind of extreme Islamophobia in a country that is itself overwhelmingly Muslim and whose military leadership affirms its private devotion to Islam. Such an inner/outer confusion is even more distressing than the Orwellian manipulations of our feelings by inversions of language: calling the peaceful demonstrator a terrorist and treating the terrorist acting on behalf of the state as a bastion of public order. Why? This demonization of the "other" engenders an atmosphere of hate and fear that makes even genocide a possibility. We urgently need further insight into the disturbing discovery that the most lethal forms of Islamophobia seem currently emergent within the Muslim heartland.

Other developments point in the same direction, none more illuminatingly than the Western media's failure to observe that the new rulers of Egypt, shockingly, turned their backs on the most elemental human entitlements of the Muslim Brotherhood, whose membership and sympathies extend to at least 25 percent of the country. Recall how strident and universally endorsed was Western criticism of Morsi for his failure to establish a more inclusive form of democratic governance. Compare this with the deafening silence about the el-Sisi cabal's undisguised embrace of violent exclusivity. Somehow the repression of Muslims, even in the form of massacres, guilt by identity, and group criminalization, can be reported upon critically as an overreach by a government seeking in difficult circumstances to establish public order. El-Sisi's repressive policies and practices are rarely identified, even tentatively, as a genocidal undertaking in which the most popular and most democratically legitimate political organization in the country is, by fiat, declared an outlaw organization whose membership is fair game. Is inclusion only expected when the government is in the hands of an elected Muslim-oriented leadership? Is exclusion overlooked when the government moves against an alleged Islamist movement? What, we might ask, is el-Sisi's concept of inclusion? At present, the only plausible answer is "my way or the highway."

---

12. See David D. Kirkpatrick, "Egypt Widens Its Crackdown and Meaning of 'Islamist,'" *New York Times*, August 25, 2013.

3

Libya

Unlike Egypt, where, at the outset, I mostly felt I was sharing a transformative moment with exciting potential for the country, its people, and possibly the region—even the world—the turmoil in Libya never generated such hope. In Egypt, despite some early misgivings about overthrowing the ruler while leaving the regime in place, there was an infectious excitement that seemed to generate hope. In Libya, the uprising essentially unleashed a power struggle among unsavory alternatives for the country's future. There were, to be sure, important individual and communal exceptions: Libyans bravely dedicated to human rights and democracy who had for many years been hounded and victimized by Qaddafi's brutal minions. The posts in Chapter 3 try to capture my sense of foreboding about Libya's future. This uprising began with a confrontation between the people and the ruler, then became a regime-changing NATO intervention that eliminated the autocratic Qaddafi entourage but also emboldened a variety of ethnic, communal, and regional tendencies to establish local power fiefdoms. The unhappy outcome has produced fragmentation and the absence of a state capable of exerting effective control over the country as a whole.

In this period of ferment, Libya became one more casualty of the Arab Spring's destructive aftermath. At first, the opposition uprising seemed like a welcome democratic movement inspired by Tunisia and Egypt's successes in ridding their countries of long-term dictatorships with a minimum of violence and bloodshed. The Libyan uprising was directed at the erratic, domineering Muammar Qaddafi, who had run Libya for several decades as essentially a one-man show. Yet the uprising quickly turned violent and, linked with European political agendas, became a bloody struggle between the regime, centered in Tripoli, and the insurgent leadership, especially associated with Benghazi. Without doubt, the fact that Libya was an oil-producing country increased pressures in Europe and the United States to avoid chaos or, worse from the perspective of the West, a radical Islamist takeover. While Egypt was a *political* prize, Libya seemed to be an *economic* and *emotional* prize, an opportunity to get rid of a leader who had long annoyed the West (even if the West also flirted with him most cynically from time to time).

Against this backdrop, the temptation to reshape Libya's future became irresistible to the West. My blog posts express skepticism about validating the use of force with appeals to humanitarian motivations. Qaddafi's modest military capabilities, Libya's relatively small population, and the presumption that the overwhelming majority of Libyans opposed the regime encouraged this armed intervention. The issues posed a genuine dilemma. As the crisis deepened, it became clear that the civilian population of Benghazi was endangered by Qaddafi's announced plan to crush the opposition, but also that the internationally proposed military operation to establish a "no-fly zone" was unlikely to protect them—and disguised a far more ambitious plot to achieve regime change. As the encounter escalated, Qaddafi foolishly employed fiery genocidal rhetoric to denounce his domestic adversaries in a manner that lent the intervention advocates humanitarian credibility and diverted attention from the real motivations, associated with strategic oil interests and containing Islamic forces. It should be noted that in Syria, where the humanitarian argument had greater force than in Libya, NATO did not seriously consider intervention, which probably reflects the absence of significant amounts of oil and logistical difficulties arising from Syria's larger size, its more sophisticated military capabilities, and the Assad government's considerable support from Syrians at home and abroad.

As the posts argue, U.S. leaders were ambivalent at first about intervening in Libya, fearing being dragged into another war within a Muslim country. In 2011 the American public was weary, having failed in Afghanistan and Iraq despite enormous investment, important strategic objectives, and prolonged military operations lasting over a decade. President Obama was reluctant to accept responsibility for a major military operation in Libya. Turning to NATO and European allies to lead the military campaign and to the UN for a legitimating mandate followed quite naturally. But there were some obstacles on this path. First of all, how to get the backing of the UN Security Council given the likely opposition of Russia and China, both possessing a right of veto?

UN authorization became crucial. This gave rise to a hypocritical debate in the UN Security Council that sought to confuse the anti-intervention governments by promising to limit the use of force to the specific humanitarian danger facing the civilian population of Benghazi, with the United States "leading from behind." The argument rested on the R2P (responsibility to protect) norm the Security Council had previously accepted as a dimension of the post-Kosovo UN conception of "peace and security," avoiding the colonialist language of intervention that was not sufficiently redeemed by the adjective "humanitarian." The haunting question was why humanitarian havoc was being allowed in Syria—and in Gaza—if the UN was operating under an R2P ethos.

The pro-intervention governments insisted that atrocity was looming in Benghazi that would reinforce an impression of UN impotence if nothing effective was done by way of protection. On this basis, skeptical Security Council members were induced to abstain from the vote on authorization, giving the NATO intervention a weak UN imprimatur. As the early posts in this section argue, such an undertaking was unlikely to remain limited and, if expanded, was likely to anger the abstaining Security Council members, especially Russia and China, which would certainly have vetoed UN approval if they had been honestly informed of the operation's intended scope. The NATO mission was dedicated from its inception to regime change; when it succeeded, Libya seemed firmly on the desired path of Western-oriented constitutional democracy.

This vindication was short-lived. A much less pleasant scenario played out on the ground after the intervention changed the political landscape in Tripoli. Libya's governance became less state-centric, and depends to this day on the role of well-armed local militias, often struggling among themselves for ascendancy. The internal regional and ethnic tensions that had been suppressed during the Qaddafi era reemerged with fury to create anxieties that the country would split or be subject to long-term civil strife. As elsewhere in the region, Islamist forces were well-organized and seem determined to gain power by all available means. As of the end of 2014, the formal government seems inept and weak and chaos prevails. The situation is very unstable and no one knows what to expect. In recent weeks an Islamist coalition seized temporary control of governmental structures in Tripoli, but whether such authority will be sustained and spread beyond the capital city is highly uncertain.

The U.S. role in Libya played out badly in American domestic politics. Republicans mocked the idea of "leading from behind," treating it as an irresponsible abandonment of leadership, an expression of American decline for which Obama was blamed. After militants staged a lethal attack on an American diplomatic compound in Benghazi on September 11, 2012, killing the American ambassador, Christopher Stevens, an angry political backlash against the Obama administration followed. Anger was especially directed at the State Department, which had described the attack in misleading ways at first and had failed to mention appeals from American officials in Libya to strengthen the security of the embassy in prior months.

The outcome a few years after the intervention is a devastating interplay between chaos and strife that has left the country hovering between two dismal fates: the complex struggles that have caused such suffering and devastation, as in Syria, and the complete breakdown of legitimate governing authority, as has been the fate of Somalia and Yemen. This misadventure should have induced a revisiting of intervention as an instrument of American foreign policy, but this has not happened. The U.S. government has responded to ISIS as if Libya never happened: military intervention by way of air strikes. Again, as in Syria, there is only a nominal diplomatic and political effort to find other ways to end the strife. Surely Washington's exclusion of Iran from regional diplomacy makes it more difficult to resolve conflicts in the Middle East, as does continuing military assistance to the failed insurgency that has been seeking to overthrow the Assad regime since early 2011, with horrifying consequences for the civilian population in Syria.

Will We Ever Learn?
Kicking the Intervention Habit

March 7, 2011[1]

What is immediately striking about the bipartisan call in Washington for a no-fly zone and air strikes to help rebel forces in Libya is the absence of any concern for international law or the authority of the United Nations. None in authority take the trouble to construct some kind of legal rationalization. The "realists" in command, echoed by the mainstream media, feel no need to provide even a legal fig leaf before embarking on aggressive warfare.

It should be obvious that establishing a no-fly zone in Libyan airspace is an act of war, as would be air strikes on Qaddafi forces. The UN Charter requires member states to refrain from any use of force unless it can be justified as self-defense after a cross-border armed attack or unless mandated by the Security Council. Neither of these conditions is remotely present, yet the media and Washington circles proceed as if the only questions worth discussing pertain to feasibility, costs, risks, and a possible backlash in the Arab world. The imperial mentality is not inclined to discuss the question of legality, much less show behavioral respect for the constraints embedded in international law.

Cannot it not be argued that a "state of exception" in situations of humanitarian emergency allows a "coalition of the willing" to intervene, provided it doesn't make the situation worse? Was not this the essential moral and political rationale for NATO's Kosovo war in 1999, and didn't that probably spare the majority Albanian population in Kosovo from a bloody episode of ethnic cleansing at the hands of the embattled Serb occupiers? Hard cases make bad precedents, as is well known. But even bad precedents need to find a justification in the circumstances of a new situation of claimed exception, or else reinforce the public impression that the powerful act as they will without even pausing to make a principled argument for departing from the normal legal regime of restraint.

With respect to Libya, we need to take account of the fact that the Qaddafi government, however distasteful on humanitarian grounds, remains the lawful diplomatic representative of a sovereign state and a member of the United Nations. Any international use of force even by the UN, much less by a state or group of states, would constitute an unlawful intervention in the internal affairs of a sovereign state, prohibited by Article 2(7) of the UN Charter unless expressly authorized by the Security Council as essential for the sake of international peace and security. Beyond this, there is no assurance that

---

1. https://richardfalk.wordpress.com/2011/03/07/
   will-we-ever-learn-kicking-the-intervention-habit.

an intervention would lessen the suffering of the Libyan people or bring to power a regime more respectful of human rights and dedicated to democratic participation.

The record of military intervention during the last several decades is one of almost unbroken failure, if either the human costs or political outcomes are taken into proper account. This makes it impossible to justify intervention in Libya in some ethically and legally persuasive way.

There are also serious credibility concerns. As has been widely noted in recent weeks, the United States has had no second thoughts about supporting oppressive regimes throughout the region for decades and is widely resented for this. Qaddafi's crimes against humanity were never a secret, certainly not to European and American intelligence services. Yet high-profile British and American liberal intellectuals welcomed invitations to Tripoli during the last several years, apparently without a blink of conscience, accepting consulting fees and shamelessly praising Libya's softening authoritarianism. Perhaps Joseph Nye, one of the most prominent of these goodwill visitors to Tripoli, would call this a private use of "smart power": commending Qaddafi for renouncing his anti-West posture, making deals for oil and weapons, and most of all abandoning what some now say was at most a phantom nuclear-weapons program.

Some Beltway pundits insist that the interventionists, after faltering in the region, want to get on the right side of history before it is too late. But the right side of history in Libya seems quite different than it is in Bahrain or Jordan, where the effort is to restore stability with minimal concessions to reformist demands, a political touch-up designed to convert the insurrectionists of yesterday into the bureaucrats of tomorrow. History seems to flow along the same currents as oil!

Mahmood Mamdani points out that we are taught to distinguish "good Muslims" from "bad Muslims"; now we are being instructed to distinguish "good autocrats" from "bad autocrats," which effectively means only the pro-regime elements in Libya and Iran, whose structures must at least be shaken if they cannot be broken. What distinguishes these regimes? Their oppressiveness is not more pervasive and severe. Other considerations give more insight: access to and pricing of oil, arms sales, Israel's security interests, the regimes' relationship to the neoliberal world economy.

What I find most disturbing is that, despite the failures of counterinsurgency thinking and practice, American foreign-policy gurus continue to contemplate intervention in postcolonial societies without the slightest sensitivity to historical experience, not even recognizing that national resistance in the postcolonial world has consistently neutralized the advantages of superior hard power. The most that has been heard is a whispered expression of concern by the relatively circumspect secretary of defense, Robert Gates, that it may not be prudent at this time for the United States to intervene in yet another Muslim country. The absence of any learning from Vietnam, Afghanistan, or Iraq is startling. Technically speaking, the proposed intervention in Libya is not an instance of counterinsurgency but a pro-insurgency intervention, as with the ongoing covert destabilization efforts in Iran.

It is easier to understand military commanders' professional resistance to learning from past failures, but civilian politicians deserve not a whit of sympathy. Among the most ardent advocates of intervention in Libya are the last Republican presidential candidate, John McCain, the supposedly independent Joe Lieberman, and the Obama Democrat John Kerry. It seems many of the Republicans who focus on the deficit—although cutting public expenditures punishes the poor at a time of widespread unemployment and home foreclosures—would not mind ponying up countless billions to finance war in Libya, seemingly to show that imperial geopolitics is not yet dead despite growing evidence of American decline.

More cautious imperial voices insist that their opposition to intervention rests on feasibility concerns; in the end, I suppose we have to hope that they carry the day!

What I am mainly decrying here is three kinds of policy failure:

1. The exclusion of international law and the United Nations from national debates about international uses of force.
2. The absence of respect for the dynamics of self-determination in societies of the South.
3. The refusal to heed the ethics and politics appropriate for an increasingly multipolar, de-Westernized postcolonial world order.

A Critical Postscript to "Will We Ever Learn?" Contra Intervention

March 8, 2011[2]

It has been suggested that a no-fly zone would enable rebel forces to deal more effectively with the foreign militias the Qaddafi regime relies upon to do much of its dirty work. It is difficult to know how this would affect the battlefield. We are speculating on the basis of radical uncertainty; in such circumstances,

---

2. http://richardfalk.wordpress. com/2011/03/08/a-short-postscript-to-"will-we-ever-learn-contra-intervention".

it is almost always better to refrain from coercive action than to engage in it. Furthermore, there is a wide spectrum of no-fly-zone scenarios, depending on the governments that take initiative, the degree of dependence on correlated air strikes, and the options available to the rebels and Qaddafi to either take advantage of its effect or to circumvent them. For instance, it is *politically* more palatable to establish and administer a no-fly zone under the auspices of the Arab League or as a joint Egypt/Turkey undertaking than NATO or a U.S.–led "coalition of the willing." The UN as sponsor is out of the question, given Russian opposition and Chinese reluctance. At the same time, given the logistical and technological demands, it is more likely that the *effectiveness* of a no-fly zone would be greater under NATO/U.S. control. A failed no-fly zone would embolden Qaddafi and likely improve his prospects in the internal struggle.

Furthermore, the tactics and character of the rebel movement seem dramatically different than uprisings elsewhere in the region, particularly in Egypt and Tunisia. In Libya, the movement lacks the inspiring qualities of nonviolence, solidarity, and social/political demands for justice. It was violent from the outset, tribalist in spirit, received weaponry from external actors, and was preoccupied with control over the oil-producing areas, with an indistinct political outlook (flying the pre-Qaddafi flag of the Libyan monarchy) and uncertain links to private-sector international oil interests. This looks more like a struggle for control of the state, or possibly an effort to establish a secessionist second state if a stalemate emerges. It would seem that if feasibility hurdles could be overcome, the political climate in the United States and Britain would support a large-scale intervention, possibly with Arab regional acquiescence.[3]

With these considerations in mind, I think the case for nonintervention remains overwhelmingly persuasive from moral, legal, and political perspectives. Roger Cohen stated perhaps the most compelling rationale, that of "the moral bankruptcy of the West with respect to the *Arab world*. Arabs have no need of U. S. or European soldiers as they seek the freedom that America and the European Union were content to deny them."[4]

Perhaps there is another way to exhibit the shabbiness of the argument being made on behalf of a protective no-fly zone. Why no comparable proposal on behalf of the civilian population of Gaza, trapped behind a

---

3. See the illuminating analysis by Michel Chossudovsky, "Insurrection and Military Intervention: The US-NATO Attempted Coup d'Etat in Libya?" Centre for Research on Globalization, March 8, 2011, www.globalresearch.ca/insurrection-and-military-intervention-the-us-nato-attempted-coup-d-etat-in-libya/23548.

4. Roger Cohen, "Libyan Closure," *New York Times*, March 7, 2011, www.nytimes.com/2011/03/08/opinion/08iht-edcohen08.html.

merciless blockade for more than three years? Aside from issues of nonintervention, always important, here is the paramount relevance of support for dynamics of self-determination. This does not assure the triumph of justice: Qaddafi may win, or the rebels may prevail and prove just as distastefully oppressive. On balance, what means most in the twenty-first century is to allow the peoples of the world to make their own history. Western military paternalism and economic exploitation have been deservedly discredited.

As suggested, there is no way to seal the borders of territorial states. Neither pure noninterventionism nor insulated self-determination are ever possible given the porousness of borders and the incentives for a range of outsiders to intervene. Various low-profile "interventions" are likely already taking place: weapons are being supplied, perhaps, or special forces are covertly present as advisors or even fighters. In this respect, the most that can be done is to oppose gross forms of overt governmental intervention, as well as limiting assistance to governments, including the Tripoli regime, that violate the fundamental human rights of their own people. In this respect, sanctions are appropriate if they are authorized by the UN, are not coupled with intervention, and take responsible account of competing moral, legal, and political claims.

Keep in mind that Libya has over 3.5 percent of the world's oil reserves, twice the amount present in the United States. One does not need to be an economic determinist to see that oil certainly helps explain the preferential treatment being given to insurrection in Libya.

Qaddafi, Moral Interventionism, Libya, and the Arab Revolutionary Moment

March 20, 2011[5]

Long ago Muammar Qaddafi forfeited the domestic legitimacy of his rule, creating the moral and political conditions for an appropriate revolutionary challenge. Recently he has confirmed this assessment by referring to the disaffected portion of his own citizenry as "rats and dogs" and "cockroaches," employing the bloodthirsty and vengeful language of a demented tyrant. This is political abuse beyond any reasonable doubt, but does it validate a UN-authorized military intervention carried out by those old colonial partners, France and Britain, and their postcolonial American overseer?

---

5. http://richardfalk.wordpress.com/2011/03/20/
   qaddafi-moral-interventionism-libya-and-the-arab-revolutionary-moment.

From a personal perspective, my hopes are with the Libyan rebels, despite their reliance on violence and the opacity of their political identity. As many credible exile Libyan voices attest, it would seem highly likely that a rebel victory would benefit the people of Libya and be a step in the right direction for the region, but does this entail supporting Western-led military intervention? I believe not.

Let us begin with some unknowns and uncertainties. There is no coherent political identity that can be confidently ascribed to the various anti-Qaddafi forces, loosely referred to as "rebels." Just who are they, whom do they represent, and what are their political aspirations? It is worth observing that, unlike the other regional events of 2011, the Libyan rising did not last long as a spontaneous popular movement or unfold as a specific reaction to some horrific incident as in Tunisia. It seems, although there is some ambiguity in the media reports, that the Libyan movement was armed and reliant on military force almost from the start and that its political character seems more in the nature of a traditional insurrection against the established order than a popular revolution inspired by democratic values. This violent reaction to Qaddafi's regime seems fully justified as an expression of Libyan self-determination and deserves encouragement from world public opinion, including support from such soft-power instruments as boycott, divestment, and maybe sanctions. By and large, the international community did not resort to threats and actions of intervention in Libya until it appeared likely that Qaddafi would reestablish order in his favor; this international intrusion therefore represents a coercive effort to restructure a country's governing process from without.

The main pretext for the intervention was Libyan civilians' vulnerability to the wrath of the Qaddafi regime. But there was little evidence that such wrath extended beyond the regime's expected defense of the admittedly brutal established order, not unusual in situations where a government and its leadership are fighting for survival. How is this response different from those of the regimes in Yemen and Bahrain, which were responding to a far smaller threat to the status quo and in the form of political resistance, not military action? In Libya the opposition forces relied on heavy weapons, while elsewhere in the region people were in the streets in massive numbers, mostly unarmed.

It may have been the case that the rebel opposition felt that it had no choice. But it should be clear from the experiences in Iraq and Afghanistan that military intervention against a hated and brutal regime is not the end of the story; before the ending is reached, violence cascades to heights far beyond what would have likely resulted had there been no intervention. In the process heavy casualties and massive displacements cause immense suffering for the entrapped and innocent population. In effect, overall historical trends vindicate trust in the dynamics of self-determination, although short-term disillusioning disasters can and do occur from time to time. These trends underscore the inherently problematic character of intervention, even given the purest of motivations, which rarely if ever exists in world politics on the side of intervening parties.

But, it can be asked, what about Rwanda? What about Bosnia? Are not these instances where humanitarian intervention should have been undertaken and was not? And didn't the NATO war in Kosovo demonstrate that humanitarian intervention does sometimes spare a vulnerable population from genocide? With respect to Rwanda and Bosnia, the threat of genocidal behavior was clearly established, could likely have been prevented by a relatively small-scale intervention, and should have been undertaken despite the uncertainties. The facts surrounding the alleged genocidal threat in Kosovo remain contested, but there was a plausible basis for taking it seriously given what had happened a few years earlier in Bosnia. But just as the Libyan rebels raise suspicion by seeking Euro-American military intervention, so did the KLA in Kosovo engage in terrorist provocations that led to violent Serb responses, allegedly setting the stage in 1999 for NATO's "coalition of the willing." NATO went ahead in Kosovo without the benefit of a Security Council mandate, as here, for military action "by all necessary means." But with respect to Libya there is no firm evidence of genocidal intentions, no humanitarian catastrophe in the making, not even clear indications of the extent of civilian casualties. We should be asking why Russia signaled its intention to veto such authorization in relation to Kosovo but not Libya: a Russian sense of identification with Serbian interests?

One of the mysteries surrounding UN support for the Libyan intervention is why China and Russia expressed their opposition by abstaining rather than using their vetoes, why South Africa voted with the majority, and why Germany, India, and Brazil were content to abstain yet expressed reservations sufficient to produce "no" votes, which would have deprived the interventionist side of the nine affirmative votes it needed to obtain authorization. Often the veto is used promiscuously, but here it was not used when it could have served positive purposes, preventing an imprudent, destructive military action that seems almost certain to be regarded in the future as an unfortunate precedent.

The internal American debate on the use of force was more complex than usual and cut across party lines. Three positions are worth distinguishing: realists, moral interventionists, and moral and legal anti-interventionists. Most realists, who usually carry the day on controversial military issues, warned against the intervention, saying it was too uncertain in its effects and costs, that the U.S. was already overstretched in its overseas commitments, and that there were few American strategic interests involved. The moral interventionists, who were in control during the George W. Bush years, triumphantly reemerged in the company of hawkish Democrats such as Hillary Clinton and Joseph Biden. They prevailed in shaping policy partly thanks to a push from London and Paris, acquiescence of Libya's Arab neighbors, and a loss of will on the part of Moscow and Beijing. It is hard to find a war that Republicans will not endorse, especially if the enemy can be personalized as anti-American, and it always helps to have some oil in the ground! The anti-interventionists are generally reluctant to rely on force in foreign policy except for self-defense and have doubts about the effectiveness of hard-power tactics, especially under Western auspices. They were outmaneuvered, especially at the United Nations and in the sensationalist media, which treated the Qaddafi horror show almost exclusively as a question of "how" rather than "whether" and giving no attention to the anti-intervention position.

Finally, there arises the question of the UN authorization itself, by way of Security Council Resolution 1373. The Security Council vote, however questionable on moral and political grounds and in relation to the Charter text and values, resolves the legal issue *within* the UN system. An earlier World Court decision, ironically involving Libya, concluded that even when the UN Security Council contravenes relevant norms of international law, its decisions are binding and authoritative. Here the Security Council has reached a decision supportive of military intervention that is *legal*, but, in my judgment, not *legitimate*, being neither *politically prudent* nor *morally acceptable*. The states that abstained acted irresponsibly, failing to uphold either the spirit or letter of the Charter, which in Article 2(7) establishes a prohibition on UN authority to intervene in matters "essentially within the domestic jurisdiction" of member states unless there is a genuine issue of international peace and security present. Here there was no such basis.

Besides, the claim to intervene as stated was patently misleading and disingenuous. The actual goals of the intervention were, minimally, to protect the armed rebels from being defeated and possibly destroyed and, maximally, to achieve a regime change resulting in a new governing leadership for Libya that would be friendly to the West, including buying fully into its liberal economic-geopolitical policy. The missile attacks in the vicinity of Tripoli, especially the early missile hits on the Qaddafi compound, are unmistakable signatures of this wider intention. As the 1991 Gulf War demonstrated, once the Security Council authorizes military action of an unspecified character it gives up any further responsibility for maintaining operational control and accountability.

Using slightly altered language, the UN Charter embeds a social contract with its membership that privileges the politics of self-determination and is heavily weighted against the politics of intervention. Neither position is absolute, but what seems to have happened with respect to Libya is that intervention was privileged and self-determination cast aside. It is an instance of normatively dubious *practice* trumping the legal/moral ethos of containing geopolitical discretion in relation to obligatory rules governing the use of force and the duty of nonintervention. We do not know yet what will happen in Libya, but we already know enough to oppose a precedent with so many unfortunate characteristics. It is time to restore the global social contract between territorial sovereign states and the organized international community, which not only corresponds with the outlawry of aggressive war but also reflects the movement of history in support of the soft-power struggles of the non-Western peoples of the world.

If ordinary citizens were allowed to have foreign-policy doctrines, mine would be this: without high levels of confidence in a proposed course of military action, the UN should never agree to allow states to engage in violent action that kills people. If this cautionary principle is ignored, governments should expect that their behavior will be widely viewed as criminal and the UN regarded as more a creature of politics than of law and morality. For these reasons it would have been my preference for the abstainers in the Security Council to have voted against Resolution 1973. It is likely that the coalition of the willing would have gone forward in any event, but at least this would have withheld the apparent UN seal of approval.

Obama's Libyan Folly: To Be or Not to Be

April 5, 2011[6]

The outcome in Libya remains uncertain, but what seems clear beyond reasonable doubt is that military intervention has not saved the day for the shadowy opposition known as "the rebels" or for the Libyan people. It has plunged the country into a protracted violent conflict, with the domestic balance of forces tipping decisively in favor of the Qaddafi regime despite a major military onslaught managed by the U.S.-led coalition, which in recent days has been supposedly outsourced to NATO. But since when is NATO not an U.S.-dominated alliance? The best that can be hoped for at this stage is a face-saving ceasefire that commits the Libyan leadership to a vague power-sharing scheme but leaves the governing process more or less as it is, possibly

6. http://richardfalk.wordpress.com/2011/04/05/obama's-libyan-folly-to-be-or-not-to-be.

replacing Qaddafi with his son, who may offer the West the cosmetic trappings of liberal modernity and reform.

President Barack Obama finally drew a line in the sand, if a rather wavering and fuzzy line, in response to what was being called an imminent atrocity about to be inflicted upon the people of Benghazi—though there was never much evidence beyond the bombast of the dictator. On March 28 he came out clearly in support of military action, although carefully circumscribed by reference to its supposedly narrow humanitarian goals. The futility of establishing a no-fly zone should have been obvious to anyone conversant with recent political struggles for control of a sovereign state. What the world actually witnessed was not an effort to protect Libyan civilians but an unauthorized attempt to turn the tide in favor of the insurrection by destroying as many of Libya's military assets as possible, clearing the path for a rebel advance.

The character of this insurrection has never been clearly established. It is still most accurately described as a motley gathering of opposition forces. Though its military challenge seemed inept, its public relations campaign worked brilliantly. It mobilized the humanitarian hawks nesting in the White House, most prominently Samantha Power, Hillary Clinton, and Susan Rice as well as the State Department's recently departed head of policy planning, Anne-Marie Slaughter. Power, particularly, has long called upon the government to use its might wherever severe human-rights abuses occur (unless in a large country beyond interventionary ambitions), analogizing nearly every humanitarian crisis to the totally different circumstances of Rwanda in 1994, where the Clinton White House inappropriately blocked a small effort to mitigate a major genocide. In the media the celebrants of this intervention have been led by the pious *New York Times* stalwarts Nicholas Kristof and Thomas Friedman. At least Friedman, the patron saint of "wars of choice," was sensible enough on this occasion to acknowledge that Obama would need major help from Lady Luck, a welcome contrast to his cheerleading of the Iraq intervention. If lives were not at stake, it might be amusing to note the new humility of this most arrogant of journalists, forever fond of addressing world leaders by their first names while dishing out unsolicited guidance, being reduced to treating the Libyan intervention like a night out in Las Vegas!

The rebels' full-court PR press misleadingly convinced world public opinion, and several Western political leaders, that the Qaddafi regime was opposed and hated by the entire population of Libya and was therefore extremely vulnerable to intervention. This encouraged the belief that the only alternative to military intervention was for the Western world to sit back and bear witness to genocide against the Libyan people on a massive scale. Other options, like diplomacy or a ceasefire, were never seriously embarked on or considered.

Even without the spurious wisdom of hindsight, the undertaking could be criticized as designed to fail: a questionable intervention in what appeared increasingly to be an armed insurrection against the established government, yet falling far short of what would be needed to secure the fall of the Qaddafi government. How can such a struggle, involving one more paternalistic challenge to the dynamics of self-determination, be won by relying on the bombs and missiles of colonial powers, undertaken without even the willingness to follow the attack with peacekeeping on the ground? Had this willingness been present, it would have at least connected the dots between the means adopted and the mission being proclaimed; the odds of success would still have remained small. If we consider the record of the past sixty years, very few interventions by colonial or hegemonic actors have been successful, despite their overwhelming military superiority. The only "success" stories of intervention involve very minor countries such as Grenada and Panama, where organized resistance was absent; the failures were in big, prolonged struggles such as in Indochina, Algeria, and Indonesia.

In Libya the prospects were further worsened by the rebels' incoherence, inexperience, and lack of discipline. The effort of a weak and unorganized opposition to induce foreign forces to secure an otherwise unattainable victory for them is reminiscent of the bill of goods that wily Iraqi exiles sold to neoconservative operatives such as Richard Perle and Paul Wolfowitz during the lead-up to the Iraq War in 2003. Remember those promises of flowers greeting the American troops arriving in Baghdad, or regime change being "a cakewalk" that would be achieved without notable American casualties or costs? As in Libya, the case for intervention rested on the false assumption that foreign occupiers would be welcomed as liberators and that the Saddam Hussein regime lacked any popular base of support.

Such a negative assessment was offered at the outset of the crisis by the most qualified high official in Obama's inner circle, Secretary of Defense Robert Gates. Why did Obama not heed this sensible advice? Unfortunately, Obama, even more than every other Democratic president, struggles to maintain his image as willing to use force in the pursuit of national interests. Obama has pursued a generally militarist foreign policy while still managing to collect a Nobel Peace Prize. In Libya, the risks of inaction must have seemed too great to bear. Instead he attempted to have it both ways: lead the diplomatic effort to obtain a mandate from the UN Security Council, provide most of the military muscle for the initial phase of the operation, then hastily withdraw to the background while European members of NATO supposedly take over. This middle path is littered with contradictions: to convince the Security Council and avoid a Russian or Chinese veto, it was necessary to portray the mission in the narrowest humanitarian terms, while protecting the rebels (who are not legally "civilians") required a much more ambitious scale of attack than a no-fly zone. If the unconditional goal was to eliminate the Qaddafi regime, the intervention would have to go far beyond the boundary set by the Security Council decision. It would have to tip the balance. As has become clear, the approved military objectives were dramatically exceeded in the flawed effort to help the rebels, but seemingly to no avail.

Of course, the abstaining members of the Security Council also have blood on their hands. China, Russia, India, Brazil, and South Africa went along with a mandate to use force that seemed inconsistent with the Charter assurances of refraining from UN intervention in matters essentially within domestic jurisdiction, as this struggle surely was and is. They also allowed the backers of the Security Council to insert the mission-creep-permitting clause "by all necessary means." They should be ashamed of their posture: criticizing before the vote, abstaining to assure that authorization would be provided, then resuming criticism afterward. The vote was ten in favor, none opposed, and five abstaining.

Such disregard for the limits of the UN Security Council authorization, which the Security Council then failed to enforce, has once again weakened the UN as a body operating within the constitutional framework of the UN Charter. It makes the UN appear to be more an agent of geopolitical and neoimperial forces in the West than an objective body seeking to implement the rule of law in relation to the strong and weak alike. We all should remember that when the UN was established in the aftermath of World War II, it was assigned the primary responsibility of *minimizing* the role of war in human affairs. The inspirational opening words of the Preamble to the UN Charter should be recalled and solemnly reaffirmed: "We the peoples of the United Nations determined *to save succeeding generations from the scourge of war.*" To allow these words to be overridden by the recently endorsed norm of "responsibility to protect" is to provide a selective tool with shameless double standards. Where were those humanitarian and paternalistic voices when the civilian population of Gaza was subjected to a murderous three-week land, air, and sea attack by the Israel Defense Forces in 2009?

Throughout this period of revolutionary ferment in the Arab world Obama's paternalism has been pronounced. While intermittently celebrating these popular risings, he has unblushingly felt entitled to pronounce on which leaders should stay and which should go, as if he is indeed the firs designated global chief executive. These pronouncements lack even the pretense of coherence and consistency unless measured from an exclusively geopolitical standpoint. The White House was fine with Mubarak until the popular movement made his continued presence untenable, and then he was instructed to leave. Yemen's leader was told to step down after he failed to quiet the protests, while in Bahrain Washington supports the al-Khalifa royal family's absolute monarchy, which has not only recently relied on extremely violent means to quell unarmed demonstrators but has even invited its stronger neighbor, Saudi Arabia, to send military forces across the border to help restore order (that is, to thwart robust popular calls for a new political order based on democracy and human rights).

These maneuvers in and out of the limelight reveal the current American dilemma: it is not yet ready to shed the mantle of imperial overseer in the postcolonial regions of the world, but it is faced with the contradictory pressures of imperial decline and overstretch. This fledgling patriarch can lecture the world and even manage a military thrust or two, but nothing is sustained and little achieved. Obama seems to be auditioning to play Hamlet in this unfolding global tragedy.

The International Criminal Court Plays Politics? The Qaddafi Arrest Warrants

June 29, 2011[7]

The International Criminal Court has formally agreed that warrants should be issued for the arrest of Col. Muammar Qaddafi, as well as his son, acting prime minister Saif al-Islam Qaddafi, and intelligence chief Abdullah Senussi. These three Libyan leaders are charged with crimes against humanity involving the murder, injury, and imprisonment of Libyan civilians between February 10 and 18, 2011, the first days of the uprising, prior to NATO's military involvement. ICC judge Sanji Mmasenono Monageng of Botswana authorized the issuance of the arrest warrants, explaining that sufficient evidence of criminality existed to proceed with the prosecution, but issuing the warrants was not intended to imply guilt, which must be determined by the outcome of a trial. The ICC assessment is likely to withstand scrutiny so far as the substance of the accusations is concerned. Qaddafi clearly responded with extreme violence, reinforced by genocidal rhetoric, to the popular challenges

---

7. http://richardfalk.wordpress.com/2011/06/29/
the-international-criminal-court-plays-politics-the-qaddafi-arrest-warrants.

directed against the Libyan government, which certainly seems to qualify as crimes against humanity. But I am led to question why an effort to arrest and indict was pushed so hard at this time.

The timing of the indictment, and now the arrest warrants, arouses strong suspicions—and not just of bad judgment! It is relevant to recall that in the course of NATO's Kosovo war, the Serbian president, Slobodan Milošević, was indicted by the special ad hoc International Criminal Tribunal for the Former Yugoslavia. Are we now to expect that whenever NATO has recourse to war, the political leader heading its opposition will be charged with international crimes while the fighting ensues? How convenient! *Lawfare* in the service of *warfare!*

In both of these instances, NATO itself has resorted to war unlawfully, engaging in what was designated at Nuremberg as a "crime against peace" and held to be the greatest of war crimes, embracing both crimes against humanity and gross violations of the laws of war (war crimes). In the Kosovo war, NATO acted without a UN mandate. In Libya there was initial authorization to protect civilians by establishing a no-fly zone, but the mission grossly exceeded the original mandate almost immediately and did little to hide its unmandated goal of regime change. In both of these wars, the leader of a country attacked by NATO was targeted for criminal prosecution before hostilities had ended. Even in World War II the Allies waited until after the end of combat before trying to impose "victors' justice" on surviving defeated German and Japanese leaders.

A somewhat similar manipulation of criminal accountability occurred in Iraq a few years ago. There the American-led war was quickly followed by a carefully orchestrated criminal prosecution, stage-managed behind the scenes by the U.S. occupation commanders, followed by the execution of Saddam Hussein and his close associates. The trial was circumscribed to exclude any evidence bearing on the close and discrediting strategic relationship between the United States and Iraq during the period of Saddam Hussein's most serious instances of criminality (genocidal operations against Kurdish villages), as well as disallowing any inquiry into American criminality associated with the attack on Iraq and subsequent allegations of criminal wrongdoing in response to Iraqi resistance to military occupation.

What converts these separate instances into a pattern is the West-centric selectivity evident in most recent efforts to enforce international criminal law, with impunity accorded to European, American, and Israeli leaders. These pervasive double standards undermine the authority of law, especially in relation to a subject as vital as war and peace. Unless equals are treated equally most of the time, what is called "law" is more accurately treated a "geopolitics."

The geopolitical nature of the ICC's arrest warrants was unintentionally confirmed when NATO officials acknowledged that it will not be possible to arrest Qaddafi unless he is captured by rebels, which is unlikely. Governmental representatives in Washington admit this but say the warrants will nevertheless be useful in forthcoming UN debates about Libya, presumably to push aside any objections based on NATO's failure to limit military operations to the no-fly zone initially authorized by the Security Council. In effect, to overcome any impression of unlawfulness on NATO's part it is useful to demonize the adversary, and an opportune way to reach this goal is to put forward premature accusations of severe criminality.

There are further technical reasons to challenge the timing of the arrest warrants, which seem legally and politically dubious: legally dubious because the Qaddafi regime's most serious criminality occurred after the ICC cutoff date of February 18 (the siege of Misrata). Why this rush to prosecute? The warrants are also politically dubious because there is now a new obstacle to diplomacy in a situation where the alternative seems likely to be a prolonged civil war. Negotiating space for an accommodation is definitely reduced by this implication of Qaddafi's criminality, which creates incentives for the Tripoli leadership to fight on as long as possible.

Cynics would argue that law always reflects power, and of course they are correct to a certain extent. Progress in human affairs arises from struggling against such pretensions. The locus and nature of power is changing in the world: the West is losing its capacity to shape history; high-technology warfare, upon which the West depends to enforce its will, is losing its capacity to produce political victories (e.g., anti-colonial wars, Vietnam, Iraq, Afghanistan). This politicized use of the ICC offers an opportunity for those dedicated to global justice, especially in the Arab world, to insist that international law should no longer serve as a plaything for those who intervene with hard power from the comfort zone of NATO headquarters.

Libya After Muammar Qaddafi's Execution
October 30, 2011[8]

The death of the despised despot who ruled Libya for forty-two years naturally produced celebrations throughout the country. Muammar Qaddafi's end was bloody and vindictive, but we should remember that his rants against his own people—and his violent repression of what was initially a

8. http://richardfalk.wordpress.com/2011/10/30/
libya-after-muammar-el-qaddafi's-execution.

peaceful uprising—invited a harsh popular response. Recall W.H. Auden's famous line: "Those to whom evil is done / do evil in return."[9] It is almost inevitable, in the absence of strong moral and political discipline, that when a leader refers to his opponents as "rats" and pledges to hunt them down house by house the stage is set for the unacceptable kind of retribution that played out recently in Sirte, where NATO air strikes leveled the city and anti-Qaddafi forces executed at least fifty-three Qaddafi loyalists. It is an ominous sign that this massacre, along with the execution and burial of Qaddafi, exhibited such vengeful and undisciplined behavior. It raises renewed doubts about the character and approach of the National Transitional Council's (NTC's) leadership, although it is still possible to redeem this loss of confidence.

These unfortunate happenings make overall accountability for war crimes an early test of whether the NTC will prove capable of managing the formation of a political and morally acceptable governmental structure. Will it investigate the alleged wrongdoings of its own forces in a manner that corresponds with international standards, or will such inquiry be avoided because such an international confidence-raising process would clearly fuel internal factionalism in which any finger-pointing will seem like an encouragement of ethnic and tribal conflict? Will the NTC cooperate with the ICC to ensure that those charged with war crimes in the service of the Qaddafi regime will receive fair trials? At the same time, there is reason to view with a cynical eye the demands of self-righteous Western NGOs that seem to expect from Libya what the liberal democratic regimes of the West refuse to do. The United States goes to extraordinary lengths to exempt its soldiers and leaders from potential criminal accountability while it pushes hard to subject its enemies to the harsh severity of international criminal law. Double standards pervade. As with so much that involves North Africa after the glories of the Arab Spring, all roads to the future seem destined to have many twists and turns, as well as treacherous potholes.

The leadership vacuum in Libya is not likely to be filled anytime soon. We don't know whether tribal or regional loyalties will emerge as primary political identities now that the great unifier—hostility to the Qaddafi regime—can no longer suppress antagonistic goals and ambitions. The NTC lent the anti-Qaddafi forces *international* credibility, but much of the fighting in the last stages of the struggle was under the control of semiautonomous militia commanders who seemed a law unto themselves. We will soon learn whether the NTC can sufficiently represent the collective will of Libyans during the interim process that is needed before establishing

9. W.H. Auden, "September 1, 1973," in *Another Time* (New York: Random House, 1940), available at www.poets.org/poetsorg/poem/september-1-1939.

an elected government and drafting a new constitution. Its first attempt to establish a new unity was premised on a call to implement political Islam. The chairman of the NTC, Mustafa Abdul-Jalil, made the following strong assertion along these lines at the victory celebration in Benghazi: "We are an Islamic country. We take the Islamic religion as the core of our new government. The constitution will be based on our Islamic religion."[10]

Some pessimists have contended that Libya's future is prefigured by the chaotic violence that befell Somalia after the overthrow of dictator Mohamed Siad Barre in 1991, a tragic set of national circumstances that have persisted ever since. But on a more hopeful note, it is worth observing that the fall of Qaddafi—unlike that of Hosni Mubarak, whose overthrow has not yet altered the power structure in Egypt—gives the victorious Libyan opposition a seemingly clean slate that could allow for genuine democratic nation-building if such a political will emerges. Libyans have given themselves an opportunity that rarely comes along in history, to achieve a real revolutionary transformation of their political, economic, and cultural life. Thus, it could turn out, paradoxically, to be helpful that Qaddafi left no institutional infrastructure upon which to construct a modern state. What has happened in Libya, unlike Egypt, is for better or worse a total regime change.

Libya starts out on this new path with some additional major advantages, most obviously oil and a relatively small population. An important test in the months ahead will be the extent to which the new leadership restores economic normalcy without mortgaging the national wealth to foreign predators—corporate, financial, and governmental. Of course, in the background is the sense that NATO was integral to Qaddafi's overthrow and may expect more than a thank-you note. Already there are media murmurs about great business opportunities for the West in the new Libya, including the challenge of rebuilding what NATO destroyed, which seems like a disturbing vindication of Naomi Klein's groundbreaking *The Shock Doctrine*, a devastating critique of the contemporary logic of the neoliberal world economy.

Against such a background, we can only wish that the Libyans will defy pessimistic expectations and manage to establish a viable and independent democratic state that is respectful of human rights and energetic in its efforts at reconstruction, without becoming overly hospitable to foreign investors and companies. After a devastating air campaign of some twenty

---

10. Adam Nossiter and Kareem Fahim, "Revolution Won, Top Libyan Official Vows a New and More Pious State," *New York Times*, October 23, 2011, www.nytimes.com/2011/10/24/world/africa/revolution-won-top-libyan-official-vows-a-new-and-more-pious-state.html.

thousand sorties, the NATO countries should have the decency to stand aside and respect the Libyans' inalienable right of self-determination. It is a sad commentary on the global setting that to set forth these hopes for the future of Libya and its long-suffering population seems like a utopian indulgence!

Post-Intervention Libya: A Militia State

October 12, 2013[11]

Two apparently related—and revealing—incidents have turned public attention briefly back to Libya just after the second anniversary of the NATO intervention that helped rebel forces overthrow the Qaddafi regime: a U.S. Special Forces operation that seized the alleged al-Qaeda operative Abu Anas al-Libi on October 5, supposedly with the knowledge and consent of the Libyan government. The second incident, evidently a response to the first seizure, was the kidnapping a few days later of Libyan prime minister Ali Zeidan while he slept in his hotel in the center of Tripoli. He was easily captured by a squadron of twenty militia gunmen, who arrived at the hotel around six a.m. and proceeded, without resistance from security guards, to carry off the head of the Libyan state. Such a bold assault on the state's essential character as the sole purveyor of legitimate violence (according to Max Weber's famous conception) is a telltale sign of a political system of shadow governance—that is, without security.

Zeidan's capture was reportedly prompted by anger at the government's impotence in the face of such an overt violation of Libyan sovereignty by the United States, as well as serving to warn Libya's political leadership that any further effort to disarm militias would be resisted. The act was largely symbolic: Zeidan's captors released him after only a few hours. Nevertheless, the ease of the kidnapping sent shivers down the spines of the Western leaders who had been so proud two years ago of their regime-changing intervention under NATO auspices. The incident also reinforced the impression in the West that prospects for lucrative foreign investment and substantial oil flows would have to be put on hold for the indefinite future.

According to journalistic accounts, which should perhaps be discounted as unreliable rumors, the militia responsible for this daring challenge to governmental seems to have formed recently and is headed by Nouri Abusahmain, the speaker of the General National Assembly, but there are reasons to doubt the veracity of this account. Abusahmain sa

11. http://richardfalk.wordpress.com/2013/10/12/post-intervention-libya-a-militia-state

serenely beside Zeidan as he addressed the nation shortly after regaining his freedom. For those conscious of Libyan realities, if such a juxtaposition were accurate, it would be a further indication that the capabilities of the elected government in Tripoli are modest compared to those of the militias and can be overridden at will by recalcitrant civil-society forces. Perhaps more to the point, there appears to be a seamless web in Libya between the government and the militias, between what is de jure and what is de facto, between what is lawful and what is criminal. Of course, it was also highly disturbing that a prominent al-Qaeda operative was roaming freely in Libya, seemingly enjoying some level of national support.

Libya is so pervasively armed that even the National Rifle Association might find it excessive. It is rumored that every household is in possession of weapons either distributed to Libyans supportive of the Qaddafi government during its struggle to survive or acquired from NATO benefactors. Unlike several of the other countries experiencing a troubled aftermath to the Arab Spring, Libya is a rich economic prize, with the world's fifth-largest oil reserves generating a cash flow that could be a boon to the troubled economies of Europe. The countries that carried out the intervention have acted subsequently as if they are entitled to a fair market share of the economic opportunities for trade and investment.

Two years ago, the concerns that prompted NATO to act were overtly associated with Qaddafi's bloody crimes against his own people. Security Council Resolution 1973 was premised on protecting the entrapped civilian population of Benghazi against imminent attacks by the regime, primarily through the establishment of a no-fly zone. The non-Western members of the UNSC were skeptical and suspicious at the time of the debate about authorizing military action, fearing that more would be done than claimed, but agreed to abstain.

As it turned out, almost from day one of the intervention it became clear that NATO was interpreting the UN mandate in the broadest possible way, engaging in military operations obviously intended to cause the collapse of the Qaddafi government in Tripoli and only incidentally protecting the people of Benghazi. This maneuver was understandably interpreted as a betrayal of trust by those Security Council members who had been persuaded to abstain, especially Russia and China. One effect of such an action was to weaken, at least in the short run, the UN's capacity to form a consensus in responses to humanitarian crises, as in Syria, and may also have undermined prospects for stable governance in Libya for many years to come.

The Libyan future remains highly uncertain, with several scenarios plausible: partition based on fundamental ethnic and regional enmities, essentially creating two polities, one centered in Benghazi, the other in

Tripoli; a perpetuation of tribal rivalries taking the form of cantonization of the country with governing authority appropriated by various militias, likely producing low-intensity warfare that would create chaos and preclude both meaningful democracy and successful programs of economic development; or "a failed state" that becomes a sanctuary for transnational extremist violence, then a counterterrorist battlefield in the manner of Pakistan, Yemen, Somalia, or Mali, the scenes of deadly drone attacks and covert operations. There is even talk of Saif al-Islam Qaddafi returning to power; he might indeed provide the only road back to political stability. The seizure of al-Libi and the subsequent kidnapping of the prime minister may be metaphors for what "governance" in Libya has come to signify.

The European media and political leaders worry aloud about these disturbing scenarios, but rarely reassess the imperial moves of 2011 that were at least partly designed to restore European influence and create economic opportunities. It is one more instance of postcolonial unwillingness to respect the sovereign autonomy of states, or at least to limit their interference to operational undertakings of genuine emergency actions truly restricted to preventing and mitigating humanitarian catastrophes within a UN mandate. The dynamics of self-determination may produce ugly strife and terrible human tragedy, but nothing can be much worse than what Western intervention produces. The logic of a state-centric world order needs to be complemented by regional and world community institutions and procedures that can address the internal failures of sovereign states and the global private-sector manipulations of domestic tensions that have contributed so insidiously to massive bloodshed in sub-Saharan Africa.[12]

There are obviously no easy answers, but there is no shortage of obscurantist commentary. For instance, the image of a "failed state" is one that poses a threat to Western interests or fails to govern in a manner that precludes its territory from being used to mount hostile violence directed at the West or its property. But is not Egypt as much, or more, a failed state than Libya? Yet it is not so regarded. A strong and oppressive state, especially if not anti-Western, is seen as compatible with geostrategic interests even if it commits terrible crimes against humanity, as has been the case with the el-Sisi coup in Egypt.

We can only wonder whether Libya, as of 2013, is not better understood as a "militia state" than a "failed state," which seems like an emerging pattern for societies that endure Western military intervention. Libya's parallels with Iraq and Afghanistan are uncomfortably suggestive.

---

12. See Noam Chomsky and Andre Vltchek, *On Western Terrorism: From Hiroshima to Drone Warfare* (London: Pluto, 2013) for a convincing elaboration of this latter contention.

4

Syria

My effort in these posts is to make some sense of the Syrian developments that epitomized the darkest shadows cast by the Arab Spring. To an extent not present elsewhere in the Middle East, the depth of suffering resulting from the criminality of the Syrian government has tested my opposition to military intervention. If intervention could have stopped the violence, which is clearly being fueled by deep internal opposition and reinforced by external financial and military assistance, then it would seem to be the lesser of evils.

I could never convince myself, however, that this is the case. The balance of internal and external forces was such that I believe a large-scale military intervention on the insurgent side would further magnify the violence, without any realistic prospect of ending the strife. So, as unsatisfactory as it felt, my posts acknowledge the anguishing dilemma, yet never achieve clarity about what outside forces could do to make the situation better—with or without the UN's blessing—other than making a maximum effort to explore diplomatic paths and take all possible steps to reduce suffering by providing humanitarian relief, including to refugees. The diplomatic path is not explored in an imaginative and dedicated manner, mainly because of American geopolitical ambivalence and Israeli and Saudi opposition to including Iran and Hezbollah in negotiations.

Of all the troubling fallout from the original upheavals that were greeted with the hopeful label of "Arab Spring," none has been more horrifyingly disillusioning than the events that have transpired in Syria since early 2011.

At first perceived as the regional reverberations of the tumultuous events in Tunisia and then Egypt, Syria's popular anti-authoritarian demonstrations were immediately met with extreme violence by the government of Bashar al-Assad. His regime arrested and tortured protesters, including many children, initially in the western town of Daraa; from then on, the fires of opposition spread throughout the country. The Assad government responded with pronounced disregard for the well-being of the Syrian population, committing atrocity after atrocity. On the opposition side, there were also severe problems associated with achieving unity, coherence, leadership, and program.

Worse, regional and global actors intervened with weapons and money in what became a proxy war of increasing magnitude, with Turkey, Saudi Arabia, and Qatar on the insurgent side and Iran on the regime side. Global actors also weighed in, with the United States acting in solidarity with the opposition while Russia supported the government. Further complicating perceptions was the participation of jihadist factions employing extremist tactics, fighting against other insurgent groups as well as against the established order. The confusion of different political agendas and the difficulty of clearly discerning the goals and agenda of the disparate elements of the opposition invited an array of differing interpretations of what was happening and what might best be done.

At first, perceptions in the West were that the Assad regime was doomed, teetering on the brink of collapse, and that it was just a matter of time before the insurgents prevailed. This understanding proved woefully wrong, misleadingly analogizing the isolation of the Qaddafi regime in Libya to the situation in Syria. The Damascus government and armed forces were not nearly as isolated as had been initially supposed, with support from an array of Syrian minorities and elements of the urban business communities. Also, unlike the authoritarian regimes in Tunisia, Egypt, and Yemen, the leadership in Syria was unwilling to accommodate opposition demands even to the extent of having al-Assad give up power. What ensued was bloody civil strife, fought without regard to the constraints of international humanitarian law, exacting an enormous price from the civilian population in terms of death and injury, as well as producing massive internal and refugee displacement.

Many questions were posed, but none more agonizing than the challenges directed toward the international community, which focused initially on the United Nations. In the background of such concerns were persistent anger and understandable distrust on the part of some members of the UN Security Council, especially Russia, over NATO's failure to confine its 2011 intervention in Libya within the terms of its mandate, proceeding without authorization to pursue the goal of regime change, which was not endorsed even indirectly by the Security Council. This distrust was heightened by the aftermath of NATO military operations in Libya: the vigilante execution of Qaddafi followed by the discrediting sequel of violence and chaos, intolerable conditions that continue with no end in sight. This experience constrained the UN's response to what was taking place in Syria and gave military intervention and R2P diplomacy a deservedly bad name.

The UN consensus, such as it was, supported seeking an end to the violence, a goal that all sides rhetorically accepted. But this agreement was superficial and misleading: it papered over the unresolved split as to whether the violence could only end if al-Assad stepped down prior to a transition process that included an electoral process to select a new government. Two distinguished UN special envoys, Kofi Annan and Lakhdar Brahimi, struggled to find common ground, and Brahimi did manage to arrange diplomatic gatherings in Geneva in 2012 and 2014 that brought the Syrian government together with opposition representatives with the mission of finding a political path to resolving the conflict. These diplomatic initiatives failed, at least partly because Saudi Arabia and Israel successfully insisted that Iran was not a welcome participant. Nor were Islamic nonstate actors represented. Without Iran's participation and support it seems impossible to end the civil strife, so we witness the appalling spectacle of ongoing violence and a mass refugee exodus from the country without the political will or capacity to put regional and global geopolitics to one side for the sake of ending the tragedy.

As the war proceeded, extremist elements began to dominate the opposition, a dynamic that accentuates the role of nonstate actors on both sides of the conflict. Hezbollah fighters crossed the border from Lebanon to help turn the tide in Damascus's favor, while the al-Nusra Front (considered in the West to be an al-Qaeda affiliate) emerged as the core of the anti-Assad opposition. These complicated factors were dramatically overshadowed by the emergence of ISIS in 2014 as a major player occupying large portions of Syria as well as Iraq. So threatening is ISIS to the West that a new approach to the entire conflict was initiated and continues to evolve, premised on treating ISIS as the principal and common enemy, a political actor independently targeted by the global War on Terror waged by Washington since the 9/11 attacks. Again, without any evidence of lessons learned, a U.S.-led coalition of countries embarks upon military intervention from the air with locals bearing the burden of ground fighting. In this context the Syrian war, despite continuing to inflict death and destruction, is regarded as a subsidiary concern; since ISIS is against al-Assad, Turkish and U.S. opposition to the Syrian government has again become muted.

The selections in this section address various facets of this predicament, which seems to make both action and inaction unacceptable. What is highlighted is the layering of conflict in the Middle East, with a struggle among various national religious, ethnic, and secular tendencies on the level of the state, with conflict intensified by a vicious sectarian struggle between Sunni- and Shi'a-led countries, overlaid with a global rivalry that pits Russia against the United States in what many are beginning to regard as a slide toward

Cold War II. In this latter sense, events surrounding Ukraine are both distinct from and connected with developments in Syria.

At least three dimensions of this reality reveal the difficulties of overcoming such strife and conflict in the Middle East:

- The structure of world order continues to be primarily based on the territorial sovereignty of states, which renders both international law and the UN marginal in sustained civil conflicts.
- The absence of high geopolitical stakes (e.g., oil reserves, the security of Israel) makes any politically viable form of intervention unlikely to be effective.
- The complications of resolving state/society conflicts are greatly intensified by both regional sectarian conflicts and the rise of nonstate extremist actors that are religiously motivated and capable of altering the balance of forces.

The Arab Spring had an extraordinary regional resonance that has led to unrest and upheaval in many countries and various ongoing confrontations between state and society. Yet the patterns that have unfolded also disclose the originality of each country in the Middle East, both internally and in relation to broader regional conflict configurations and global rivalries. More than anywhere else, Syria has proved to be the eye of a perfect storm: so many factors have been brought to bear in ways that magnified the violence and made efforts to end it so far futile. As the posts that follow seek to show, what has transpired in Syria is in the first instance a tragedy but can be more broadly conceived as a microcosm of the disappointing secondary effects of the initially promising Arab Spring.

Geopolitical Mentoring versus Rehab for Addicted Geopolitical Leaders

August 19, 2011[1]

On August 18, 2011, President Barack Obama rendered judgment and gave guidance, affirming that "the future of Syria must be determined by its own people" but that "the time has come for President Assad to step aside."[2] This advice was orchestrated to coincide with the release of a joint statement along similar lines by the leaders of Germany, France, and Britain that instructed President Assad to "leave power in the greater interests of Syria and the unity of its people." Sanctions against Syria were imposed and tightened, involving energy imports, business connections, and weapons. Other countries were urged to stop supporting the regime and "get on the right side of history." Such words seemed appropriate given the violent behavior of the regime toward its people, except that the source of this utterance was Secretary of State Hillary Clinton, who could well have been sent the same message, given the course of U.S. foreign policy during the Obama presidency.

The Republicans attacked Obama for waiting so long. With a perfect ear for geopolitical mentoring, the leading Republican presidential hopeful, Mitt Romney, modeled the proper American role: "America must show leadership on the world stage and work to move these developing countries toward modernity." Of course, decoding "modernity" suggests the U.S. model of government and economy: be like us and you will be modern and successful. Not a message likely to get a favorable hearing in the global South, but maybe such "modernity" is what the people of Alabama and Arizona desire.

But it's not only Republicans who believe the United States offers the world the best model of humane and legitimate governance. Clinton made clear that governments sharing American values should join together in opposing the Syrian regime through the use of what she called "smart power," "where it is not just brute force, it is not just unilateralism," but behavior shaped by shared commitments to "universal freedom, human rights, democracy, everything we have stood for and pioneered over 235 years."[3] Clinton seems

---

1. http://richardfalk.wordpress.com/2011/08/19/
   syria-geopolitical-mentoring-versus-rehab-for-addicted-geopolitical-leaders/.

2. Barack Obama, press release, August 18, 2011, www.whitehouse.gov/blog/2011/08/18/
   president-obama-future-syria-must-be-determined-its-people-president-bashar-al-
   assad.

3. Associated Press, "Clinton: US Using "Smart Power" for Libya,
   Syria," CBS News, August 16, 2011, www.cbsnews.com/news/
   clinton-us-using-smart-power-for-libya-syria.

to be proposing another "coalition of the willing." But she appears unaware of how starkly these sentiments contradict America's record throughout those 235 years; the ongoing interventions in Afghanistan, Iraq, and Libya are displays of brute force and, if not unilateralism, then at least West-centric interventions that superimpose a West-oriented, secular governing process onto the internal workings of the politics of self-determination. President Obama's guidance on Syria is equally, if less blatantly, suspect. What does it mean to tell the established leadership in Damascus to step aside while affirming the role of the Syrian people in shaping their own future? Such policy incoherence must be hiding something deeper!

This theatrical exhibition that I am describing as "geopolitical mentoring" seems both regrettable and discrediting. To begin with, these ideas emanate directly from the good old days of undisguised colonialism. The language suggests an ideological regression that forgets the very flow of the history that Secretary Clinton was keen to invoke while discouraging countries like Russia, China, India, and Iran from maintaining normal relations with the Damascus regime—the familiar imperial trait of talking endlessly about what others should do but never listening to what others tell us to do. A half-century ago, Adlai Stevenson made a similar observation when he quipped that "the item of technology that America most needs is a hearing aid." Without genuine listening there is no learning.

Geopolitical mentoring sounds condescending even when it is sincere. It is relevant that none of the emerging geopolitical actors, including Brazil, China, and India, have joined the American-led choir and told al-Assad to move on. Even Turkey, which has pressured al-Assad in recent weeks to stop state violence, provide reforms, and abide by human rights, has refrained from joining in the call for his removal from power. Instead of geopolitical mentoring, it is time for some kind of geopolitical rehab program that might allow the United States to grasp the character and full extent of its actual role in the world and its addictive relationship to military solutions. Why else linger in Iraq and Afghanistan? Why kill babies in Libya? There are better ways of exhibiting empathy for the victims of state violence and brutality!

The architects of grand strategy in Washington know that smart power in world politics is all about manipulating double standards. How else can their silence about Israel's oppressive occupation of the West Bank and East Jerusalem be explained, or about the unlawful collective punishment of the people of Gaza? Why their indulgence of Saudi Arabia's systemic suppression of women? Our current political leaders are either not smart or they are merely running moral interference for an ethos of *raison d'état*, which entails that law and morality be damned.

I do not deny that state atrocities of the sort the world has been witnessing in Syria and Libya are unacceptable and should not be tolerated. Moral globalization is incompatible with viewing the boundaries of sovereign states as absolute or treating their leaders as situated beyond legal and moral standards of accountability. Yet it is a sorry commentary on present global conditions if the best we can do is either mount an airborne military intervention that destroys much of what is to be saved or engage in self-satisfied exercises in geopolitical mentoring.

Of course, the future should not be entrusted to the political leaders representing sovereign states. It is up to the peoples of the world to propose and demand better solutions. Populist complacency is part of what gives this geopolitical posturing a semblance of credibility in our postcolonial era. A benign human future, whether in relation to state/society relations and human rights or the abatement of climate change, depends ultimately on a struggle for peace and justice mounted by energized and dedicated transnational movements from below. Only a global populism of as-yet-unimaginable intensity and vision can provide us with that possibility. It is too soon to say whether the Arab Spring is this first glimmering of a Global Spring or just another thwarted challenge to an exploitative and oppressive established order.

Tragedy and Impotence

May 31, 2012[4]

The Houla massacre a week ago in several small Muslim villages near the Syrian city of Homs underscores the brutal violence of a criminal government. Reliable reports confirm that most of the 108 civilians who died in Houla were executed at close range in cold blood, half of whom were children under ten.[5] It is no wonder that the Houla Massacre is being called "a tipping point" in the global response to this latest horrifying outbreak of Syrian violence. The chilling nature of this vicious attack does seem like a point of no return. What happened in Houla, although the details are still contested, seems mainly the work of the Shabiha, the notorious militia of thugs employed by Damascus to deal cruelly with opposition forces and their supposed supporters. This massacre also represents a crude repudiation of

4. http://richardfalk.wordpress.com/2012/05/31/
   what-can-be-done-about-syria-tragedy-and-impotence..

5. Elizabeth A. Kennedy, "Syria Massacre Victims in Houla Executed, Says UN," Associated Press, May 29, 2012, www.huffingtonpost.com/2012/05/29/syria-massacre-victims-in_n_1552070.html.

UN diplomacy, especially the ceasefire that 280 unarmed UN observers have been monitoring since April 12. It reinforces the impression that the Assad regime is increasingly relying on state terror to destroy the movement against it. Such defiance also creates new pressure on the UN and the international community to do something more than bemoaning and censuring, or face being further discredited as inept and even irrelevant.

But is not the Syrian situation better treated as a "tragic predicament" of contemporary world order rather than as a "tipping point" that might justify military intervention? The phrase "tipping point" raises misleading hard-power expectations that external, coercive initiatives can redeem the situation. What kind of UN or NATO action could hope to stop the violence and change the governing structure of Syria for the better? There has long existed an international consensus that the Syrian response to the popular uprising should be vigorously opposed, but this awareness was coupled with a growing realization that there are no good options to choose from; the Assad regime defies international censure and media exposure. Even those who supported Kofi Annan's six-point peace plan acknowledged that it represented a desperate effort with almost no prospect of succeeding. Critics claimed that Assad "accepted" the plan in bad faith to gain breathing space while he went forward with his own efforts to crush the opposition. In truth, the opposition may also have been unwilling to live within the limits of the Annan approach, which meant giving up its primary goal of controlling a new governance structure in Syria.

There is a widely shared sentiment that "something more must be done," but what? Remembering the awful failure of the world to address the 1994 genocide in Rwanda and the 1995 massacre at Srebrenica, many feel that developments in Syria are heading toward a comparably "unspeakable humanitarian catastrophe." Already more than ten thousand Syrians have died, and it seems likely that far worse may still occur if the Assad leadership is not removed.

Diplomacy has been arduously pursued since the outset of the turmoil originally by Turkey, then the Arab League, and finally by Annan, with each phase greeted in Damascus by deceptive welcoming gestures without any intention to abandon or even mitigate reliance on indiscriminate violence. Government officials sweet-talked international emissaries, announced their willingness to stop the killing and other abuses, and even accepted monitoring arrangements. On occasion after occasion, before negotiators had left the country, the regime resumed its fierce combat tactics as if nothing had happened; for this, the opposition, led by the Free Syrian Army, deserves a share of the blame. Diplomacy has been given multiple chances and continues to be put forward as the only way to make a difference in the conflict, yet it clearly lacks the authority and capability to stop the blood-shed and suspend the political struggle for control of the Syrian state.

This frustration of diplomacy naturally turns our attention to more coercive options. Secretary of State Clinton blames Russia for preventing the stronger action the UN Security Council endorses, arguing that this is pushing Syria into a prolonged civil war. Whether Russia will alter its stance remains uncertain, but there is a definite call for new initiatives inside and outside the UN. There are intimations of the formation of a new "coalition of the willing" prepared to engage in military intervention. Even NGOs are demanding a stronger stand: Amnesty International, for instance, has issued an appeal to the Security Council to call upon the International Criminal Court to indict Syrian leaders for their role in severe crimes against human-ity, culminating in the Houla massacre. Some irresponsibly belligerent politi-cal figures in the United States have been advocating military intervention for several months, most notably John McCain, the Republican senator who lost the presidential election to Barack Obama in 2008. So far there seems little appetite for such an undertaking, even at the Pentagon, and certainly not among the American public. Unlike Libya, Syria has no substantial oil reserves to swing the balance.

The logistics and politics surrounding any proposed military inter-vention in Syria make it an unrealistic option. There is no political will to mount the kind of major military operation on the ground that would have reasonable hopes of combining regime change with an enforced stability until normalcy could be established by a new national leadership. NATO's reliance on air power without ground troops was able to turn the tide deci-sively, if destructively, in favor of rebel forces in Libya, but such a scenario is inapplicable to Syria, where the regime commands more public support and more substantial military and paramilitary resources, especially if it continues to receive military assistance from Iran. All in all, the military option would likely make matters worse for the Syrian people, increasing the magnitude of internal violence without bringing the conflict to an end.

There is radical uncertainty surrounding the nature of the anti-Assad forces within Syria and the motivations of their external backers. Such uncer-tainty is particularly prevalent among Syrian minorities, who seem to fear the collapse of the present regime in Damascus more than they dislike some of its oppressive behavior. Such circumstances should warrant humility. What is certain is the bloody nature of the conflict, the indiscriminate tactics, and the efforts to terrorize the civilian population. While it is correct at this point to hold the government in power responsible and accountable, both sides have acted ruthlessly and in a manner that casts a dark cloud over Syria's future.

The dilemma exposes the weakness of empathetic geopolitics in a world dominated by territorially supreme sovereign states with insecure and antagonistic minorities. It is unacceptable to remain a passive spectator when events are reported visually almost as they occur; there is no way to avert the gaze of an outside world that is both compassionate and untrustworthy. It is morally unacceptable to stand by, watch, and do nothing. But the UN lacks the authority, capability, and legitimacy to impose the collective will of international society, except in those rare instances when it is able to mobilize an effective *geopolitical* consensus. For reasons explained above, plus the lingering resentment due to the deception of Russia and China regarding Libya, no such consensus favoring military intervention in Syria has emerged, and none seems likely.

What is left to fill the gap between the unacceptable and the unrealistic is diplomacy, which has proved to be futile up to this point, but hanging on to the slim possibility that it might yet somehow produce positive results is the only conceivable way forward. It is easy to deride Kofi Annan and the frustrations arising from Damascus's repeated failures to comply with the agreed framework, but it remains impossible to find preferable alternatives. If diplomacy is finally admitted to be a dead end, as seems almost certain, it raises serious questions as to whether the absence of stronger global institutions of a democratic character is not a fatal flaw in the twenty-first-century structure of world order. Moral awareness without the political capacity to act responsively points to a desperate need for global reform, but the grossly unequal distributions of power and wealth in the world make such adjustments unfeasible for the foreseeable future. The peoples of the world, and of Syria, seem destined to go on living in this tragic space between the unacceptable and the impossible.

Killing and Dying: Persisting Syrian Dilemmas
October 12, 2012[6]

In appraising political developments most of us rely on trusted sources, our overall political orientation, what we have learned from past experience, and our personal hierarchy of hopes and fears. No matter how judicious, we still reach conclusions in settings of radical uncertainty, which incline our judgments to reflect *a priori* and interpretative biases. As militarists tend to favor

---

6. http://richardfalk.wordpress.com/2012/10/12/hope-wisdom-law-ethics-and-spirituality-in-relation-to-killing-and-dying-persisting-syrian-dilemmas.

force to resolve disputes, so war-weary and pacifist citizens will seek to resolve even the most dire conflict situations through nonviolent diplomacy.

In the end, even in liberal democracies, most of us are far too dependent on untrustworthy and manipulated media assessments to form judgments about unfolding world events. How then should we understand the terrible ongoing ordeal of violence in Syria? The polarized perceptions of the conflict are almost certain to convey one-sided false impressions: that the atrocities and violence are the work of a bloody regime with a history of brutal oppression or that this hapless country has become the scene of a proxy war between irresponsible outsiders with strong Sunni/Shi'a sectarian overtones, further complicated by geopolitical alignments and the undisclosed ambitions of the United States, Russia, Israel, Iran, Saudi Arabia, Turkey, and others. Undoubtedly the truth lies at some point between the two poles, with ambiguities and unknowns leading many to discount the extremely dirty hands of all the major participants, seen and unseen.

If we seek to interpret the conflict from all angles with as much detachment as possible, the result is likely to be paralyzing. There is too much uncertainty, secrecy, and complexity to give rise to the clarity needed to shape policy with any confidence, and without confidence, either in killing or allowing the killing to continue, no responsible conclusion can be reached. In effect, only oversimplification is capable of overcoming passivity, but at a high cost. Passivity, here, thus functions as a political virtue: the lesser evil.

Assuming we repudiate proxy and geopolitical agendas as the desired bases for determining Syria's future, for what should we hope? A rapid end to the violence, some sort of now-unimaginable accommodation between the sides, a recognition by "interested" third parties that their goals cannot be attained at acceptable costs, the abdication of Bashar al-Assad, a uniformly enforced arms embargo, perhaps the completely implausible emergence of constitutional democracy, including respect for minority rights. Merely composing such a wish list underscores the seeming *hopelessness* of resolving the situation, yet we know that eventually it will somehow be resolved.

From the perspective of the Syrian participants, so much blood has been spilled that it probably seems unacceptable to be receptive to any offer of reconciliation: the only *hope* is for either an unconditional victory for the self or the extermination of the other. It is therefore not surprising that the bodies keep piling up. What are we to do when every realistic trajectory adds to an outcome that is already tragic?

My approach in these situations of internal conflict has been to oppose and distrust the humanitarian and democratizing pretensions of those who counsel intervention under the alluring banner of the "responsibility to protect" (R2P) and other liberal rationales supportive of military interven-tion, or what Noam Chomsky tellingly calls "military humanism." Yet to counsel a passive international response to the most severe crimes against humanity and genocidal atrocities would seem to deny the most elemental ethical bonds of human solidarity in a networked, globalized world, bonds that may turn out in the near future to be indispensable if we are to achieve environmental sustainability before climate change burns us to a crisp.

There are structural issues arising from the statist character of the post-colonial world order that make political choices in such situations of bitter internal conflict a tragic predicament. On one side is the statist logic that endows territorial governments with unconditional authority to sustain their unity in the face of insurgent challenges, a political principle given con-stitutional backing in Article 2(7) of the UN Charter, which prohibits UN intervention in internal conflicts. This statist logic is deeply challenged and contradicted by legitimizing the inalienable and emancipatory right of self-determination conferred on every "people" and not on governments. In the background as well are the various non-Western collective memories, uni-formly bad, of colonial rule, and well-founded contemporary suspicions that humanitarian interventions represent attempted colonialist revivals, both ideologically and behaviorally.

On the other side of the policy fence is an odd coalition of liberal interna-tionalists who sincerely regard intervention as an essential tool for the promo-tion of a more humane world, along with more cynical geopolitical strategists who regard conflict zones, especially ones with large oil reserves, as targets of opportunity for extending Western interests. Further, normative confu-sion arises from the UN's tendency to vest in the Security Council unlimited competence to interpret the Charter as it wishes.[7] In this regard, the rhetoric of human rights has been used to circumvent the Charter limits on address-ing conflicts internal to states: see the previous chapter on Libya, for example.

In evaluating our positions for or against a given intervention, should our sense of strategic motivations matter? For instance, the Kosovo inter-vention was at least partially motivated by the desire in Washington and among many European elites to show that NATO was still useful after the Cold War. Do such strategic considerations matter if indeed the people of Kosovo were spared the kind of ethnic cleansing endured not long before by the people of Bosnia? Might it not be claimed that only when strategic incen-tives exist will an intervention be of sufficient magnitude to be effective? In effect, this position holds that altruism alone will not produce effective form

---

7. See the World Court decision in the *Lockerbie* case, which coincidentally involved Libya. "Questions of Interpretation and Application Arising from the Aerial Inciden at Lockerbie (*Libya v. United Kingdom*)," ICJ Reports, February 27, 1998.

of humanitarian intervention. Do double standards matter? Certain crimes against humanity generate intervention response while others are overlooked, such as in Gaza. Should we drink from a glass that is only half full?

There are other ways of evaluating what has taken place. For example, should the consequences of intervention or nonintervention color our assessments of the policy choice? Let's say that Kosovo evolves in a constructive direction of respect for human rights, including those of the Serbian minority, or that it becomes repressive toward its minority population. Should we retrospectively reexamine our earlier view on what it was preferable to do back in 1999? Finally, should we give priority to the postulates of human solidarity, what might be called "moral globalization," or to the primacy of self-determination as the best hope that peoples of the world have of achieving emancipatory goals, recognizing that the grand strategies of the geopolitical actors are at best indifferent and often hostile to such claims?

In such a global setting we cannot avoid making disastrous mistakes, but we should not withdraw from politics and throw up our hands in frustration. We can expose false claims, contradictions, and double standards and side with those who act on behalf of emancipatory goals, while not being insensitive to the complexity and even contradictions of "emancipation" in many political settings. There are often "right" and "wrong" sides from the perspective of international morality, international law, and global justice—but not always. When all sides seem deeply "wrong," as in Syria, the only responsible posture may be one of humility and acknowledgment of radical uncertainty. In such circumstances, the most salient moral imperative is to refrain from acts that are likely to intensify the violence, suffering, dying, and killing. This may not be a heroic political posture, but it offers the most constructive response to a particular mix of circumstances, minimizing prospects of further escalation.

Finally, it is not very helpful to observe that "time will tell." Perhaps in the future we can learn about factors that might have altered our assessment, but we base decisions on what we know and perceive at the time. In some situations, such as the many struggles of oppressed and occupied peoples, it seems desirable to be hopeful even though the eventual outcome could bring deep disappointment. We should, I feel, as often as possible be guided by our hopes and beliefs—even when, as nearly always, we are confronted by dilemmas of radical uncertainty. We should also do our best not to be manipulated by those media-savvy "realists" who stress fears, claim a convergence of benevolence and interests, exaggerate the benefits of military superiority, and (especially in America) serve as the self-appointed chief designers of exploitative patterns of geopolitically shaped security.

With hope we can often overcome uncertainty with desire and engage in struggles for a just and sustainable future. Without hope, we fall victim to despair and will be carried along with the historical current that is leading our nation, society, civilization, species, and world toward catastrophe.

The Wrong "Red Line"

May 11, 2013[8]

At an August 2012 press conference, President Obama was asked about the consequences of a possible future use of chemical weapons by the Assad regime. Obama replied that such a use, should it occur, would be to cross "a red line." This assertion was widely understood as a threat either to launch air strikes or to provide rebel forces with major, direct military assistance, including weaponry. There have been sketchy reports that Syria did use chemical weapons, as well as allegations that the reported use was a "false flag" operation designed to force Obama's hand. The *New York Times* described Obama as "in a geopolitical box, his credibility at stake with frustratingly few good options."[9] This policy dilemma raises tactical issues about how to intervene in the Syrian civil war without risking costly and uncertain involvement in yet another Middle Eastern war. Not responding also raises delicate questions of presidential leadership in a highly polarized domestic political atmosphere, already shamelessly exploited by belligerent Republican lawmakers backed by a feverish media that always seem to be pushing Obama to pursue a more muscular foreign policy in support of alleged U.S.'s global interests, as if hard-power geopolitics still is the key to global security.

What is missing from the debate on Syria, and generally from the challenge to American foreign policy, is a more fundamental "red line" that the United States once took the lead in formulating—namely, the unconditional prohibition of the use of international force by states, other than in cases of self-defense against a prior armed attack. This prohibition was the core idea embodied in the United Nations Charter, is embedded in contemporary international law, and was a natural sequel to the prosecution and punishment of surviving German and Japanese leaders after World War II for their commission of "crimes against peace," the international crime associated with

8. http://richardfalk.wordpress.com/2013/05/11/rethinking-red-lines.

9. Peter Baker, Mark Landler, David E. Sanger, and Anne Barnard, "Off-the-Cuff Obama Line Put U.S. in Bind on Syria," *New York Times*, May 4, 2013, www.nytimes com/2013/05/05/world/middleeast/obamas-vow-on-chemical-weapons-puts-him-in-tough-spot.html.

ngaging in aggressive warfare. The only lawful exceptions are uses of force onsistent with the terms of prior authorization by the UN Security Council. his consensus among the winners in World War II was the key hope for vorld peace: that aggressive war and acquisition of territory by force, even in he exercise of self-defense, must be outlawed without exceptions. The West btained Security Council authorizations in the 1991 Gulf War and again n Libya in 2011, but in each instance the scope and intensity of the actual ndertaking far exceeded the UN mandate. The resulting loss of trust on the art of China and Russia has become evident in the gridlocked debate about vhat to do in Syria, where the conflict combines internal strife with external roxy involvements that threaten to expand the war zone in a variety of menacing ways.

The Charter's red line has been surprisingly well respected since 1945, at east in clear instances of border-crossing, sustained violence. The UN authorized the defense of South Korea in response to an armed attack by North Korea in 1950, and even exerted effective pressure in 1956 on the United Kingdom, France, and Israel, with surprising U.S. support, to withdraw from erritory seized after their attack on Egypt: the sole prominent example of *law* revailing over *geopolitics* at the UN. In 1991 the UN successfully authorized orce that followed sanctions and succeeded in restoring the sovereignty of Kuwait after Iraq's aggressive occupation and annexation the previous year. The UN red line held up reasonably well until the end of the last century, but ts interpretation was subject to geopolitical manipulations and evasions associated with claims of humanitarian intervention, as well as a variety of strategically motivated covert interventions (such as Iran in 1953 and Guatemala n 1954). This pattern of evasion was a prominent feature of the Cold War, as oth sides intervened in foreign states or in their respective spheres of influnce (South Vietnam, Eastern Europe, Afghanistan, Central America). Such ses of international force by rival superpowers without engaging the UN ramework definitely eroded the authority of the red line and its stature in nternational law, but did not lead political actors to call for its abandonment though some antilegalist, realist international-law specialists felt that, in ffect, the red line had been erased, at least for the top tier of sovereign states). Although not explicit, the American position was increasingly exhibiting the sychological characteristics of geopolitical *bipolarity* (also sometimes called American exceptionalism"): no red line for U.S. foreign policy but a bright ed line for others, especially adversary states.

What weakened this red line even more decisively was undoubtedly the American-led attack on Iraq in 2003 after the Security Council rebuffed an American plea for UN permission to use force, despite a concerted effort o convince its members that Iraq's supposed possession of weapons of mass destruction was such a great menace to world peace as to justify what amounted to a "preventive war." The United States stood in undisguised defiance not only of this most fundamental red line of international law but also of world public opinion, expressed in the most massive antiwar demonstrations in all of history, held in some eighty countries on February 15, 2003. Richard Perle, often touted as the most astute of the Bush-era neocon intellectuals, was exultant about this seemingly definitive breach of the red line, celebrating American aggression against Iraq in a *Guardian* article aptly headlined "Thank God for the Death of the UN."[10] Although its authority was definitely flouted, the UN is far from dead as an organization. Its manifold efforts to address the concerns of the world continue and even its red line, although covered with dust, has not yet been erased. Maybe we should really thank God that the collective global consciousness has partly ignored such disabling precedents as the Iraq experience!

What is baffling about Obama's approach is that it purports to be very mindful of the importance of international law. Just last September, in a speech to the General Assembly, he said, "We know from painful experience that the path to security and prosperity does not lie outside the boundaries of international law."[11] In arguing on behalf of collective action against states that violate international law, he told the Nobel Peace Prize audience in Oslo that "those that claim respect for international law cannot avert their eyes when those laws are flouted."[12]

Yet, when reflecting on Syria (or Iran's nuclear program), Obama is silent about the relevance of international law, although in neither instance could force be justified as self-defense. It is true that the Clinton presidency, in participating via NATO in the 1999 Kosovo war, proceeded also to embark on a nondefensive war without prior authorization, setting a precedent that generated worries about nondefensive military undertakings lacking a legal foundation. These were offset in the belief that a humanitarian catastrophe had been averted.

The question raised is whether the red line of international law at stake in Syria is more like Iraq or like Kosovo or Libya. It is unlike Iraq in the sense that there is an ongoing unresolved civil war that is actively destabilizing

10. Richard Perle, "Thank God for the Death of the UN," *Guardian,* March 20, 2003, www.theguardian.com/politics/2003/mar/21/foreignpolicy.iraq1.

11. Barack Obama, remarks to the United Nations General Assembly, New York, New York, September 25, 2012, www.whitehouse.gov/the-press-office/2012/09/25/remarks-president-un-general-assembly.

12. Barack Obama, remarks at acceptance of Nobel Peace Prize, Oslo, Norway, December 10, 2009, www.whitehouse.gov/the-press-office/remarks-president-acceptance-nobel-peace-prize.

the region and spilling over national borders to cause unrest in neighboring countries. Syria is also the scene of severe crimes against humanity by the regime, and no end to the violence is in sight. It is, however, unlike Kosovo or Libya in that proxy states are acting as participants on both sides, and in that the Damascus regime maintains considerable internal support. It is essential that each conflict be assessed within its own distinctive context, which should raise for discussion whether the red line should be crossed in this instance on behalf of the "blue line" of legitimacy (saving a vulnerable people from a humanitarian catastrophe) or the "white line" of feasibility (likelihood of success with minimum loss of life and high probability of positive net effects).

Finally, it has been argued that the changing nature of conflict has made the red line obsolete since 9/11. Traditional ideas of deterrence, containment, and territorial defense seem almost irrelevant in relation to global security regimes when the perceived assailants are individuals who cannot be deterred and are operating in nonterritorial networks. As matters proceed, policy about force is being formulated without bothering with international law and the UN, regressively producing a world of unregulated sovereign states and extremist nonstates essentially deciding on their own when war is permissible. The recent Israeli air strikes on Syrian targets are illustrative: unprovoked and nondefensive, yet eliciting scant criticism in the media or even commentary about the dangers of such unilateralism. Such normative chaos, in a world where nine countries possess nuclear weapons, seems like a prescription for eventual species suicide, an impression reinforced by our failure to address the menace of global warming. Never has the world more needed red lines to be drawn and upheld by major states out of the realization that national interests increasingly coincide with the global interest. Arguably the Charter needs to be modified in light of the rise of nonstate actors and nonterritorial warfare, but such an undertaking is nowhere on the agenda—so the world drifts back to the pre–World War I era of unrestricted warfare.

Obama talks the talk, but seems unwilling to walk the walk. Such a disjunction invites cynicism about law and morality and induces despair in those of us who believe the world we inhabit badly needs red lines—the *right* red lines. Redrawing them to fit the realities of our world and keep hopes for peace and justice alive should be the great diplomatic challenge of our time.

Contra Attacking Syria

August 30, 2013[13]

Informed opinion agrees that the proper response of the West to the Assad regime's presumed responsibility for the use of chemical weapons on August 21 in Ghuta, a neighborhood east of Damascus, is intended to be *punitive* and at the same time to deny any ambition to alter the course of the internal struggle for power in Syria or to assassinate Bashar al-Assad. If it achieved some larger goal unexpectedly, this would likely be welcomed—although not necessarily—by Washington, Ankara, Riyadh, and Tel Aviv.

Why not necessarily? Because there is a growing belief in influential Western circles that it is better for the United States and Israel if the civil war goes on and on with no winners.[14] Accorded to this warped reasoning, if al-Assad wins, it would produce significant regional gains for Iran, Russia, and Hezbollah; if the Free Syrian Army and its al-Nusra Front and al-Qaeda allies win, it is feared this would give violent extremist forces a base of operations that would work strongly against Western interests. Only Turkey, the front-line opponent of the Assad regime, and Saudi Arabia, the regional champion of Sunni sectarianism, stand to gain by resolving the conflict in favor of the Sunni-led opposition forces: as Ankara and Riyadh see it, this would contribute to greater regional stability, augment their preferred sectarian alignment, and inflict a major setback on Iran and Russia.

Turkey and Saudi Arabia are split on whether a regime that has repeatedly committed crimes against humanity against its own people should ever be protected. Their contradictory responses to the el-Sisi coup and massacres in Egypt are illuminating on this score: Turkey adhered to principle despite a sacrifice of its short-term material and political interests in the Middle East, while Saudi Arabia rushed in to provide massive economic assistance and a show of strong diplomatic support for a military takeover that is crushing the leading Muslim political organization in the country.

Another way of thinking about the grand strategy of the United States in the Middle East is suggested by the noted Israeli peace activist and former Knesset member Uri Avnery, who portrays the United States as frantically at work behind the scenes to restore the function of governance to military dictators, with Egypt the new poster child. Avnery attributes these Machiavellian machinations to CIA masterminds swimming in dark waters,

13. http://richardfalk.wordpress.com/2013/08/30/contra-syria-attack.

14. For a representative approach, see Edward N. Luttwak, "In Syria, America Loses If Either Side Wins," *New York Times*, August 24, 2013, www.nytimes.com/2013/08/25/opinion/sunday/in-syria-america-loses-if-either-side-wins.html.

entrapping Obama by overriding his strong rhetorical support for democracy in the Arab world.[15]

The rationale for an American-led attack on Syria is mostly expressed as follows:

- America's credibility is at stake after al-Assad crossed Obama's "red line" by launching a large-scale lethal chemical weapons attack; doing nothing in response would undermine U.S. global leadership.
- America's credibility makes indispensable and irreplaceable contributions to world order and should not be jeopardized by continued passivity; inaction has been tried for the past two years and failed miserably not clearly tried—Hillary Clinton was an avowed early supporter of the rebel cause, including arms supplies; recent reports indicate American-led "special forces operations" are being conducted to bolster the anti-Assad struggle.
- A punitive strike will deter future uses of chemical weapons by Syria and others, teaching al-Assad and other leaders that serious adverse consequences will follow a failure to heed American warnings.
- Even if the attack does not shift the balance back to the insurgent forces, it will restore their political will to persist in the struggle for an eventual political victory over al-Assad and operate to offset their recently weakened position.
- It is possible that an attack would enhance prospects for a diplomatic compromise, allowing a reconvening of the Geneva diplomatic conference, the preferred forum for promoting the transition to a post-Assad Syria.

Why is this rationale insufficient?

- It does not take account of the fact that such a punitive attack would lack any foundation in international law.
- It presupposes that the U.S. government rightfully exercises police powers on the global stage and, by unilateral (or "coalition of the willing") decision, can give *legitimacy* to another *unlawful* undertaking.
- U.S. foreign policy under President Obama has similarities to that of George W. Bush in relation to international law, despite differences in rhetoric and style: Obama evades the constraints

---

15. Uri Avnery, "Poor Obama," *Outlook India*, August 30, 2013, www.outlookindia. com/article/Poor-Obama/287653.

of international law by the practice of "reverential interpretations," while Bush defied as matter of national self-assertion and
the meta-norms of grand strategy; as a result Obama comes off
as a hypocrite while Bush is critically portrayed as an outlaw
or cowboy. In an ideal form of global law both would be held
accountable for their violations of international criminal law.

- A punitive strike could generate harmful results, weakening
diplomatic prospects; increasing spillover effects on Lebanon,
Turkey, Jordan, and elsewhere; complicating relations with Iran
and Russia; producing retaliatory responses that widen the combat zone; and causing a worldwide rise in anti-Americanism.

There is one conceptual issue that deserves further attention. In the aftermath of the Kosovo war the Independent International Commission argued
that the attack was "illegal but legitimate"—illegal because nondefensive and
unauthorized by the Security Council, but legitimate because of compelling moral reasons coupled with considerations of political feasibility.[16] Such
claims were also subject to harsh criticism as exhibiting double standards
(why not Palestine?).

None of these elements are present in relation to Syria: an attack would
be manifestly unlawful and also illegitimate, harming innocent Syrians without achieving proportionate political ends benefitting their well-being. The
principal justifications for using force relate to geopolitical concerns such as
"credibility," "deterrence," and "U.S. leadership."[17]

Questioning Obamacare for Syria

September 5, 2013[18]

There is something particularly distressing about the ongoing debate on
authorizing an internationally illegal and immoral military attack on Syria:
a show of political support from the right. Such a "coming together" of some

16. Independent International Commission on Kosovo, *The Kosovo Report of the
Independent International Commission on Kosovo* (London: Oxford University Press,
2000), 163–98.

17. For an intelligent counterargument, see Ian Hurd, "Bomb Syria, Even if it is Illegal,"
New York Times, August 27, 2013, www.nytimes.com/2013/08/28/opinion/bomb-
syria-even-if-it-is-illegal.html; also Ian Hurd, "Saving Syria: International Law
Is Not the Answer," Al Jazeera, August 27, 2013, www.aljazeera.com/indepth/
opinion/2013/08/2013827123244943321.html.

18. http://richardfalk.wordpress.com/2013/09/05/questioning-obamacare-for-syria.

of the center and much of the right in Congress has been sadly absent during Obama's presidency until now. This support emerges on the rare occasion when a majority of American citizens—not known for their cosmopolitan sentiments or affection for the UN Charter—oppose attacking Syria, as do the British Parliament and public opinion throughout Europe. Supporting an attack, in such a setting, repudiates not only international law and the UN but the whole fabric of democratic accountability to law and the judgment of the people.

At least the reactionary tendency in American political life, over the course of the last decade or so, has been consistent in its adherence to irresponsible means in the pursuit of irresponsible ends. The real selling point of an attack is not saving the Syrians, but warning Iran that it is next on the hit list unless it soon surrenders to Washington's demands with respect to its nuclear program. Is this what global leadership has come to mean—reminding adversaries that the global bully means business?

What about the damage to President Obama's legacy? If an attack on Syria is truly limited and does not produce many civilian casualties, hawkish stalwarts like Senators McCain and Graham will quickly change sides, arguing that giving al-Assad a slap on the wrist is worse than nothing. The hawks' broadening of the Congressional resolution suggests that their support depends on launching a much wider attack than what Obama seemed to favor in his call to Congress for authorization. Does he heed his earlier concept of the attack or go along with his more militarist supporters?

If, as seems probable, there are casualties, retaliations, escalations, diplomatic fallout, persisting civil strife, and cross-border spillover effects, Obama is almost sure to face a grassroots protest movement expressing national and global disaffection. This movement would include some of those Democrats who will go along with the attack because a "red line," once drawn by an American president, must be respected—even if the cost of doing so is irresponsible, irrational, imprudent, illegal, and immoral. Carrying out Obama's preferred course of action would mean reverting to the once-derided "Nixon madman" approach to foreign policy—that is, making adversaries believe that the American president is trigger-happy and crazy, doing whatever it takes to make sure America is feared around the world. This iron-fist style of "keeping of the peace" is totally divorced from adherence to international law and support for the UN.

If the only way America can seem strong is to cast itself in the role of global bully, supplanting the somewhat more understandable imperial cover of *pax Americana*, then the wise and virtuous will conclude, if they have not already, that America is actually *weak*. In this century true strength will not be measured by degrees of military dominance and battlefield victories, but by helping to solve the growing problems endangering the future of humanity.

Such a constructive path can only be taken if the major states respect international law and the UN Charter as the foundational premises of a sustainable world order. Interpreting history from the militarist perspectives of those who base human and societal security on a global war machine places us all on a slippery slope that leads to nothing less than species extinction. We need to fear more a clash of rationalities than a clash of civilizations, although both should be transcended.

Any attack on Syria is likely to be over in several days (although the current language of the resolution extends authorization to 90 days). The reaction by Syria and its friends, if any, will probably be muted, and life in America, the Middle East, and the world will return to what passes for normalcy. Even so, the effect would be deeply destructive. It would enable most of us to remain ignorant of the frightening underlying reality that our body politic suffers from the crippling disease of "martialitis" for which there is no known cure. Indeed, the disgraceful edifice of global surveillance may have as its primary task suppressing knowledge that our political leaders suffer from severe versions of this disease. Edward Snowden, Chelsea Manning, and Julian Assange were attempting to remove the geopolitical cataracts clouding our vision of such a distressing political reality, and for these good works the government is poised to criminalize and punish rather than learn and honor.

Resolving the Syrian Chemical-Weapons Crisis: Sunlight and Shadows

September 15, 2013[19]

This is Vladimir Putin's moment.

Putin explains coherently in a *New York Times* op-ed (published on September 11 (without invoking the symbolism of the twelfth anniversary of the 9/11 attacks) that his approach to Russian foreign policy relies on two instruments: soft power and economic diplomacy.[20] He acknowledges American leadership, but only if exercised within a framework of respect for

19. http://richardfalk.wordpress.com/2013/09/15/
   resolving-the-syrian-chemical-weapons-crisis-sunlight-and-shadows.

20. Vladimir Putin, "A Plea for Caution from Russia," *New York Times*, September 11, 2013, www.nytimes.com/2013/09/12/opinion/putin-plea-for-caution-from-russia-on syria.html?_r=0.

international law and the UN Charter. He also appropriately takes issue with Obama's sentiments, expressed a night earlier, to the effect that America has a unique entitlement to use force to overcome injustice in situations other than self-defense, even without Security Council authorization. Putin, perhaps disingenuously, claims (quite correctly) that such a prerogative is "extremely dangerous." He rejects Obama's pretense that unilateral discretion with respect to the use of force can be inferred from American exceptionalism. Whether disingenuous or not, requiring Security Council authorization for non-defensive uses of force, while sometimes preventing UN peacekeeping responses to certain tragic situations, overall contributes to finding diplomatically agreed-upon solutions for conflict and enables the UN (unlike the League of Nations) to persist despite severe tensions among its dominant members.

Not only has Putin exhibited a new, constructive role for Russia in twenty-first-century statecraft and spared Syria and the Middle East from another cycle of escalating violence, but he articulated this in the form of a direct appeal to the American people. Not since Nikita Khrushchev helped save the world from nuclear war in the Cuban missile crisis of 1962, by backing down and agreeing to a face-saving formula for both superpowers, has Moscow distinguished itself in any positive way in international relations. For Putin to be so forthcoming, without being belligerent, was particularly impressive given Obama's rather ill-considered cancellation only a few weeks ago of their planned bilateral meeting, supposedly out of anger at Russia's refusal to turn Edward Snowden over for criminal prosecution. Considering that Putin has much blood on his hands, it is hard to expect anything benevolent during his watch. So Putin is emerging as a virtual "geopolitical black swan," making major, unanticipated moves that could transform the character of conflict management and resolution. Putin could have stayed on the sidelines as Obama sank into the Syrian quagmire; instead he stepped in with a momentous move that seems to have served the regional and global interest.

Let us hope that this virtuoso exhibition of creative diplomacy prompts Putin's counterpart in the White House to explore soft-power opportunities that will better protect American national interests while simultaneously serving the global interest. Doing so might even reverse the steady decline of American credibility as a benevolent global leader.

Syria: What to Do Now

February 26, 2014[21]

There is a new mood of moral desperation, as the ongoing strife in Syria has resulted in at least 135,000 deaths, 9.3 million displaced, and countless atrocities, including urban sieges designed to starve civilians perceived to be hostile and Palestinian refugee communities in Syria being attacked, blockaded, and dispersed. As the second round of negotiations in the Geneva II Conference on Syria ended as fruitlessly as the earlier round, there is a sense that diplomacy is a performance ritual without any serious intent to engage in conflict-resolving negotiations. Expectations couldn't be lower for the planned third round of the Geneva II process.

The Damascus regime wants an end to armed opposition, while the insurgency insists upon setting up a transition process that is independently administered and committed to the election of a new political leadership. The gap between the parties is too big and getting bigger, especially as the Damascus government correctly perceives the tide of combat to be turning in its favor, leading the main opposition forces to seek to achieve politically and diplomatically what they appear unable to do militarily. Also, it is unclear whether the opposition presence in Geneva has the authority to speak on behalf of several opposition groups in the field in Syria.

In light of these frustrations, it is not surprising to observe an acrimonious debate between American interventionists who believe that only force, or at least its threat, can thread the needle of hope. Invoking the R2P norm, they suggest that such an approach should be used in Syria either to establish a no-fly zone, opening a corridor that will allow humanitarian aid to flow to besieged cities, or to achieve regime change.

The anti-interventionists point out that the Libyan precedent of 2011 is tainted by the deliberate expansion of the humanitarian authorization by the UN Security Council to undertake a much wider campaign with the clear intent of regime change, which in fact ended with the capture and execution of Muammar Qaddafi. It is also somewhat tarnished by the post-Qaddafi realities of widespread militia violence and the failure to develop a coherent and legitimate governance structure. They also argue that introducing external military force almost always makes matters worse—more killing, more devastation, and no politically sustainable outcome—and there is no good reason to think this will not happen in Syria. Furthermore, without a Security Council mandate, such force would once again violate the UN Charter and international law.

---

21. http://richardfalk.wordpress.com/2014/02/26/syria-what-to-do-now.

Providing humanitarian relief in a situation mainly free of internal political struggle should be sharply distinguished from realities amid serious civil strife. The 1992 response to the Somali breakdown of governability is illustrative of a seemingly pure humanitarian response to famine and disease, characterized by a posture of political noninterference and the shipment of food and medical supplies to people in desperate need. This contrasted with the supposedly more muscular response to a troubled Somalia during the early stages of the Clinton presidency in 1993, when the humanitarian mission was fused with anti-"warlord" and political reconstruction goals. Difficulties soon emerged as robust national armed resistance was encountered, culminating in the Blackhawk Down incident that resulted in the deaths of eighteen American soldiers. This prompted Washington to pull out from Somalia almost immediately, under intense criticism of the diplomacy of "humanitarian intervention" within the United States. This led the supposedly liberal Clinton White House to discourage even a minimal humanitarian response to the onset of genocide in Rwanda in 1994, which might have saved hundreds of thousands of lives. In Rwanda the U.S. government discouraged even a modest upgrade of the UN peacekeeping presence in the country, whose commander urged reinforcements and authority to protect the targets of genocidal massacres. This failure to act remains a terrible stain on America's reputation as a humane and respected world leader, and is frequently interpreted as a racist disregard of threats confronting an African population when no major strategic Western interests were present on the side of the victims.

The Syrian conflict has been dominated by a political uprising, later an insurgency demanding regime change in Damascus, a leadership deficit, and factionalism that has only become worse with the passage of time. It is further complicated and confused by its proxy dimensions, both in relation to the supply of arms and to diplomatic alignment.

The humanitarian relief argument, to be credible, much less persuasive, needs to deal with the complexities, as with Somalia circa 1993, and not act as if the humanitarian response can be addressed in detachment from the political struggle, as was the case in Somalia in 1992. When political objectives become intertwined with a humanitarian rationale, forces of national resistance are activated on the reasonable assumption that the real goal of the mission is the political one, with humanitarian relief as a cover. This complexity makes for a more difficult burden of persuasion, although not an impossible one. Indeed, against the background of recent failed interventions, every proposed intervention confronts such a burden at some level. The Syrian case makes this burden more formidable, given the record of past interventions in the region and the mixture of forces that make up the "opposition," which is far from unified.

The Syrian political struggle is more acute and vicious than was the case in 1993 Somalia. The humanitarian crisis is also deeper, and this horrifying war is both internal and contains regional proxy elements, making the probable effects of threats and uses of force on behalf of genuine humanitarian goals more confusing.

There are no easy answers at this stage, and dogmatic discourse for or against intervention misses the deeply tragic nature of the policy predicament for all political actors. I would feel more comfortable about the intervention debate if it were expressed in a discourse that accords prominence to the virtue of humility. Too much in Syria remains unknowable for us to have any confidence that a clear line of advocacy will be historically vindicated.

I remember hearing the senior State Department diplomat George Ball speak just weeks after he left the government, in the closing years of the Vietnam War. His primary message was that he only began to understand the war when he stopped reading the cables—that is, the highly classified messages sent by military commanders and their civilian counterparts in the war zone. It is easy to explain why. Those in the field were committed to achieving victory and determined to provide reassurance, however false, to the leaders back in Washington so that they could deal with growing antiwar pressures, which in turn stemmed from a combination of public fatigue (after almost a decade of engagement) and skepticism (based on the "credibility gap" between claims of continuing progress in the war and the reality in Vietnam). Rather than making policy more transparent, the counterintuitive effect of these messages was to shroud the reality of Vietnam in greater obscurity.

For me, the fundamental question is what it is best to do or not do in such a desperate situation of radical uncertainty. It is not only that the interventionists, and perhaps the anti-interventionists, are motivated by a convergence of humanitarian/moral considerations with geostrategic ambitions, but that these hidden calculations are discussed behind locked doors and transcribed in secret policy memoranda. Until we address these questions of consequences and secret goals in the context of uncertainty and unknowability, the public discourse on what to do about Syria offers limited insight into how best to evaluate policy options. I hope that such a discussion will replace the dogmatic, self-righteous indignation of both interventionists and anti-interventionists.

The Obsolescence of Ideology:
Debating Syria and Ukraine
March 23, 2014[22]

I have been struck by the unhelpfulness of ideology to my own efforts to think through the complexities of policy in relation to Syria and, more recently, Ukraine. There is no obvious "left" or "right" posture to be struck; a convincing policy proposal depends on sensitivity to context and the particulars of the conflict. This is not the same as saying that the left/right distinction is irrelevant to the public debate. In the American context, to be on the left generally implies an anti-interventionist stance, while being on the right is usually associated with being pro-intervention. Yet these first approximations can be misleading, even ideologically. Liberals, who are deliberately consigned to the left by the mainstream media, often favor intervention if the rationale for military force is primarily humanitarian.

Likewise, the neoconservative right is often opposed to intervention if it is not persuasively justified on the basis of strategic interests, which could include promoting ideological affinities. The neocon leitmotif is global leadership via military strength, force projection, friends and enemies, and the assertion and enforcement of red lines: when Obama failed to bomb Syria in 2013, after declaring that al-Assad's use of chemical weapons would be treated as a red line, this supposedly undermined the credibility of American power. Ideology remains a helpful predictor of how people line up with respect to controversial uses of force, although relying on ideology is lazy if the purpose is to decide on the best course of action, which requires sensitivity to the concrete realities of a particular situation. Such an analysis depends on context and may include acknowledging the difficulties of intervention and the moral unacceptability of nonintervention. To assess particularities requires a genuine familiarity with the specifics and the changing dynamics of a conflict, if persuasive policy recommendations are to be grounded in relevant knowledge rather than knee-jerk reactions. No matter how expert the recommenders, however, core uncertainties will persist, and the responsibility is huge.

A caveat: In the last fifty years military intervention has rarely worked out well for the target society or for the intervener. Historical experience would seem to call for what lawyers call a "presumption against intervention." This is not intended as an absolute prohibition, but it does impose a burden of persuasion on the advocates of intervention. Evidence, also, is often doctored and manipulated one way or another to reflect the views of the government or

2. http://richardfalk.wordpress.com/2014/03/23/
the-obsolescence-of-ideology-debating-syria-and-ukraine.

of special interests. This was spectacularly illustrated in 2003, when governmental efforts to strengthen the public case for intervention in Iraq produced notorious fabrications.

The best solution in such situations might be procedural—that is, leaving the final policy decision in each instance up to the UN Security Council. If the Bush administration had accepted the outcome of the Security Council vote that withheld approval for intervening in Iraq, it would have been spared a humiliating strategic defeat that damaged America's status as a world leader. Allowing the Security Council to decide whether or not international force is required and justified also is consistent with the presumption against intervention, since any of the five permanent members casting a negative vote counts as a veto.

Beyond this issue of trust are questions of geopolitical alignment, especially encounters that align the United States and NATO on one side and Russia and/or China on the other. Fortunately, there is no second Cold War yet, although the neocons (and some in Europe), are beating the war drums in relation to Ukraine in such a way as to point in that most unwelcome and totally unjustified direction. Russia's sensitivity to hostile developments on its borders, previously expressed a few years ago in the 2008 crisis over Georgia, is now more potently evident in relation to Ukraine and breakaway Crimea, which contains a strategic naval base at Sevastopol, the only Russian warmwater port, as well as the home of Russia's Black Sea naval fleet.

American exceptionalism, or the geopolitical asymmetry that generates one set of rules for the United States and another for secondary geopolitical actors such as Russia, pushes the United States to claim a license to act against Russian borderland encroachments that would never be tolerated in reverse. If, say, a radical anti-American takeover took place in Mexico and Russia was audacious enough to object to American extraterritorial interference, dire consequences would follow. Recall America's readiness to risk World War III to prevent the deployment of Soviet missiles in Cuba back in 1962. The problems of both Syria and Ukraine are intensified by geopolitical antagonism that restricts the UN's role to the margins and prevents a diplomatic consensus that would move the parties away from violence and toward a political settlement.

The question of what is to be done is daunting in the very different challenges posed by Syria and Ukraine. Syria's horrifying humanitarian catastrophe is also destroying some of the country's ancient and most cherished cities. The opposition to the regime is disunited and guilty of its own atrocities, and the governing authorities and insurgency are both supported by external actors that treat the civil strife as a proxy war and seem unlikely to yield regardless of the humanitarian ordeal being inflicted on the Syria people. In this respect, Syria illustrates regional and global geopolitics in its most cynical and destructive form. One revealing aspect of this disheartening complexity is that the anti-Assad governments have excluded Iran from the ongoing Geneva diplomacy. Iran's exclusion seems irresponsibly submissive to the views of America's regional allies, Saudi Arabia and Israel, and works against surmounting an admittedly difficult set of diplomatic obstacles.

The geopolitical realities of Ukraine are totally different, raising risks of a new Cold War or at least renewed great-power rivalry, and threaten to produce a militarily uneven encounter between Russia and Ukraine over Moscow's moves to annex Crimea on the basis of a hastily arranged referendum that, as expected, went Russia's way by an overwhelming 95 percent of the vote. Even if the lopsided outcome partly reflected pro-Russian intimidation, there is little doubt that the people of Crimea strongly prefer being part of Russia to remaining an autonomous province of Ukraine. The Western media gives little attention to the strong historical and cultural affinities between Russia and Crimea. It should be remembered that Crimea was long part of Russia, its population is mostly Russian speaking, and its shift to Ukraine was accomplished through a capricious 1954 Kremlin decree by Nikita Khrushchev, who was himself part Ukrainian. From an international-law standpoint, the applicability of self-determination is ambiguous in light of this background. From a Ukrainian point of view, the transfer of Crimean sovereignty was a valid legal act sixty years ago and the population of Crimea does not seem to qualify as "a people" entitled to claim a right of self-determination. Besides, self-determination is not applicable if its exercise fragments an existing state, in this case Ukraine. But as we have seen, when self-determination is asserted successfully, as in the former Yugoslavia, the *political* outcome will be generally accepted, although maybe not formalized immediately.

Putting aside the geopolitical dimension, there are other problems with action in the Syria setting (granting the unacceptability of inaction). First of all, the regime is not isolated from popular support, although the breadth and depth of that support is controversial and probably unknowable. Second, because the regime is well armed, it would require a major undertaking to produce regime change, security, and political transition rather than escalation. As demonstrated over and over again in the postcolonial era, a Western intervention is likely to provoke prolonged and, in the end, effective national territorial resistance, with highly unpredictable political consequences. In Syria, with minimal strategic U.S. interests at stake, the difficulties of achieving regime change by intervention seem too great.

We are left, then, with the other part of the challenge: the unacceptability of doing nothing in relation to Syria, and a debate about what could be done to promote a more sustainable and satisfactory outcome in Ukraine. A no-fly zone in Syria has been proposed to protect a humanitarian corridor to allow deliveries of food and medicine to beleaguered communities. Such a course of action is beset with problems, stemming from a lack of trust, control of the scope and magnitude of the forcible action once undertaken, and the genuine difficulties of making such a zone secure without expanding the scale and scope of the use of force.

In Ukraine, there seems to be no constructive role for the West to play at this stage. Granting that anti-Russian sentiments prevail in the Ukrainian-speaking, Catholic portions of the country, it seems that the upheaval that led the Viktor Yanukovych government to collapse can be viewed as consistent with the internal sovereignty of the country, although not without some inappropriate Western encouragement of a destabilizing political opposition. Even this interference does not justify Russian intervention, regardless of the degree to which the new leadership includes a strong fascist component. Fortunately, there is no current prospect of a Russian intervention designed to break up Ukraine, but the impact of Western anger, expressed by the imposition of sanctions personally directed at Putin and some of his close associates, seems designed to hurt Russian investment and trade. Such hostile moves could easily trigger Russian retaliation and give rise to an unpredictable and dangerous escalation of tensions. Given the statist logic on which the world is organized, reinforced by geopolitical zones of influence, it would be a major move in the direction of global hegemony if the West were to mount a provocative challenge to Russia's relationship to its "near abroad" or threatened vital Russian security interests.

In relation to both Syria and Ukraine, there are internationalist frustrations because of the inability to protect vulnerable people in severe distress. At stake are opposing principles of respect for sovereignty and human rights as well as the hostile interplay of dangerous geopolitical rivalries. The effort to uphold the collective rights of weaker countries and their peoples is opportunistically manipulated by a variety of external state and nonstate actors making current frustrations mainly a reflection of the dysfunctional operations of a structure of hard-power world order that accords primacy to state sovereignty, the pursuit of national interests, and the hegemonic claims and conflicts of geopolitical actors with varying ambitions, claims under international law, and diplomatic and military capabilities.

Further in the background lie the nuclear arsenals that make hardly any political or moral goal worth risking major intergovernmental military encounters. Until the main countries in the world are prepared to reorien their political priorities around a *species*-based sense of identity and solidarity, we are stuck with this territorially delimited structure, a relic of seventeenth-century Europe. This world order is being challenged by functional considerations of sustainability, climate change, and weaponry of mass destruction as well as by normative considerations associated with human rights, equity, and species survival. The breakdowns in Syria and Ukraine are emblematic failures of this system, but also human tragedies entailing massive suffering and trauma.

Prosecuting Syrians for War Crimes Now
June 5, 2014[23]

The victorious powers in World War II imposed individual criminal accountability upon political and military leaders for alleged crimes committed during wartime. A tribunal convened by the victors gave the accused surviving German and Japanese leaders a fair opportunity to present a defense at trials held in Nuremberg and Tokyo. This was hailed at the time as a major step in the direction of a "just peace." International law was treated as binding upon sovereign states and their representatives, and was conceived to be a major step toward the global rule of law. The final decisions of these tribunals also produced a narrative as to why World War II was a necessary and just war. This outcome both vindicated the victory on the battlefield and punitively repudiated those who fought and lost. Significantly, this criminal process was formally initiated only *after* the combat phase of the war had ended and Germany and Japan had surrendered.

There were skeptics in 1945 who whispered "victors' justice" and insisted that the "Nuremberg experience" was a partisan exercise in truth-telling. Above the courtroom hung an invisible sign reading "only losers need enter here." The Nuremberg goddess of "war justice" wore no blindfold, assessing with one eye the crimes of the losers and averting her other eye so as not to see the crimes of the winners. In the actual trials, those whose criminality was being assessed were not accused of any crimes that resembled the practices of the winners and were not allowed to bring up any of the winners' alleged crimes in their own defense.

Many wanted to overlook this flaw and move on to create a justice system that would indeed operate on the basis of the nature of the *act* as criminal or not, without making criminality depend on the identity of the *actor*.

23. http://richardfalk.wordpress.com/2014/06/05/
prosecuting-syrians-for-war-crimes-now.

But moving toward the ideal of equality before the law has not been easy. It requires elevating international criminal law above the precepts of geopolitics. The impulse to do so in *form* has surfaced strongly in the aftermath of the Cold War, but we have yet to see any corresponding *substantive* transformation, which must occur if equals are to be treated equally in international criminal law.

Against such a background, the attempts to hold individuals, whether acting on behalf of governments or insurgencies, individually accountable for war crimes is treated as a core element of global justice. The International Criminal Court (ICC), established in 2002, is a global institutional mechanism for applying international criminal law in an objective and authoritative manner. There is convincing proof that horrifying atrocities have been committed in the course of the Syrian civil war, principally by the government and armed forces of Syria and, to a far lesser extent, by various factions among the fragmented rebel forces. It would certainly seem appropriate to charge both Syrian government officials, including military commanders, and members of the insurgent opposition with such crimes.

France presented a resolution to the UN Security Council on May 22, 2014, calling upon the ICC to investigate allegations of war crimes in Syria and to proceed with prosecutions to the extent possible. The resolution was supported by a 13–2 vote, but failed to pass because the two dissenting votes were cast by Russia and China. According to the Russian delegate, the French initiative was nothing more than a "publicity stunt" that would hamper, or even preclude, the difficult search for a diplomatic end to the strife.[24] The Western reaction, significantly endorsed by the UN Secretary General's office, declared that such a use of the veto was "disastrous."[25] It amounted to a de facto grant of impunity to the worst perpetrators of state crime active on the planet.

I believe that both of these contrasting reactions are understandable and can be given a qualified endorsement, despite seeming to contradict one another. The Russian reaction reflects a view that the main motivations for such a resolution is to weaken the legitimacy of the Damascus regime in the midst of an unresolved struggle for control of the country, and in this sense is better interpreted geopolitically as an irresponsible propaganda move rather than as a genuine attempt to promote criminal justice. Moscow has insisted

24. Michele Kelemen, "Russia, China Block U.N. Effort To Investigate Syrian War Crimes," National Public Radio, May 22, 2014, www.npr.org/2014/05/22/314925036/russia-china-block-u-n-effort-to-investigate-syrian-war-crimes.

25. Julian Borger, Luke Harding, Chris McGreatl, and Peter Walker, "Ban Ki-moon: UN's Failure to Agree on a Syrian Resolution Is Disastrous," *Guardian*, February 9, 2012, www.theguardian.com/world/2012/feb/09/un-ban-ki-moon-syria.

all along that the only way to end the violence in Syria is by way of diplomatic compromise. Thus, any attempt to indict Syrian leaders as war criminals while the fighting persists weakens the already dim prospects of resolving the conflict by diplomacy. It gives al-Assad and other Syrian leaders, those who would likely be indicted, strong incentives to rely on combat rather than take their chances with diplomacy.

The French approach, strongly supported by the Western powers, focuses on the clear evidence of criminality attributable to the Damascus regime. Such behavior deserves to be formally criminalized, and the fact that the Assad regime remains in power enhances the urgency of doing so. There is no need to look beyond these facts; taking such action may increase the pressure on the Syrian government to seek accommodation. Further, they posit that the argument that recourse to the ICC will end diplomatic efforts to end the violence is specious. Conventional diplomacy has been given many chances and has failed. To act as if diplomacy might succeed in the future is mainly a diversionary tactic to discourage immediate steps that might bring the war to an end in ways that would be helpful to the majority of Syrians. Supporters of the French resolution argue that activating the ICC would produce public indignation, swing support to the insurgent side, and produce a more politically and morally desirable endgame by discrediting the Damascus regime and empowering the opposition within Syria, the region, and the world. There are many uncertainties exposed by this debate. It is difficult to reach a clear conclusion as to which side is more persuasive, but there are considerations that add weight to those who voice skepticism about the French initiative.

Motivation. There are reasons to think that this effort at this time is mainly an expression of frustration and desperation and, as such, a misuse of the ICC by Western powers. True, the crimes of the insurgent rebels were also included in the proposed resolution, but the motivation was to delegitimize the Damascus government. Yet initiating a criminal investigation directed at the leadership of all participants in the midst of a civil war seems like a misdirected move in the face of the failure of earlier Western efforts to produce regime change.

Timing. To use the ICC in the midst of an ongoing civil war in Syria is to take sides, and thus to interfere with an ongoing internal struggle for control of the state and society. Even the Allied powers waited until the guns of World War II fell silent before initiating any criminal process. Acting in the present setting interferes with Syrians' right of self-determination; yet, since there has been already considerable interference through funding and material support, the preconditions for self-determination do not exist, making an end to the violence a primary goal. Would criminal indictments while the war rages hasten or delay an ending to the conflict? Since neither side has shown the ability to prevail, the Russians seem right that, despite disappointments with earlier efforts, diplomacy continues to be the only path forward.

Justice. Is justice served when the authority of the ICC is invoked to influence the outcome of a civil war? There are reasons to worry about the discrediting impact of double standards. Why was there never any initiative to pursue leaders of the United States and United Kingdom during the Iraq War, which included many incidents that seemed to qualify as crimes against humanity? This question takes on greater weight when added to earlier criticisms of the ICC, which has pursued a variety of sub-Saharan African leaders but few others. It is also relevant to recall that the Serbian leader Slobodan Milošević was indicted in the midst of the Kosovo war, undertaken without UN authorization by NATO, again seemingly motivated by the urge to strengthen public support for a legally controversial military effort. In the NATO-led military operation against the Libyan regime, the ICC issued arrest warrants for the Qaddafi leadership while NATO planes were bombing Tripoli. Critics of such war-crimes prosecutions allege that the whole undertaking has been politicized in ways that lead to a selective application of the law that seems inconsistent with claims of justice. In effect, the criticism of Nuremberg still applies—only losers and the weak are accountable. For the others, impunity.

Feasibility. The unlikelihood of obtaining personal jurisdiction in relation to the principal perpetrators of war crimes in Syria, especially Bashar al-Assad and major political officials and military commanders, also makes the claimed rationale for seeking indictments at this stage suspect. Proceeding now seems to have as its main justification adding moral weight to the position of pro-insurgency governments that something more should be done to stop al-Assad. Reinforcing this reasoning is a consensus that, since military intervention is not feasible and diplomacy has failed, the only option left is to charge Syrian leaders with crimes against humanity. The ICC provides a venue to mobilize pressure for giving additional help to the rebels and, at the same time, depriving the Damascus government of whatever is left of its legitimacy. The fact that the French resolution calls also for an investigation of possible crimes against humanity by the opposition, while not frivolous, would nevertheless certainly have received far less attention had the Security Council given the ICC a green light.

There is a serious question as to whether it is appropriate to use the ICC to gather evidence and prepare an indictment in circumstances where prospects of prosecution are remote and an ongoing struggle for control of the Syrian state remains unresolved. Such limitations also reinforce concerns about the timing of this initiative. It makes recourse to ICC not only ineffectual as a means to pursue criminal justice, but damaging to the credibility of this fledgling international institution—which was created, it should be remembered, to overcome the vagaries of geopolitics, not to serve as an instrument for engaging in maneuvers.

There are two intertwined concerns: First, is seeking indictments of Syrians accused of crimes against humanity, on balance, helpful or harmful to the search for peace? Secondly, would this strengthen or weaken the ICC, with its need to overcome the strong impression of operating on the basis of double standards? So far all efforts to use the ICC in response to crimes alleged against Western countries have been rebuffed; Western leaders have enjoyed impunity and have minimized their own participation in the activities of the ICC except when it serves their interests. A tiny opening is the recent indication that the ICC is formally investigating criminal charges relating to occupying UK forces' abuse of Iraqi detainees in the years after 2003. Perhaps the times are changing after all, although far too slowly and modestly.

5

Turkey

My relationship to Turkey is far closer than it is to any of the other countries in the Middle East. My wife is Turkish, we have made long annual visits to Turkey for the past twenty years, and I have had the opportunity to know a wide range of Turkish political personalities quite closely. This helps explain why the chapter on Turkey is by far the largest in this book.

I have also been motivated to write about the Turkish government and its leadership because it has so often been misunderstood. Western perceptions of Turkish political life are distorted by several interacting factors: the hostility of Turkey's secular establishment to the governing AKP (Justice and Development Party) and its dominant leader, Recep Tayyip Erdoğan; Turkey's tensions with Israel and the United States; and the global media exhibiting hostility to Turkey due to the influence of these political forces. While I share some of the criticisms directed at the AKP and Erdoğan, especially since 2011, I am also much more appreciative of their political, economic, and ethical performance than their harsh detractors. The following posts express this orientation in reaction to various tumultuous developments since 2010.

Turkey's relationship to the Middle East is particularly layered and complex. It neither belongs to the Arab world nor to the European Christian world, yet is deeply implicated in the history, culture, economic and politics of both. Since 2002, Turkey has had dramatic ups and downs internally, regionally, and internationally. During this entire period it has been governed controversially by the AKP, which has been attacked as both authoritarian and trending toward Islamism. Its supporters emphasize tradition, social justice, and rapid economic development.

After the upheavals of the Arab Spring in early 2011, Turkey was popularly viewed as a model of stability and development throughout the region, a country that had managed to reconcile secularism and religion. Its prime minister (now president), Recep Tayyip Erdoğan, was the most popular leader in the Middle East; its foreign minister, Ahmet Davutoğlu, became one of the most influential diplomats in the world, admired for his energetic efforts to promote peaceful conflict resolution and compromise and to enlarge Turkey's political horizons in all directions.

Yet there were many bumps in the road. At home, the secular opposition has never been willing to accept the legitimacy of the AKP leadership, despite its extraordinary record of economic growth. At the same time this opposition was frustrated by its inability to produce either a credible alternative program or interesting potential political leaders. As a result, the AKP has won election after election and the opposition became more and more embittered. Since 2011, Erdoğan has relied on his electoral mandate and grassroots popularity to govern in a more overtly authoritarian style. He has especially agitated the secular ranks of "white Turks" with his rants about such social issues as abortion, alcohol, education, the role of women, and the desirability of population increase. Erdoğan seems increasingly to be abandoning any effort to lead in a manner that is inclusive of opposition concerns. To some extent, this is a reasonable reaction to the inflammatory behavior of the main opposition parties and media.

The demonstrations in Gezi Park in 2013 showed the anti-Erdoğan fury that exists in Turkey, with its contradictory interpretations exhibiting the polarization ripping the country apart. There is no doubt that the Turkish police overreacted in a brutal manner and that Erdoğan handled the incident awkwardly, endorsing the use of excessive force. It is also the case that after the initial phase of the protests against turning an historic Istanbul park into a shopping mall, the second phase of the events in Gezi were more confrontational, apparently seeking to imitate the anti-Morsi street politics that created a crisis of governability in Egypt.

In the last year or so, the domestic scene in Turkey has been further roiled by conflict between the government and the Hizmet movement, led by an Islamic scholar and preacher living in Pennsylvania named Fethullah Gülen. The AKP accuses Hizmet of setting up a "parallel state" by deliberately infiltrating its loyalists into the bureaucracy, especially the police and judiciary. Hizmet accuses Erdoğan of corruption, crony capitalism, and authoritarianism. As with the displaced secular opposition, Hizmet's defection from the AKP cause has so far not diminished the AKP's level of popular support

In recent years, Turkey has experienced a series of setbacks internationally. The AKP's approach to Syria has been problematic in several ways that have weakened the overall credibility of Turkish relations with the region. Davutoğlu's signature approach of "zero problems with neighbors" was launched with fanfare as Turkey embraced al-Assad's Syria, ending years of tension. When the Arab Spring arrived and Syrians rose up against the authoritarianism of the Assad regime in Damascus, Turkey first tried to urge democratic reforms. When these failed to materialize, Ankara sided with the rebels and especially the Muslim Brotherhood component of the many-sided Syrian opposition, perceiving the conflict as certain to be quickly resolved in favor of the anti-government side. Damascus accused Turkey of intervening on behalf of the insurgency and promoting Sunni sectarianism.

A second vector of difficulty arose when Turkey criticized Israel after the breakdown of Turkey's effort to mediate a solution to the conflict between Israel and Syria over the Golan Heights. The initial criticisms focused on Israel's behavior in Gaza, especially the military operations known as Cast Lead that began at the end of 2008. These tensions reached their climax in 2010 when Israeli commandos attacked the Turkish civilian ship *Mavi Marmara* in international waters, killing nine Turkish passengers. The ship was the lead vessel in a flotilla of small, unarmed ships seeking to challenge Israel's unlawful blockade of Gaza by delivering humanitarian goods directly to the beleaguered Gazan population.

The problems with Israel overlapped with and reinforced some tensions with the United States. It seemed that the U.S. government expected Turkey to be as submissive after the Cold War as it had been during it. The AKP clearly sought to maintain its role in NATO as part of the Western alliance. It also sought continuity in its relationship with the United States, but felt entitled to act as an independent player in the region. This posture came up against Washington's insistence on having a free hand in the Middle East. When Turkey, in collaboration with Brazil, sought to defuse nuclear tensions with Iran in 2010, Washington reacted angrily, reminding Turkey not to get out of line, as President Obama called for strengthened sanctions as the centerpiece of its reliance on coercive diplomacy to gain its goals in relation to Iran's nuclear program. The Turkish initiative, designed to lower tensions, ran directly counter to the belligerently anti-Iranian approach being advocated by Israel.

What followed was a worldwide campaign to discredit the AKP leadership, portraying Erdoğan as a second Putin. In my view, the AKP deserves a more balanced treatment. Turkey's achievements since 2002 far outweigh its shortcomings. Erdoğan is skilled in surrounding himself with highly capable officials and advisors, especially in key positions. Turkey's economic development has been sustained far more successfully than that of other countries in the region, or in Europe for that matter. Perhaps the greatest of the AKP's achievements has been eliminating the "deep state" as a force that had lurked below the surface of Turkish politics ever since the republic was established in 1920. Gaining civilian control over security policies repudiated the Atatürk tradition, which allowed the armed forces to play a custodial role in relation to the elected government and had seemed a permanent feature of Turkish political life, producing periodic military coups as well as supervision over the behavior of political leaders. Challenging this structure required great political skill and commitment as well as accepting the risk of provoking a coup, which nearly happened in the early years of AKP governance. Turkey also did its utmost to bring greater stability and prosperity to the region, through diplomacy, cultural exchanges, and trade/investment relations. Beyond this, Davutoğlu and Erdoğan were innovative in encouraging diplomatic and economic relations with Africa and Latin America, regions Turkey had previously ignored.

As with so many countries in this period, Turkey's fundamental problem has been the polarization of beliefs and affinities within its own population, which has created intense negativity in the political atmosphere. It is rather remarkable that the AKP has so far been able to ride this unruly horse of polarization without worse mishaps. The Turkish leadership is being daily challenged by a defamatory campaign by its opponents at home and abroad designed to undermine the legitimacy of the state, an undertaking aided by the international media.

The 2014 emergence of ISIS near Turkey's borders has added yet another destabilizing and daunting challenge, one further complicated by Ankara's search for a peaceful resolution of its own long, violent conflict with its large Kurdish minority. Turkey finds itself pulled in opposite directions. ISIS is an effective force in the ongoing effort to topple the Assad regime, but is also guilty of massive atrocities and is the target of an American-led intervention. ISIS poses a difficult dilemma for Turkey—to give priority either to sectarian objectives or to the defeat of extremist challenges to the status quo.

These posts seek to explain AKP's political strength at home and the innovativeness of its foreign policy while taking due account of its mistakes and setbacks. All political actors, within the region and beyond, made mistakes during this turbulent period; while Turkey made important miscalculations, its intentions were constructive and its record stands up well compared to other main players in the region, including the United States.

I anticipate two notable challenges for Turkey in 2015. The first is to respond to the worldwide Armenian campaign associated with observing the centennial anniversary of the 1915 massacres. The Erdoğan leadership has been more forthcoming in acknowledging these tragic events than its predecessors, but has not been willing to accede to the Armenian demand that they be acknowledged as "genocide." One post tries to interpret this open wound and how it might be treated for the benefit of both sides. The second challenge involves the December 2015 UN climate-change conference in Paris, expected to be a make-or-break occasion with respect to heeding scientific warnings about global warming. To date Turkey has been extremely passive about international limits on carbon emissions and gives the impression of being unwilling to burden its economic ambitions by acting in an environmentally responsible manner.

Ahmet Davutoğlu: Turkey's Foreign Minister

September 2, 2009[1]

It has been my privilege to know Ahmet Davutoğlu since he was a young professor teaching in Malaysia in the early 1990s. At that time I was immediately struck by his keen understanding of the importance of culture and civilization to the proper conduct of international relations. Mr. Davutoğlu was definitely not just one more realist foreign-policy analyst with a good grounding in the mainstream tradition of Western political thought covering the conceptual ground that connects Machiavelli to Kissinger. This tradition was preoccupied with the management of power, and there is no doubt that Davutoğlu had a sophisticated understanding about how to cope with power and conflict in world politics. Yet what made him more intriguing and distinguished him from many other intelligent interpreters of the changing global scene was his recognition of the significance of non-Western thought as forming an *essential* basis for shaping historically relevant policy that had become necessary to enable governments to meet the challenges of the contemporary world.

Davutoğlu returned to Turkey a few years later and began teaching university courses. More impressively, he founded and led a voluntary program of advanced studies for doctoral students in the social sciences and humanities from all over the country, an exciting and innovative learning community that combined an intrinsic love of knowledge and ideas with a search for practical wisdom that would enable Turkey to fulfill its potential as a national, regional, and global actor. Davutoğlu emphasized the importance of history, culture, and what is sometimes called "macro-history" or the comparative study of civilizations, examining the broad sweep of the rise and fall of civilizations through time and space, interpreting Turkey's role within a wider cultural and historical context of past, present, and future. This approach acted as a corrective to a narrowly conceived nationalism that never looked back further than the sacrosanct ideas and guidance of the founder of the modern Turkish state, Mustafa Kemal Atatürk.

It was Davutoğlu's particular insight that Turkey, to move creatively forward into the future, needed to recapture an understanding of and a pride in the achievements of its past, especially the Ottoman Empire's extraordinary capacity to encompass diverse peoples while respecting distinct cultures and religions. I found this way of thinking congenial. It represented a refreshing enlargement upon the nonhistorical forms of strategic thought so prominent at the time in Turkey, and was almost entirely derivative from the way

---

1. www.todayszaman.com/op-ed_davutoglu-turkeys-finest-foreign-minister-of-republican-era-by-richard-falk-_185835.html.

world politics was conceived in the United States. Davutoğlu, as a scholar, was striving for an approach that came directly to terms with Turkey's hopes and aspirations for the future and to expose students and the intelligent public in Turkey to similar styles of global thinking from other parts of the world. His academic foundation organized several conferences in the last decade of the twentieth century that brought leading thinkers from all over the world to Turkey. Such events exhibited his commitment to the establishment of a cross-cultural community of scholars dedicated to a universalizing vision of a peaceful and just world.

Davutoğlu's book *Stratejik Derinlik,* on "strategic depth" as the foundation of a constructive approach to security, is one of the outstanding formulations of the way sovereign states should pursue their interests. Although the book is now about ten years old and is not available in English, it has gone through many printings, and is being translated into a variety of foreign languages. It is one of the most significant contributions to the literature of international relations; although imprinted with the geopolitics of the Cold War and its globalization sequel, it retains great relevance to the relations of Turkey to an evolving world order. Davutoğlu has expressed frustration that his public duties have prevented him from either revising or following it up with additional books on "cultural depth" and "historical depth" that would have given his published work a more accurate reflection of his intended approach to international relations in our time.

Against such a background, it may seem surprising that Davutoğlu has had such a major impact on Turkish foreign policy, initially as chief advisor to the top AKP leadership and, since 2009, as foreign minister. Usually there is not a very good fit between professors and successful government service. What has made Davutoğlu an exception is his unusual combination of social and diplomatic skills and an absence of political ambition. Staying aloof from party politics yet aligned with the AKP policy outlook has managed to give him a unique place on the Turkish scene, at once independent and exceedingly influential with political leaders, the public, and in foreign capitals.

Even before becoming foreign minister, Davutoğlu was widely appreciated in the media and diplomatic community as the architect of Turkish foreign policy since 2002. His initial portfolio focused on achieving membership for Turkey in the European Union, which Davutoğlu's held was not only beneficial to Turkey, including establishing a stronger foundation for genuine democracy at home, but also would present Europe with a unique opportunity to become a dynamic force enjoying multicivilizational legitimacy in a world order where the West could no longer play an effective role unless it could claim an identity and recruit the participation of the rising peoples of the East. Although Davutoğlu's hopes for greater European receptivity to Turkey have undoubtedly been disappointed by the unanticipated surge of Islamophobia in several European countries, as well as the unfortunate admission of Cyprus to EU membership in 2004, he continues to believe that the goal of membership is attainable and desirable. This quest continues and has had its own benefits, providing strong support for domestic moves to strengthen democracy and human rights.

As foreign minister, Davutoğlu has exhibited the qualities of energy, intelligence, political savvy, moral concern, self-confidence (without arrogance), and historically grounded vision that one encounters in his scholarship and lectures. It is hard to think of a world figure who has had a more positive impact in a shorter time. His signature approach of "zero problems with neighbors" has been consistently successful in establishing better relations throughout the region and posed a challenge to Egypt for regional leadership, even among Arab governments. Less noticed, but as important, is Davutoğlu's tireless search for nonviolent approaches to conflict management based on identifying and maximizing the common ground between adversaries. This brings an urgently needed stabilizing influence to the inflamed politics of the Middle East, but also brings Turkey respect, stature, and expanding economic and diplomatic opportunities. Perhaps most notable in this regard are growing economic links with Russia and Iran, countries that have often in the past been at odds with Turkey.

It is particularly notable that Turkey embarked on these controversial initiatives without harming its strategically central relationship with the United States. Quite the contrary. Turkey is more than ever treated by Washington as an important ally, as exhibited by President Obama's visit to Istanbul shortly after becoming president, but to a far greater extent than in the past, Turkey is now also respected as an independent actor with its own agenda and priorities that may diverge from those of the United States in particular instances. This new mutuality led Richard Holbrooke, the U.S. special envoy for Afghanistan, to say that it was up to Turkey to decide whether to send additional troops to Afghanistan. This contrasted with the heavy-handed approach of the Bush years, when American officials, most prominently Paul Wolfowitz, lectured Turkish leaders in public on their responsibility to do whatever the White House desired. This change reflects a more multilateralist U.S. foreign policy but it is also a recognition that Turkey is now an independent force in world affairs, not just an appendage of NATO or the West. Davutoğlu deserves major credit for conceptualizing this change as well as for its application to practical, day-to-day foreign policy decisions.

Davutoğlu took career risks while serving as chief foreign-policy advisor that showed a willingness to put principle ahead of personal ambition. He tried very hard to find and enlarge the common ground and dormant mutual interests in the most intractable, sensitive, and dangerous regional conflict, that between Israel and Palestine and the Arab world. He did his best to broker Israel/Syria negotiations, encouraging an agreement that would end Israeli occupation of the Golan Heights and establish some kind of diplomatic normalcy between the two countries. More controversially, but not less constructively, he tried hard to soften Hamas's posture as an uncompromising and violent element in the Palestinian struggle, and at the same time encouraged Israel to treat Hamas as a political actor, not a terrorist organization, after it gained political power through the 2006 elections in Gaza and declared its intention to establish a ceasefire. Israel (as well as the United States and EU) refused to drop the terrorist label and instead put a deadly squeeze on the 1.5 million Palestinians living in Gaza. A devastating humanitarian ordeal has resulted. So much suffering might have been avoided if Davutoğlu's approach had succeeded; the outlook for peace would have been far brighter than it is today. In this sense, Davutoğlu's foreign-policy disappointments during the past several years are as deserving of our admiration as are his successes.

There is no doubt in my mind that Turkey is extremely fortunate to have Ahmet Davutoğlu as its foreign minister, and it is a tribute to the elected leadership in Ankara that so much responsibility has been entrusted to someone without any formal party affiliation,[2] of independent character, and of scholarly temperament. Much has been made of Davutoğlu's emphasis on "strategic depth," but I believe he will be in the end most remembered for his "moral depth"—his dedicated search for peaceful conflict resolution through mediation and compromise, based on mutual respect for legal rights and a commitment to justice. Although it is far too early in his tenure to make any final appraisal with confidence, it is not too soon to think that fusing strategic depth with moral depth will turn out to be a memorable dimension of his legacy. If so, it is likely to underpin an eventual judgment that Ahmet Davutoğlu should be regarded as Turkey's finest foreign minister of the republican era.

---

2. Prior to the 2011 national elections in Turkey, Davutoğlu did join the AKP and won a seat in Parliament, which he retains even since he became prime minister in 2014.

Interpreting the AKP Victory in Turkey (with Hilal Elver)

June 13, 2011[3]

Turkey's elections have not aroused such widespread international interest since the founding of the republic. The AKP is celebrating its landslide victory on June 12, a vindication of its overall economic and political approach over the past nine years. Its win is also an endorsement of the creative foreign policy that has given Turkey such a prominent place on regional and global diplomatic maps for the first time in its republican history.

The afterglow of electoral victory should not obscure the challenges that lie ahead for the AKP. The most important of these involves finally providing the large Kurdish minority with secure cultural and political rights, which, to be trusted, would need to be vested in a new constitution. There is wide agreement in Turkey that the existing 1982 constitution, drafted by oppressive leaders of a military coup, needs to be replaced, but there are serious divisions with respect to the substantive content of a new constitution. The secular opposition, as represented by the Republican People's Party (Cumhuriyet Halk Partisi, or CHP), remains particularly worried about an alleged danger the Turkish government becoming "Putinized" if it switches from a parliamentary to a presidential system. More concretely, the opposition believes that Recep Tayyip Erdoğan harbors authoritarian dreams that could be fulfilled if Turkey were to follow the French presidential model.

Yet there should be less worry, for two main reasons. First, the AKP, while winning 327 seats in Parliament, fell well short of securing the 367 seats needed for the supermajorities that would have allowed it to decide on its own the contents of a new constitution, or even the 330 seats necessary for it to be able to write a constitution that would become law if approved by a national referendum. Without this degree of parliamentary control, the AKP will not be able to produce a constitution without the cooperation of the other parties, especially the CHP, and that bodes well—particularly if the opposition acts responsibly by offering constructive cooperation.

Second, Erdoğan, in his victory speech, went out of his way to reassure the country that constitutional reform would be a consensual process that would protect diverse lifestyles and strive to achieve acceptance and justice for the entire society. Erdoğan seemed unexpectedly sensitive to criticism of his supposedly arrogant political style, and took the high road of moderation and humility. He seemed intent on convincing the public that he respects the

---

3. http://richardfalk.wordpress.com/2011/06/13/interpreting-the-akp-victory-in-turkey

secular principles that have dominated political life since the time of Atatürk, and that the country will become more pluralistic than ever, in an atmosphere of mutual respect.

It is not just Turks who should welcome this AKP victory. It provides an extremely positive example of dynamic democracy at a time of unresolved internal struggles throughout the region. Turkey's steady and helpful diplomatic hand offers an attractive alternative to anxieties associated with American and European interventions and alignments in the region. Turkey is a vibrant society with a flourishing economy that has managed to follow a democratic path to political stability and an independent course in foreign policy, and that offers an inspiring example.

There are many uncertainties. Turkey faces the consequences of an unresolved bloody conflict in neighboring Syria, including a massive inflow of refugees. There are also the risks of an escalated confrontation with Iran arising from the Israel/U.S. hard-power response to Iran's nuclear program. This could ignite a war that engulfs the entire region. In addition, tense relations between Ankara and Tel Aviv are likely to be further stressed in coming weeks as preparation for a second Freedom Flotilla go forward.

Yet the sun shines brighter on the morning after these Turkish elections. Voters have affirmed an inclusive approach to peace, justice, and rights. To build on this mandate will create progress in the country and hope for the region. There will be mistakes and setbacks, but the orientation and vision of the AKP leadership is one of the most encouraging political developments of this still-young twenty-first century.

The prime minister's victory address was the culmination of the long and steady rise of the AKP over the past decade—from 34 percent of the vote in 2002 to 47 percent in 2007, and now almost 50 percent in 2011. This latest result did *not* give the AKP more seats, due to recent changes decreed by the Higher Election Board, a part of the state bureaucracy known to be hostile to the AKP. This restructuring, hardly noticed when it took place, hurt the AKP (327 seats rather than 341), while it helped the CHP (rising from 112 to 135) and the Peace and Democracy Party (Barış ve Demokrasi Partisi, BDP) which helped elect Kurdish independent candidates. The rightist Nationalist Movement Party (Milliyetçi Hareket Partisi, MHP) also won 13 percent of the vote and 53 seats in the new parliament.

The prime minister interpreted these results sympathetically, telling the public that he heard the voice of people as demanding consensus rather than bestowing unitary power on one party: "Our nation assigned us to draft a new constitution. They gave us a message to build the new constitution through consensus and negotiation. We will seek the broadest consensus."[4] He used the word "compromise" three times.

Erdoğan also tried to calm the political waters, declaring that "incendiary speeches given during the campaign should be forgotten." This is an encouraging start for the next phase of constructing a democracy that responds to the realities of the diverse peoples living in Turkey. At one point he promised that the constitution "will address everybody's demands for freedom, democracy, peace and justice, and each identity and each value." The last phrase indicates a resolve to move beyond the unitary Kemalist ideas that still animate the ultranationalist MHP: "one identity (Turk), one state (Turkey), and one language (Turkish)."[5] Such a rigid position seems impossible to reconcile with Erdoğan's consensus approach, explicitly directed at Turkish minorities' quest for distinct cultural and political rights, most significantly the Kurds. Erdoğan also mentioned Arabs, Circassians, Georgians, Roma, Alevis, and Laz. The prime minister insisted that hereafter "all citizens will be first class," which seems to be a historic commitment to equality between Turks and non-Turks in all phases of national life.

There are additional hopeful signs for Turkey's future. Seventy-eight women were elected to Parliament, significantly more than ever before. Perhaps, finally, the headscarf issue will be resolved in the direction of freedom of religion and the rights of women. Religiously observant Muslim women have suffered the punitive effects of the headscarf ban in public-sector activities, including institutions of higher learning, for far too long. The discriminatory nature of the current policy is dramatized by the unassailed freedom of the AKP men, who lead the government despite being as religiously observant as their wives.

Moreover, this parliament will be robustly diverse because of the many new faces, including a left-wing former student leader who spent many years in jail (Ertuğrul Kürkçü); several CHP members who are incarcerated, accused of antistate activity in the Ergenekon case[6]; and Leyla Zana, the internationally known Kurdish parliamentarian who, upon being originally elected in 1991, arrived in Parliament wearing a Kurdish flag bandana and refused to

---

4. Jonathan Head, "Turkey Election: Victorious Erdogan Pledges 'Consensus,'" BBC News, June 13, 2011, www.bbc.com/news/world-europe-13744972.

5. See the MHP's English-language website: www.mhp.org.tr/mhp_dil.php?dil=en.

6. Ergenekon was the name given to an alleged secret organization in Turkey with an ultranationalist and hypersecularist outlook whose members were accused and prosecuted for a variety of violent crimes. The organization was particularly threatening to the AKP as it had links to the armed forces and security services in the Turkish government.

take an oath of loyalty to the Turkish state. After many years, some of them in jail, Zana is again in Parliament. A few days ago on TV she joked: "Perhaps this time I will come with a headscarf"—implying that the individual rights of those who wear headscarves should not be excluded from protection.

As the most popular and admired leader in the region, Erdoğan did not forget to send a message to peoples of the Middle East, mentioning several cities and countries by name—including places in occupied Palestine—and suggesting rather dramatically that these places would be considered under the same banner of concern as Turkish cities. In a rhetorical flourish Erdoğan insisted that the outcome of the elections in Turkey was a victory "for Bosnia as much as Istanbul, Beirut as much as Izmir, Damascus as much as Ankara."[7] While somewhat hyperbolic, such a display of internationalism is new in Turkish politics and signifies Turkey's rise as a diplomatic force beyond its borders. Of course, critics treat such rhetoric as disclosing the AKP's dreams of an Ottoman revival throughout the Middle East.

Erdoğan somewhat unexpectedly also recalled a dark episode in Turkey's past, specifically what happened in 1960 when a military coup not only ousted a democratically elected government headed by the Democratic Party, but executed three of its political leaders, including Prime Minister Adnan Menderes, for daring to challenge the supremacy of the military by reducing its budget. Menderes had governed Turkey for three consecutive terms, winning elections by overwhelming majorities. Erdoğan was conveying his sense that the struggle to achieve Turkish democracy has been long and painful. He was also indirectly reminding his audience that the "deep state" is no longer in a position to frustrate the will of the people. All in all, the message was upbeat, as befits an electoral victory of this magnitude.

A final observation: June 12 was also the day on which Iranian elections were held two years ago. What is so startling is the contrast between the joyful expectations of the majority of the Turkish people after the electoral results were announced, compared to the anger and despair of the Iranian majority, who believed for good reason that the regime in Tehran had fraudulently deprived them of an electoral victory. This difference between a governing process that periodically legitimates itself through free and fair multiparty elections and a governing process that lacks the consent of the public and must rule by fear and force may be the most basic fault line in domestic politics—and will serve as the litmus test of the Arab Spring in the near future.

---

7. Ibid.

Turkey, the Region, and the West
(with Hilal Elver)
June 23, 2011[8]

There has been a dramatic shift in critical international responses to the current Turkish political leadership, highlighted by reactions to the resounding AKP electoral victory of June 12. The concern was first expressed as variations on the theme that Turkey was at risk of becoming "a second Iran," that is, an antidemocratic, theocratic state in which sharia law would dominate. Such a discrediting approach has itself been discredited, to the extent that it is all but abandoned in serious discussions of the Turkish governing process.

The new mantra of criticism is focused on the alleged authoritarian goals of Prime Minister Recep Tayyip Erdoğan. He is widely accused of seeking to shift the whole constitutional order of Turkey from a parliamentary to a presidential system, coupled with a little-disguised scheme to become Turkey's first president under the new constitution, and then look forward to being reelected the leader of the country for a second five-year term. Some of these anxieties have receded since the AKP did not win the needed two-thirds majority that would have enabled it to adopt a new constitution without needing to gain the consent of the citizenry through a referendum. In his election victory speech Erdoğan went out of his way to reassure Turkish society, including those who voted against the AKP, that he will seek the widest possible participation in the constitution-making process, with the aim of producing a consensus document that will satisfy a wide spectrum of Turks. Such a process would likely preclude any shift to a presidential system, and would certainly make politically impossible the adoption of the strong French version, which does give a president extraordinary powers.

From outside Turkey, this new line of criticism seems to reflect American and Israeli priorities and perspectives, and is not too closely related to Turkish realities. The tone and substance of this line was epitomized by a lead *New York Times* editorial published the day after the Turkish elections. After acknowledging some AKP achievements, including giving it credit for the flourishing Turkish economy and for successfully reining in the deep state, the editorial moved on to criticize "Mr. Erdoğan's increasingly confrontational foreign policies, which may play well at the polls, but...have proved costly for the country's interests."[9] Such a comment by the supposedly authoritative

---

8. http://richardfalk.wordpress.com/2011/06/23/
turkey-the-region-and-the-west-after-the-elections.

9. *New York Times* editorial board, "Reading Turkey's Elections," June 13, 2011, www.nytimes.com/2011/06/14/opinion/14tue3.html.

and balanced *New York Times* is quite extraordinary for its ignorance and slyly disguised bias. After all, the hallmark of Turkish foreign policy during the Erdoğan years, as developed under the inspired diplomatic leadership of the foreign minister, Ahmet Davutoğlu, has been "zero problems with neighbors." It is possible to argue that this nonconfrontational foreign policy has gone too far in some instances—most notably Syria, and possibly Libya—and as a result has generated some serious challenges for Turkey.

The only exception to this pattern of zero problems has been Israel, but here the *Times* once again displays a uninformed and opinionated outlook: "Once-constructive relations with Israel have yielded to tit-for-tat provocations and, if they continue, could threaten Turkey's substantial trade with Israel."[10] It would be hard to compose a more misleading description of the deterioration of Turkish/Israeli relations. It should be remembered that prior to the Israeli attack on Gaza at the end of 2008, Turkey was doing its best to promote peace between Israel and Syria by acting as an intermediary, a role seemingly appreciated at the time by both parties. It is also quite outrageous to speak of "tit-for-tat provocations" when it was Israeli commandos who boarded in international waters a Turkish ship, the *Mavi Marmara*, carrying humanitarian goods for the long-blockaded people of Gaza and killed nine Turkish citizens in cold blood. Even then Turkey tried its best to calm the waters, asking Tel Aviv only for an apology and compensation to the families of the victims as preconditions for the restoration of normal relations with Israel. It has been Israel defiantly refusing to make even these minimal gestures of reconciliation. Recently Davutoğlu has gone further, perhaps too far, in his dedication to peaceful relations by openly discouraging Turkish participation in plans for a second Freedom Flotilla at the end of June, asking activists to wait to see if the blockade is broken due to changes in the Egyptian approach at the Rafah crossing. The latest indications are that the *Mavi Marmara* will join the second Freedom Flotilla.

The *Times* goes even further in its Orientalist approach to Turkey, writing that "Ankara must discourage private Turkish groups from initiating a second blockade-running Gaza flotilla."[11] Why must it? Is the blockade, approaching its fourth anniversary, not widely condemned as cruel and unlawful, a flagrant violation of the legal prohibition on collective punishment set forth in Article 33 of the Fourth Geneva Convention? Should not such a demand at least be balanced by a call on Israel to end the blockade? Given the failure of the UN or neighboring governments to protect the people of Gaza, should

---

10. Ibid.
11. Ibid.

members of civil society not feel a duty to do so, and in democratic societies not be hampered by their governments?

The other foreign policy complaint in the editorial deals with Iran. Here, of course echoing complaints from Washington as well as Tel Aviv, Turkey is blamed for playing "cozy games with Iran" that have "only encouraged Iran's nuclear ambitions." Perhaps wrongheaded, but hardly an example of Erdoğan's allegedly confrontational style! What the *Times* obviously favors, not surprisingly, is confrontation, urging the Turkish government to "press Turkish companies and banks to enforce international sanctions against Iran." What is at stake here is the foreign-policy independence of Turkey. Its efforts to find a peaceful resolution of the dispute surrounding Iran's nuclear program are clearly designed to lessen the tensions surrounding the present coercive diplomacy of the U.S.-led, UN-backed coalition, which is based on sanctions and military threats. It is in Turkey's clear national interest to avoid a military encounter that could eventuate in a damaging regional war that would be disastrous for Turkey and dash the hopes raised by the Arab Spring, while also using its diplomatic leverage to discourage Iran from developing nuclear weapons.

Another Western criticism of Erdoğan's approach is to blame Turkey for the diminishing prospect of its accession to membership in the European Union. The *Financial Times,* in a far more reasonable postelection editorial, nevertheless appears to blame Turkey for "neglected relations with the EU."[12] On what basis is not disclosed. What was not even discussed, but is the main explanation for the strained relations, is the rise of Islamophobia throughout Europe reflected in governmental skepticism in Paris and Berlin about whether Turkey is a suitable candidate for membership, given its large Muslim population. Islamophobia in Europe, while resurgent, is not new. Recently it has been associated with Turkophobia, in reaction to the Turkish guest workers who stayed on and became a strong presence often unwanted, in Germany. In the two centuries prior to the twentieth Europeans feared and loathed an invading Ottoman Empire; even earlier, of course, were the Crusades with their marauding militarism.

What emerges overall is this American-led reluctance to accept Turkey as an independent regional force in the Middle East, one that has achieved enormous influence in recent years by relying on its own brand of soft-power diplomacy. A dramatic indicator of this influence is the great popularity of Erdoğan throughout the region, including among the youth who brought about the uprisings throughout the Arab world. It is an encouraging sign of

---

12. Delphine Strauss, "Time to Make the Most of the Limelight," *Financial Times,* June 27, 2011, www.ft.com/intl/cms/s/0/0bc58584-a070-11e0-a115-00144feabdc0. html#axzz3U2WFimYg.

1e times that these new Arab champions of democracy are coming to Ankara
nd Istanbul—not Washington, Tel Aviv, or Paris—for guidance and inspira-
on. Whether through NATO intervention in Libya or crude efforts to intim-
late Iran, the West, under faltering American leadership, remains addicted
o hard-power statecraft, which no longer achieves its goals, although it con-
nues to cause great suffering on the ground. It is time that the West stops
cturing Turkey and starts learning better what succeeds and what fails in
venty-first-century foreign policy. A good place to start learning and listen-
1g might be Ankara!

'urkey's Foreign Policy:
:ero Problems with Neighbors Revisited
ebruary 8, 2012[13]

undits in Europe and North America have delighted in citing, with a liter-
:y smirk, "zero problems with neighbors," which has been the centerpiece
f Ahmet Davutoğlu's agenda since he became foreign minister. They point
o Turkey's heightened tensions with Syria and Iraq, its persisting inability to
vercome the hostile fallout from the *Mavi Marmara* incident with Israel, and
ven the revived salience of the long-unresolved dispute with the Armenian
iaspora, sparked by a new French law that makes the denial of genocide
ssociated with the 1915 massacres a crime and has led to a dramatic worsen-
1g of Turkish-French relations.

Troubles, to be sure, but should these be interpreted as "failures," or
1ore precisely as "Turkish failures"? Perhaps Davutoğlu was insufficiently
1utious (or, alternatively, too optimistic) when he articulated the zero-
roblems diplomacy, but was it not *at the time* an accurate way of signaling
 new dawn for Turkey's approach to neighbors and the world as a whole?
avutoğlu implemented his lofty vision with a dizzying series of initiatives
1at opened long-locked doors. He also made it clear that the "neighbor-
ood" was not to be understood in a narrow geographical sense, but rather
 a broad sense disclosed by cultural and historical affinities and mutual
rategic interests. Davutoğlu was eager not only to banish lingering bad
1emories of Ottoman rule over much of the Arab world but to renew con-
ections with countries that share Turkic and Muslim identities.

Turkish foreign policy began charting this new course years before Davutoğlu became foreign minister, and this shift in worldview was shared with Recep Tayyip Erdoğan and Abdullah Gül, the two dominant political leaders during the past decade. Both men deserve some of the credit, and a share of the responsibility, for steering the Turkish ship of state into such uncharted waters of diplomatic initiative.

In an important sense, the turning point came in 2003 when the Turkish government, after sending some mixed signals to Washington, refused to allow the United States to use its territory to stage an invasion of Iraq. The anti-AKP domestic opposition challenged this unprecedented act of geopolitical insubordination as the biggest mistake in the whole of Turkish republican history. In retrospect, opting out of the invasion of Iraq constituted a transformational moment for Turkey that demonstrated to its neighbors and the world, and even to itself, that Turkey could and would think and act for itself, that the hierarchical alliances of the Cold War period were over, and that Washington should no longer take Ankara's collaboration for granted. This move did not mean, as some critics in both Turkey and the United States wrongly claimed, a turn toward Islam and away from the West or from continuing involvement in Western security arrangements; Turkey did allow American combat aircraft to use Incirlik Air Base, including for bombing missions. As recently shown, Turkey still values its NATO ties, even to the extent of allowing radar stations to be deployed on its territory that are linked to a missile-defense system.

By now it is almost forgotten that it was Turkey that encouraged peace talks between Syria and Israel. The talks seemed to be headed for success but broke down abruptly, a development that was attributed at the time to the Israeli attacks on Gaza but in retrospect had more to do with Israel's unwillingness to give up the Golan Heights. Turkey also sought to do the seemingly impossible, bringing Bosnia and Serbia together in a manner that moved them closer to normalization and at least a cold peace. Even more ambitiously in collaboration with Brazil, Turkey used its new stature as an independent regional player in May 2010 to persuade Iran to accept an arrangement to store a large portion of its enriched uranium in Turkey, thereby demonstrating the plausibility of a peaceful alternative to sanctions and warmongering.

To be sure, the earlier sensible effort to have friendly relations with Syria badly backfired, but not until the Damascus regime started shooting its citizens and refusing to meet the demands of its people for far-reaching reforms. Arguably, the same reversal of outlook in Ankara occurred in relation to Libya after Qaddafi threatened to massacre his opposition, leading eventually to some Turkish humanitarian support for the UN-backed NATO intervention. Also, there is no doubt that the EU's refusal to shift i one-sided stance on Cyprus has had some serious consequences, souring relations with Greece. Together with the recent wave of Islamophobia in Europe, this perceived unfairness to Turkey with respect to Cyprus weakened Turkey's commitment to qualifying for membership in the EU.

Despite the Turkish public's strong sympathies with the Palestinian struggle, the AKP leadership has done its best to restore normalcy to the relationship with Israel. After all, the attack on the *Mavi Marmara* was not only a flagrant breach of international law but resulted in the death of nine Turkish passengers. Turkey demanded an official apology and compensation for the families of the victims, a reasonable set of expectations that Tel Aviv was apparently on the verge of accepting, but this initiative collapsed at the last hour when challenged by the internal political opposition to Netanyahu.

Turkey has consistently tried to avert intervention and war in the Middle East and to promote diplomatic approaches that rely to the greatest extent possible on soft power. It has, to be sure, experienced several geopolitical rebuffs, as in relation to its efforts to end the confrontation with Iran. Davutoğlu has correctly affirmed Turkey's resolve to act on the principled basis of its values and convictions as well as strategic calculations of its interests, and not blindly follow directives from Washington. Iran is a striking case where the Turkish approach is both wiser and more likely to achieve the goal of reassuring the world that Tehran means what it says when it insists that it does not intend to acquire nuclear weapons. As in every other foreign policy setting, Davutoğlu is exhibiting his belief that, in the twenty-first century, *persuasion* works better than *coercion*.

In sum, the "zero problems with neighbors" approach needs to be understood as an *aspiration* and *strong preference* rather than as an invariable guide to *practice*. There are too many contradictions embedded in the political realities of the contemporary world to be slavishly tied to a rigid foreign-policy doctrine without taking account of context. For instance, in Syria and Libya the Turkish government was forced to choose between siding with a regime slaughtering its own people and backing a disorganized opposition. "Zero problems" needs to be understood as a preferred framework for addressing the relations between countries, not just governments; in situations of strife, choices must be made. One can argue that Turkey went too far when it backed NATO in Libya or not far enough when it failed to show support for the Green Revolution in Iran. These are difficult interpretative choices that do not invalidate the principled positions that Davutoğlu has affirmed as being as important as realist calculations in shaping foreign policy in complex situations.

Davutoğlu, on more than one occasion, has expressed enthusiastic support for the 2011 upheavals known collectively as the Arab Spring. He calls these upheavals great and irreversible historical transformations, expressions of young people's thirst for dignity and democratic freedoms.[14] Turkey has done nothing to thwart these high ideals.

Turkish foreign policy has charted a course of action based to the extent feasible on soft-power diplomacy, taking initiatives to resolve its conflicts with neighbors but also to mediate conflicts to which it is not a party. Its credibility has become so great that Istanbul has often replaced European capitals as a preferred venue for conflict resolution. Despite annoyance with Ankara regarding Iran or Israel, the U.S. government seems to favor Istanbul as the most propitious site for any prospective negotiations with Iran concerning its nuclear program.

As Syria and Libya show, it is not always possible to avoid taking sides in response to internal struggles, although Turkey has delayed doing so to give governments in power the opportunity to establish internal peace. In a globalizing world, boundaries are not absolute and sovereignty must give way if severe violations of human rights are being committed by the regime, but armed intervention should be a last resort undertaken only in extreme instances, on behalf of known opposition forces, and in a manner that has a reasonable prospect of success at acceptable costs for the targeted society. Such conditions almost never exist, so intervention is rarely if ever, in my judgment, justified, although conditions may quite often create strong pressures to do so.

We can only hope that Turkey stays the course. Rather than viewing "zero problems" as a failure, we should reaffirm its creativity. This soft-power diplomacy, supplemented by Turkey's economic success, political stability and cultural vitality, helps us understand Erdoğan's great popularity throughout the region and the world.

---

14. *Today's Zaman*, "Davutoğlu Offers Turkish Perspective on Arab Spring in UN Address," January 15, 2012, www.todayszaman.com/diplomacy_davutoglu-offers-turkish-perspective-on-arab-spring-in-un-address_268645.html; Sevil Kücükkosum, "Arab Spring Was Inevitable, Says Davutoğlu," *Turkish Weekly*, December 17, 2011, www.turkishweekly.net/news/128272/arab-spring-was-inevitable-says-davutoglu.html.

Ten Years of AKP Leadership in Turkey

August 25, 2012[15]

Nothing better epitomizes the great political changes in Turkey over the course of the last decade than a seemingly minor report that Prime Minister Recep Tayyip Erdoğan and his wife Emine Erdoğan attended a private iftar dinner (the ritual meal breaking the Ramadan fast each evening) by invitation of the current Turkish chief of staff, General Necdet Özel, at his official residence. Only a few years earlier, the military leadership had come hair-trigger close to pulling off a coup to get rid of the AKP leadership. Of course, such a military intrusion on Turkish political life would have been nothing new. Turkey hasexperienced a series of coups during its republican life that started in 1923.

The most recent example of military interference with Turkey's elected leadership took place in 1997, when Prime Minister Necmettin Erbakan sheepishly left office under pressure amounting to an ultimatum, outlawed his own political party, and withdrew from political activity for five years in what amounted to a bloodless coup, prompted by his alleged Islamic agenda. Unlike the prior coups of 1960, 1971, and 1980, when the military temporarily seized power, after 1997 bloodless coup politicians were allowed to form a new civilian government. Really, looking back on the period shortly after the AKP came to power in 2002, the big surprise is that a coup did *not* occur. We still await informed commentary that explains why. For the present, those who value the civilianization of governance can take comfort in the receding prospect of a future military takeover of Turkish political life, and this iftar meal is a strong symbolic expression of a far healthier civil-military relationship.

Improving Turkish Civil-Military Relations

Shortly after the AKP gained control of the government in 2002, it was much publicized that the elected leaders' wives were not welcome at the annual Victory Day Military Ball, the major social gathering of top military officers, because they wore headscarves. A similar issue arose a few years later when ardent Kemalists insisted that Abdullah Gül should not be allowed to serve as Turkey's president because his wife's headscarf supposedly signaled to the world that he did not represent the secular community. Recent court testimony by former Turkish chief of staff Hilmi Özkök confirms what many had long suspected: in 2003 and 2004, many high-ranking military officers supported plans to overrule the will of the Turkish electorate by removing the AKP from leadership and imposing martial law. These

---

5. http://richardfalk.wordpress.com/2012/08/25/ten-years-of-akp-leadership-in-turkey.

grim recollections should help us appreciate the significance of this iftar dinner between the Erdoğans and Özels as a strong expression of accommodation between military institutions and political leaders in Turkey. Such an event helps us understand just how much things have changed for the better, with respect to civil-military relations.

This event, first of all, indicates a more relaxed attitude on the part of the military toward Turkish women who wear a headscarf in conformity to Islamic tradition. Although this sign of normalization is a definite move in the right direction, Turkey has a long way to go before it eliminates the many forms of discrimination that continue to restrict their life and work options. Second, crucially, these developments show that the military seems finally to have reconciled itself to the popularity and competence of AKP leadership. This is significant, as it conveys willingness to accept a reduced role for the military in a revamped Turkish constitutional system, as well as trust in the sincerity of AKP pledges of adherence to secular principles, including respect for the autonomy of the military. This latter achievement is quite remarkable, a tribute to the skill with which Erdoğan in particular has handled the civilianization of the Turkish governing process, for which he is given surprisingly little credit by the international media and almost none by the Turkish media. Such an outcome was almost inconceivable ten years ago, but today it is taken for granted.

In 2000 Eric Rouleau, Le Monde's influential lead writer on the Middle East and France's former distinguished ambassador to Turkey (1988-1992), writing in Foreign Affairs, emphasized the extent to which republican Turkey's system, "which places the military at the very heart of political life," poses by far the biggest obstacle to Turkish entry into the European Union. Indeed Rouleau and other Turkish experts believed that the Turkish deep state (consisting of its security apparatus, including the intelligence organizations), was far too imbued with Kemalist ideology to sit idly by while the secular elites were displaced by the conservative forces that support the AKP. Not only were the Kemalist elites displaced, but their capacity to pull the strings of power from behind closed doors was ended by a series of bureaucratic reforms that have made the National Security Council a part of the civilian structure of government, not a hidden and unaccountable policymaking authority.

Continuing Political Polarization within Turkey

Despite these accomplishments, the displaced "secularists" are no happier with Erdoğan's leadership than they were a decade ago. (It needs to be understood, though, that the AKP's orientation and policy guidance have been consistently secularist, despite the personal religious beliefs and practices of its leaders. Indeed, quite unexpectedly, Erdoğan, visiting Cairo after the 201

Tahrir uprising, urged Egyptians to opt for secularism rather than Islamism, a message not appreciated at the time by the leadership of the Muslim Brotherhood.) Those who identify with the opposition to the AKP, and that includes most of the TV and print media, can never find a positive word to say about its domestic and foreign policy, although, as noted above, the line of attack has drastically shifted.

There are certainly valid complaints about Erdoğan's tendency to express his strong and sometimes insensitive personal opinions on socially controversial topics, ranging from abortion to advocating three-child families. He made an offhand remark recently that seemed to insult Alevi religious practices. As well, journalists, students, political activists, and non-AKP mayors are being held in Turkish prisons in fairly large numbers, without being charged with crimes and for activities that should be treated as normal in a healthy democracy. It is difficult to evaluate this disturbing trend; there are strong rumors that the AKP is not in firm control of parts of the bureaucracy, including the police. Although this may be true, it does not relieve the AKP from ultimate responsibility. As mentioned, there are many allegations that Erdoğan is laying the groundwork to become president in a revised constitutional framework that would give the position much greater powers than it now possesses. In my judgment, on the basis of available evidence, Erdoğan is opinionated, but not seeking to enthrone himself as head of a newly authoritarian Turkey.

This persisting polarization extends to other policy domains, perhaps most justifiably in relation to the unresolved Kurdish issues, which have violently resurfaced after some relatively quiet years. It is reasonable to fault the AKP for promising to resolve the conflict, then failing to offer the full range of inducements likely to make such a positive outcome happen. It is difficult to interpret accurately the renewal of PKK violence; many segments of Turkish elite opinion see it as removing all hope for a negotiated solution. The ferocity of the latest stage of this thirty-year struggle is not easily explained. To some degree it is a spillover of growing regional tensions with the countries surrounding Turkey, particularly the Kurdish movements in Iraq and Syria. There is also the strong possibility that elements of the Kurdish resistance see the fluidity of the regional situation as a window of opportunity to achieve national self-determination.

Also serious is some deserved criticism of Turkey's Syria policy as an imprudent and amateurish shift from one extreme to the other: first an ill-advised embrace of al-Assad's dictatorial regime a few years ago, followed by a questionable alignment with anti-regime rebel forces without knowing their true character. Ahmet Davutoğlu's positive initiatives in Damascus were hailed early on as the centerpiece of "zero problems with neighbors," an approach that his harshest critics now find totally discredited given the deterioration of relations not only with Syria, but with Iran and Iraq. Again such criticism seems greatly overstated by an opposition that seizes on any failure of governing policy without considering either its positive sides or offering more sensible alternatives. Whatever the leadership in Ankara during the last two years, the changing regional circumstances would require the foreign-policy establishment to push hard on a reset button. Mr. Davutoğlu has done his best all along to offer a rationale for the changed tone and substance of Turkish foreign policy, especially in relation to Syria, which I find generally convincing, although coordinating Syria policy with Washington seems questionable.

In the larger picture, there were few advance warnings that the Arab Spring would erupt and produce uprisings throughout the region. Prior to this tumult, the Arab world seemed ultra-stable, with authoritarian regimes in place for several decades and little indication of domestic challenges. In these conditions it seemed sensible to have positive relations with neighbors and throughout the Arab world, based on a mixture of practical and principled considerations. There were attractive economic opportunities to expand Turkish trade, investment, and cultural influence, and it was reasonable to suppose that conflict-mediation efforts could open political space for modest moves toward democracy and the protection of human rights.

Foreign Policy Achievements

It should also be pointed out that Foreign Minister Davutoğlu has been tireless in his efforts to resolve conflicts within an expanding zone of activity and influence. Even when unsuccessful, such attempts are bold and responsible efforts to find ways to improve the political atmosphere, and to find better diplomatic options than permanent antagonism, or worse, threats or use force to resolve conflicts and enhance security. His initiatives have helped Turkey become a major player in the region and beyond, almost alone in the world in constructing a foreign policy that neither continues Cold War deference to Washington nor adopts an alienated anti-Western posture. Turkey has continued its role in NATO, persisted with its attempts to satisfy the many demands of the EU accession process, and even participated militarily, in my view unwisely, in the failed NATO War in Afghanistan. Fairly considered, the Davutoğlu approach yielded extraordinary results and, even where it faltered, was consistent in exploring every plausible path to a more peaceful and just Middle East, Balkans, and Central Asia, as well as reaching into Africa, Latin America, and Asia, making Turkey for the first time in its history a true global political presence. Turkey has also displayed a principled commitment to international law and morality on key regional issues, especially the Israel Palestine conflict.

There were other international initiatives, none more spectacular than the major effort to engage with Somalia when the rest of the world had written it off as the worst example of "a failed state." Not only did Turkey offer material assistance in reconstructing the infrastructure of governance, it also more impressively ventured where angels feared to tread: organizing a high-profile, courageous visit by the prime minister, his wife, and other notables to Mogadishu at a time when the security situation there was known to be extremely dangerous. Such a show of solidarity to a struggling African nation was unprecedented in Turkish diplomacy and has been followed up with a range of projects to improve the economic and humanitarian situation in this troubled country. In a similar spirit of outreach, Turkey hosted a UN summit on behalf of the Least Developed Countries (LDCs) in May 2011 and formally accepted leadership responsibility within the UN to organize assistance to this group of states, considered the most impoverished in the world.

More recently, Mr. Davutoğlu, together with Ms. Erdoğan, visited the Muslim Rohingya minority in the western Myanmar state of Rakhine. This community had been brutally attacked in June by the local Buddhist majority, who claimed the Muslims were unwanted illegal immigrants from Bangladesh and should leave the country. Bangladesh officially denied such allegations, insisting that the Rohingya people had been living in Myanmar for centuries. This high-level mission delivered medical aid, displayed empathy that could only be interpreted as a genuine humanitarian gesture far removed from any calculations of national advantage, and above all conveyed a sense of how important it was for Turkey to do what it can to protect this vulnerable minority in a distant country. Mr. Davutoğlu also met with local Buddhists in a nearby town to express his hope that the two communities could live in peace and mutual respect. This is one more example of how Turkey combines a traditional pursuit of national advantage in world affairs with exemplary citizenship in the wider world community. This blend of enlightened nationalism and ethical globalism gives some hope that challenges to the world community can be addressed in a peaceful and equitable manner.

Surely Turkey, like any democracy, would benefit from a responsible opposition that calls attention to failings and offers alternative policy initiatives, while being ready to give those in authority credit for constructive undertakings and achievements. Unfortunately, the polarized and demoralized opposition in Turkey is strident, bereft of the political imagination required to put forward its own policies, and lacking in balance and leadership. It is especially suspect for the most secularized segments of Turkish society to complain about an authoritarian drift in AKP leadership when it was these very social forces who, a few years earlier, were virtually pleading with the army to step in and hand power back to them in the most antidemocratic manner imaginable. Instead of taking justifiable pride in the great Turkish accomplishments of the last decade, their unrestrained hostility is generating a sterile debate that makes it almost impossible to solve the problems facing the country or to take full advantage of the opportunities available.

Turkey remains a shining success story, both economically and politically. Nothing could bring more hope and pride to the region than for the Turkish ascent to be achieved elsewhere, sharing the commitment to build an inclusive democracy in which the military stays in the barracks and the diplomats take pride in resolving and preventing conflicts.

Whither Turkey: First Thoughts after Gezi Park

June 30, 2013[16]

As the dramatic Turkish protests subside, or declare an intermission, this is a time to take stock, but cautiously.

When political reality explodes in unexpected ways, pundits suggest comparisons, reflect their biases, offer hastily constructed explanations, and cite influences and antecedents. Most "experts" do all they can to hide how little they knew about the explosive forces in society, which so often erupt without any advance notice, suppressing their surprise and stepping forth with undiminished confidence to tell us why and how it happened and why it was almost inevitable. The most arrogant even dare tell us what to expect next and why it is good or bad. Yet even the most wily intelligence agencies, with billions at their disposal and total command over mountains of secret data running roughshod over privacy and legal rights, still invariably miss the "jumps" of change that are the real stuff of history. Why? Partly for the same reasons that even the most sophisticated volcanologists cannot predict a volcanic eruption with any accuracy—as in politics, the tipping points in nature and society generally disclose themselves with unforeseeable abruptness. An appropriate level of humility goes a long way: acknowledging these limits of understanding, explaining as best we can such charismatic events when they occur, taking due account of their distinctiveness, and admitting our inability to access the deeper meanings that lie beneath the surface. We are habitually trained and experienced to look at politics from above, whether our perspective is that of elites or counterelites, but revolutionary impulses come, and when they come, almost invariably from pressures generated from below, from the "multitude," suddenly bursting forth as happenings that startle an

---

16. http://richardfalk.wordpress.com/2013/06/30/whither-turkey-after-gezi-park.

reverberate: Nelson Mandela's release from prison, the collapse of the Berlin Wall, the Velvet Revolution, the Jasmine Revolution, Tahrir Square, Occupy Wall Street.

The Gezi Park Protests

Was Gezi Park in Istanbul such a happening, as many here in Turkey hope? Did it reflect the wishful thinking of those seeking a genuinely inclusive democracy in Turkey not only respectful of the environment and cultural identity but dedicated to the rights of all, especially such habitually abused minorities as Kurds and Alevis? Asli Bâli, a highly regarded law scholar teaching at UCLA, persuasively encapsulates the struggle as an epic encounter between two models of democracy—the majoritarian entitlement claims of Erdoğan (but not necessarily all elements in the AKP) versus the participatory and populist ethos of the younger generation, which is almost as opposed to the republican (antidemocratic) ethos of the secular elders as to Erdoğan. Bâli pins her own best hopes for the political future of Turkey on a split within the AKP that will transfer control from Erdoğan to the more inclusive moderate wing, which I presume would be led by the current president of Turkey, Abdullah Gül.

This is a most unusual idea, and it underscores that a change in the leadership of the country would be beneficial, but cannot be seen as issuing from either the present arrangements of governmental authority or as a result of a successful challenge by the organized opposition. The idea of a split within the AKP producing a more moderate and inclusive leadership is attractive for three reasons. First, it validates the positive contributions of AKP governance over the past eleven years while rejecting the style and some of the majoritarian implications of Erdoğan's leadership. Second, it implicitly rejects the prospect of an electoral transfer of authority to the traditional opposition represented by the old Kemalist party, the CHP, which despite its strong presence in protests at Gezi Park and throughout the country was viewed by the core protesters as politically antagonistic to reshaping Turkish democracy and intolerant toward the religiously observant, as well as repressive toward the Kurdish regions of the country. Third, strong doubts are present as to whether the Gezi protests, without party, program, agenda, or leaders and with strong anarchist elements, could grow into an inclusive movement along the lines of what Derrida calls "democracy to come," an aspirational, liberating vision of freedom that far transcends any historical embodiment of "democracy" up to this point. If the past teaches us anything, it suggests that such revolutionary impulses, no matter how intense, will quickly dissipate or implode, either because they become institutionalized in stultifying bureaucracies; engage in revolutionary terror, losing their revolutionary authenticity; or don't institutionalize, purge enemies from within and without, and simply fade away. Of course, history is cunning and may not mimic the past.

What Future for Turkish "New Politics"?

The dust in Turkey has not yet settled. It is far too early to discern whether a new political subjectivity has been born that will fill the political vacuum formed by the absence of a credible and responsible opposition. It is uncertain whether this venting of frustration and resentment can be converted into a sustainable political movement that offers the Turkish polity a post-Kemalist alternative to Erdoğan's AKP without losing its very substantial achievements, including ending prison torture, civilianizing the military, paying off the IMF, tripling the GDP, coming forward with a promising approach to the Kurdish problem, and gaining great influence and respect for Turkey as a success story in the region and world. Istanbul's emergence as a cosmopolitan crossroads for the world and a favored site for diplomatic meetings and high-profile events symbolizes these eleven years of national ascent.

We also should not dismiss the capacity of the AKP, including Erdoğan, to learn from the Gezi Park experience. Despite inflammatory tirades about the evils of social networking, foreign provocateurs, and domestic "looters" and "terrorists," and the excesses of police force (hardly a novelty in the region, and even Europe, but no more excusable for being "the old normal"), Erdoğan did eventually pull back to a significant degree, apparently taking account of the strong objections mounted against the Gezi Park project in its original form, which would involve reconstructing Ottoman-era military barracks that would then be used to house a shopping center that would obliterate the park. Erdoğan seems now to have put the project on hold for the indefinite future, awaiting a judicial finding and possibly organizing a citywide referendum. We should not idealize the protesters: a minority did vandalize a nearby mosque with obscene graffiti and allegedly threw beer bottles on its floor, although this charge is sharply contested. Unfortunately, and unacceptably, many governments that claim the mantle of democracy use excessive force when dealing with angry protests—but no autocrat worth the name attempts to meet adversaries halfway.

The government's new approach to the Gezi controversy may yet prove to be problematic. If the referendum endorses the project, Erdoğan might be tempted to plunge ahead. A referendum in such situations can often dangerously infringe upon fundamental social values that should be protected regardless of how "the people" vote. The preservation of Gezi Park would seem to qualify for metapolitical protective treatment: as a green enclave along with its proximity to Taksim Square, it possesses a vivid resonance for the whole city of Istanbul, including the revitalized Ottoman heritage so dear to Erdoğan and the AKP generally. It seems especially precious to a younger generation of urban Turks, and for the most ardent followers of Kemal Atatürk it has always been hallowed space.

Of course, Gezi Park was about far more than Gezi Park. It was a slowly articulated repudiation of the sort of democracy being offered by the Turkish state, along with as-yet-unarticulated demands for another kind of governance based on a different understanding of politics and freedom. It was also about, although vaguely and incoherently, the cultural leveling-down associated with neoliberal globalization and the rise of the predatory private sector littering the city of Istanbul with shopping malls and high-rise towers. Other, more conventional demands include releasing journalists and other prisoners of conscience from prison, greater freedom of expression and dissent, and more public accountability for police and government. At the same time, the depth and intractability of the CHP opposition makes reconciliation a mission impossible. Polarization seems the destiny of Turkey for the foreseeable future. Most of the protest spawned by Gezi Square focused on calls for Erdoğan's resignation, in effect demanding a repudiation of democratic elections, which seems rather perverse considering the overall success of Turkey under Erdoğan.

There are, to be sure, some peculiar features in the litany of opposition complaints. For instance, there are frequent allegations that antigovernment criticism of Erdoğan and the AKP is absent from the media due to intimidation. It is true that Turkish TV seemed at first to ignore the events in Gezi Park, while international TV covered the story in real time. Yet the true situation in Turkey, as I have experienced it, is one of widespread and harsh criticism of Erdoğan from many angles, not the slightest evidence of media intimidation or self-censorship, and a greatly exaggerated contention here and abroad that voices of censure have been silenced by imprisonment. Many journalists have been imprisoned, to be sure, but apparently less for their critical views than for their supposed involvement in unlawful antigovernment activities. These charges should be investigated without any further delays, and those being held either tried or released, but that is a different matter than contending that the Turkish media are treating Erdoğan as a hothouse flower, which is manifestly untrue.

The puzzle is why so many people seem honestly to believe that freedom of expression has been so severely encroached upon when it seems at least as robust as what is found in other democracies. What can be more aptly complained about here in Turkey, but less so than in the United States, where talk radio features inflammatory voices of the extreme right, is the shrillness of the critical media, which offer no space for those with moderate views.

I find *Today's Zaman* the most consistently informed and balanced of the major media sources in Turkey, but interestingly, it is almost unavailable at most newsstands throughout Istanbul, which seem to favor the strictly secular media.[17]

A Preliminary Balance Sheet

Despite their marginalization in Gezi Square itself, the mainstream Turkish secular opposition welcomed these protests with unreserved enthusiasm, misleadingly claiming that the confrontations were their moment of supreme vindication. The spontaneous outpouring was of youth, clearly thirsting for a new form of emancipatory politics, discovering and revealing themselves as events unfolded and exemplifying their distance from traditional politics by relying on humor, satire, inclusiveness, and a political style that seemed to owe more to performance art than to bombastic political speeches. This politics of protest was fully committed in its critical posture to a "search and explore" method of doing politics, along with an extreme reflex of disgust whenever political leaders tell their citizens what to do and not do in their lives. It is this acute sensitivity to government intruding upon private autonomy that does make this new protest ethos seem to join forces with secularists in their denunciation of Erdoğan and the AKP. Imprudently, Erdoğan has gone down this road. He has backed legislation restricting where and when alcohol can be consumed, aired his opinion as to how many children mothers should produce, and told the public why lipstick and kissing in public should be discouraged. There is no doubt that Erdoğan irresponsibly fans the flames of discontent in Turkey by refusal to keep his conservative personal preferences to himself, undermining his identity as the elected leader of a diverse, modern nation. As we should all know by 2013, "the personal is political."

These traits also lend some credibility to the deeper fears that Erdoğan does harbor dreams, if not ambitions and plans, of becoming an autocratic ruler. Erdoğan should not be blamed for the acute polarization of Turkish society, of which he is in many ways an unjust and long-term victim, but his blunt communication style is also polarizing. It suggests that Turkey remains an immature political culture—but it is far from alone in this regard.

---

17. Since this post was written, *Today's Zaman*, the newspaper of the Hizmet movement has been obsessively critical of the Erdoğan leadership and more generally has adopted a strongly anti-AKP line.

Imperiled Polities: Egypt and Turkey
January 25, 2014[18]

In mid-January 2014, Egyptians approved a constitution drafted by the interim government put in place after the 2013 military coup by a 98.1 percent majority. This compares with 63.8 percent support for the constitution prepared during the presidency of Mohamed Morsi (from the 32.9 percent of Egyptians who participated in the vote). This new constitutional referendum, in which 38.6 percent of the eligible 53 million voted, was boycotted by both the Muslim Brotherhood and various youth groups at the forefront of the anti-Mubarak upheaval in 2011. The vote was further discredited by the atmosphere of intimidation, well conveyed by the pro-coup slogan: "You are either with me or with the terrorists." Not only was the MB criminalized, its assets seized, its leaders jailed, and its media outlets shut down, but anyone of any persuasion who seemed opposed to the leadership and style of General Abdel-Fattah el-Sisi was subject to arrest and abuse.

In the background here are questions about the nature of "democracy" and how to evaluate the views of people caught in the maelstrom of political conflict. On one level, it might seem that a vote of over 90 percent for absolutely anything is an expression of extraordinary consensus, and therefore el-Sisi's constitution is far more popular than Morsi's, hence more legitimate. Further reflection makes the opposite seem evident, especially when the oppressive context is to taken into account: any vote in a modern society that claims 98.1 percent support should be automatically disregarded, because it must have been contrived and coerced. In effect, we cannot trust democratic procedures to reveal true sentiments in a political atmosphere that terrorizes its opponents and purports to delegitimize its opposition by engaging in state crime. The consent of the governed can only be truly ascertained if the conditions exist for free and honest expression of views for and against what present power-wielders favor.

Maybe seeking this populist signal of approval by the ritual of a vote is itself a kind of blindfold. It would seem that a majority of Egyptians did in fact welcome the coup, believing that a military leadership would at least ensure affordable food and fuel and restore order on the streets. In other words, most citizens in crisis situations posit order and economic stability as their highest political priorities and are ready to give up "democracy" if its leaders fail to meet these expectations. In my view, what has happened in Egypt is the abandonment of the substance of democracy by the majority

8. http://richardfalk.wordpress.com/2014/01/25/
imperiled-polities-egypt-and-turkey-two-visions-of-democracy.

of the Egyptian people, reinforced by the suppression of a minority hostile to the takeover. This dynamic is hidden because the discourse and rituals of democracy are retained. In effect, the polarization of the first two and a half years following the overthrow of Mubarak has been followed by the restoration of autocratic rule—but due to the intervening embrace of political freedom, however problematic, the new autocrat is even harsher than the one rejected at Tahrir Square three years ago.

The Politics of Polarization and Alienation

Amid this political turmoil is a conceptual confusion that contributes to the acute political alienation of those who feel subject to a government and policy agenda they perceive as hostile to their interests and values. Such circumstances are aggravated by political cultures that have been accustomed to "one-man shows" that tend toward adoration and demonization. Each national situation reflects the particularities of history, culture, values, national memories, personalities, and a host of other considerations, yet there are certain shared tendencies that may reflect some commonalities of experience and intersocietal mimicry as well as the deformed adoption of Western hegemonic ideas of modernity, development, constitutionalism, and governance, as well as of course the relationship between religion and politics.

Turkey and Egypt, each in its own way, are illustrative. In both countries there are strong, although quite divergent, traditions of charismatic authoritarian leadership reinforced by quasi-religious sanctification. Very recently, however, this authoritarian past is being challenged by counter-traditions of populist legitimacy putting forward impassioned demands for freedom, integrity, equity, and inclusive democracy which, if not met, justify putting aside governmental procedures, including even the results o: national elections. Within this emergent countertradition is also a willingness to give up all democratic pretensions to restore a preferred ideologica orientation toward governance—that is, resorting to whatever instrument are effective in transferring control of the state back to the old order.

In Egypt, this circumstance led to unconditional opposition to th elected leadership, especially Morsi. The aim of this opposition, conscious o not, seemed to have been to create a crisis of governability sufficient to pro voke a crisis of legitimacy, which could then produce a populist challeng from below that brought together ideological demands for a different orienta tion and material demands for a better life. It is true that Morsi lent a certai credibility to this rising tide of opposition by a combination of incompetenc and some clumsy repressive moves, but this was almost irrelevant; his secula and *fulool* opponents wanted him to fail and never allowed him even the po: sibility of success. For them, living under a government run by the MB was k itself intolerable. In the end, many of those who pleaded so bravely for freedom in Tahrir Square were, two years later, pleading with the armed forces to engage in the most brutal expressions of counterrevolutionary vengeance. Whether this will be the end of the Egyptian story for the near future is difficult to discern; the downward spiral suggests serious risks of insurrection and strife in the foreseeable future.

In Turkey, such a collision has recently produced turmoil highlighting the dangers and passions that accompany lethal polarization: initially in the encounters of the summer of 2013 at Gezi Park and, some months later, in a titanic struggle between Recep Tayyip Erdoğan and Fethullah Gülen, generating a rising tide of mutual recriminations and accusations that threatens AKP dominance. Turkey is different than Egypt in at least two major respects. First of all, its economy has flourished in the past decade, producing a rising middle class and a business community with lots to lose if investor confidence and currency exchange rates decline sharply. This reality is complicated by the fact that some of those who have gained economically are aligned with the AKP, and by the degree to which the Turkish armed forces are also major stakeholders in the private sector. Secondly, a major achievement of the AKP leadership has been to depoliticize the role of the Turkish military, partly to protect itself against interference and partly to satisfy European Union accession criteria.

Alienation and emotional distress are more a symptom than an explanation for these strong political tensions. Better understood, these conflicts are about class, religion, status, political style, the benefits of governmental control, and the availability of capital and credit. An additional source of public antagonism is the unresolved, and mostly unacknowledged, debate about the true nature of democracy as the legitimating ideal for good governance in the twenty-first century. There is an impulse on one side to base governmental legitimacy on pleasing the citizenry, and an impulse on the other side to insist upon fidelity to law and constitutionalism. Both sides invoke powerful arguments to support their claims. There is no right and wrong, which is infuriating for polarized discourse that can only raise its voice to shout in higher decibels. Each side is motivated by unshakeable convictions and has no disposition to listen, much less appreciate, what the others are saying. In effect, good governance is impossible in the absence of *community*, and what has become evident is that societal unity is currently unattainable in the presence of the sort of alienation that has gripped the publics in Egypt, Turkey, and elsewhere.

Part of the controversy—but only part—can be reduced to these differences over the very nature of democracy. Another part, as discussed above, involves abandoning democracy in substance while insisting on its retention in form.

Varieties of Democracy

The word *democracy* itself needs to be qualified in one of two ways: majoritarian or republican. Here is the central tension: public myth in all countries that deem themselves "modern" endorses the republican tradition of limited government and internal checks and balances, while political culture is decidedly ambivalent. It can spontaneously legitimize the majoritarian prerogatives of a popular leader with strong backing on the street and among the armed forces, even at the cost of republican correctness. Because of this reality, those social forces being displaced through societal power shifts tend to view a newly ascendant leader through a glass darkly. They suddenly lament authoritarian tendencies that never troubled them when their elites held the reins. Part of the recent confusion is that sometimes the authoritarian tendency gets so corrupted that it loses support even among those who share its class and ideological outlook, and a reformist enthusiasm emerges. This happened in Egypt, but its tenure was short-lived as its adherents, drawn from the ranks of the urban educated elites, quickly realized that their interests and values were more jeopardized by the "new" order than by the excesses of the "old."

We find this pattern playing out in Egypt through wild gyrations in the perception of the armed forces as a political player. In the Mubarak era, the armed forces were the central pillar of the state, a major beneficiary of governmental corruption and neoliberal inequities, and a principal perpetrator, along with other security forces, of state crime. In the Morsi period the armed forces seemed to stay in the background until either responding to or prompting the populist mandate of the opposition, exhibited by mass demonstrations and media mobilization based on a paranoid image of Muslim Brotherhood rule and genuine distress about economic stagnancy and political disarray.

After the July 3 coup, the armed forces set aside the constitution, installed a transitional government, promised new elections, and went about drafting a new constitution that embodied the hegemony of the armed forces. What has taken place, however, is an undisguised exercise of authoritarian closure based on declaring the former choice of the citizenry, the Muslim Brotherhood, to be a "terrorist" organization. Its leadership were victims of several atrocities, imprisoned, forced underground, and fled the country. Nevertheless, despite these repressive measures, the armed forces are proceeding as if their action has been mandated by "democracy," that is, by majoritarian demands for change, eventually validated through demonstration voting, and electoral ratification. In the background of such a counterrevolutionary turn, of course, were weak institutions of government accustomed for decades to operating within a strict authoritarian political space and a governmental bureaucracy whose judiciary and police continued to align ideologically with the old order. This entrenched bureaucracy seems to have regarded the reemergence of authoritarian and militarized politics as natural, linked in their imagination with Egypt's ancient heritage of greatness.

Challenging Democracy in Turkey

The situation in Turkey is much more subtle and less menacing, yet exhibits several analogous features. Despite the AKP's initial rise to power in 2002, a development subsequently reinforced by stronger electoral mandates in 2007 and 2012, most of the opposition never accepted these results as politically acceptable and immediately sought to undermine the elected leadership in a variety of legal and extralegal ways. In the background of this alienation was the implicit and feared belief that the AKP was mounting a challenge to the hallowed legacy of Kemal Atatürk, as well as to the rigid Turkish style of secularism that was periodically reinvigorated by the armed forces that staged coups, which in 1982 had imposed a highly centralized, security-oriented constitution on the country. With political acumen, the AKP maneuvered pragmatically, creating a rapidly growing economy, playing a conflict-resolving role throughout the Middle East, repeatedly proclaiming fidelity to the secular creed as the foundation of public order, and by stages subjecting the armed forces to civilian control. Despite the magnitude of these achievements the AKP and Erdoğan never gained an iota of appreciation or respect from the anti-religious Kemalist opposition that claims to be the only legitimate guardians of Turkish "secularism." Strangely, this alienated opposition was never able to present a responsible political platform that could give the Turkish people a *positive* alternative, so the prospects of mounting an electoral challenge remained poor.

This intensely alienated opposition seemed increasingly dependent on manufacturing a crisis of legitimacy that would restore the old state/society balance that had prevailed since the founding of the republic in 1923. The Atatürk legacy included a somewhat reluctant acceptance of procedural democracy in the form of free and fair elections, with the apparent implied assumption that the outcome would remain faithful to his modernist orientation. The range of opposition was limited by a law allowing the closure of political parties that seemed to be straying from the Kemalist path. When the AKP defied these expectations in 2002, the opposition became quickly fed up with the workings of "democracy" and seemed early on to count on being rescued, as in the past, by a military takeover of government. They hoped this would be encouraged by Washington, which they assumed to be unhappy about the Islamist leanings attributed to the AKP political base and leadership. The failure of these expectations to materialize deepened the alienation and frustrations of opposition forces, which exaggerated the faults of the government and ignored its achievements.

With such considerations in mind it was understandable that there would be exhilaration among the opposition about the Gezi Park demonstrations in the summer of 2013, especially in their initial phases, which were as much a protest against the AKP's embrace of an environmentally rapacious neoliberalism as against the alleged authoritarian excesses of the Erdoğan leadership. This enthusiasm weakened when the Gezi movement was substantially hijacked in its subsequent phases by the most extreme tendencies of the alienated opposition, which seemed to believe that Gezi presented an opportunity to fashion a full-fledged crisis of governability that might force the resignation of Erdoğan, if not the collapse of the AKP. There was an attempt to take advantage of escalating public outrage about excessive force by the police. Of course, Erdoğan's harsh style of discourse was particularly alarming to an already alienated opposition, reinforcing their underlying beliefs that any alternative would be better. The situation was aggravated after the AKP's electoral success in 2011, which seemed to give Erdoğan confidence that he need no longer adhere to his earlier cautiously pragmatic approach to leadership. The swagger he adopted both frightened and disgusted an opposition disinclined to give him any leeway.

Similarly, the more recent, unexpected, and still bitter public falling out between the AKP and the Hizmet movement has injected a new virus into the Turkish body politic, posing unpredictable threats. It may turn out that this conflict represents nothing more fundamental than a struggle for relative influence and power that calmer minds will resolve before long. Perhaps Turkey is also experiencing some of the almost inevitable mishaps associated with keeping one political party with a strong leader in power for too long. In the more distant Turkish past are the memories of Ottoman times, when the country was a regional power center governed by highly authoritarian figures, a hallowed past that was secularized in the last century but not challenged in its essential role in Turkish political culture.

Majoritarian and Republican Democracy Assessed

The distinction between "majoritarian democracy" and "republican democracy," although it simplifies the actual political texture, seems important. In majoritarian democracy the leadership is essentially responsible to the electorate: if its policies reflect the will of the majority, the views and values of opposed minorities need not be respected. Critical views treat such forms government as susceptible to the "tyranny of the majority," which has subjective and objective realities distinguishing between what is perceived and what is actually taking place. Arguably, given the embittered opposition that seemed unwilling to accept the outcome of the vote, after Morsi's election the Muslim Brotherhood used the prerogatives of office in a failed attempt to impose the majoritarian will and may itself have been prepared to change the rules of the political game so as to retain control. Part of the majoritarian mentality is to locate a check on its excesses in the will of the citizenry; thus, when the people are mobilized to demand a new leadership for the country without waiting upon the niceties of the next elections, the path is cleared for the sort of military takeover that occurred last July. Of course, majoritarian dynamics are subject to manipulation by antidemocratic forces whose zeal is directed toward gaining control of the state.

"Republican democracy," in contrast, starts with a generally skeptical view of human nature and prizes *moderate* government over efficiency and transcendent leadership. The United States' self-conscious adoption of republican democracy at the end of the eighteenth century, as spelled out for the ages in *The Federalist Papers*, is a classic instance of a constitutional system that was wary of majorities and protective of minorities and of individual rights (although totally blind to the human claims of slaves and Native Americans). Delinking government from religious claims of certainty was also consistent with republican sensitivity to human flaws and the general ethos of Lord Acton's famous saying: "Power tends to corrupt, and absolute power corrupts absolutely."

Because every political system faces crises, the American founders realized that the arrangements they envisioned would only survive the tests of time if two conditions were realized: first, reverence for the constitution by both lawmakers and citizens; second, judicial supremacy to override legislative and executive swings toward either implementing the momentary passions of the mob or aggrandizing power and authority and upsetting the delicate balance of institutions. Despite this self-conscious commitment to the republican approach, in times of war and crisis, the democratic feature of accountable power-wielding tends to yield to claims of national security and public expediency. Once such departures from republicanism become entrenched (as a result of a long period of warfare or in relation to nuclear weaponry or, now, transnational terrorism), the authoritarian genie can escape from the constitutional bottle. As the American motto of "eternal vigilance" reminds us, there are no safe paths to moderate government, and its most influential advocates realized that their wishes might be so defeated that they recognized that the people enjoyed "a right of revolution" if, despite all precautions, the governing process had become despotic.

It need hardly be argued that neither Egypt nor Turkey is remotely similar to the United States or Europe, but their superficial embrace of democracy might benefit from examining more closely the menace of majoritarian democracy in a fragmented polity and the difficulties of establishing republican democracy in political cultures long dominated by militarism and authoritarianism. Egypt is experiencing the essentially antidemocratic restoration of authoritarian militarism, while Turkey is trying to preserve sufficient stability and consensus to enable the self-restrained persistence of procedural democracy and a successful process of constitutional renewal, rid itself of the 1982 militarist vision of governance, and move toward creating the institutional and procedural framework and safeguards associated with republican democracy. Beyond this, however, will be the immense educational challenge of shaping a supportive political culture that entrenches republican values in public consciousness: above all, a respect for individual and group rights and an inclusive approach to policy formation that seeks participation by and approval from stakeholding constituencies opposed to the majority. Such a vision of a democratic future implies a *process*, not an *event*, and will require an ongoing *struggle* inevitably distracted by both manufactured and authentic crises of legitimacy. The hope is that moderate minds will prevail in Turkey, serving the long-term interests of a state and its peoples that retain great potential to be a beacon of light for the region and beyond.

Armenian Grievances, Turkey, the United States, and 1915

April 26, 2014[19]

On April 10, by a vote of 12 to 5, with one abstention, the U.S. Senate Committee on Foreign Relations gave its approval to Resolution 410, calling upon Turkey to acknowledge that the massacres of Armenians in 1915 and subsequently constituted genocide. It also asks President Obama to adjust American foreign policy by advocating an "equitable, constructive, stable and durable Armenian-Turkish relationship that includes the full acknowlededgment of...the Armenian Genocide."[20] Obama, since becoming president has refrained from uttering the G-word, although he has acknowledged the

---

19. http://richardfalk.wordpress.com/2014/04/26/
   armenian-grievances-turkey-united-states-and-1915.

20. U.S. Senate Committee on Foreign Relations, 113th Congress, 2nd session, Senate Resolution 410, reported in the Senate April 11, 2014, www.congress.gov/bill/113th-congress/senate-resolution/410/text.

historical wrongs done to the Armenian people in the strongest possible language of condemnation.

Such resolutions, although widely understood to be symbolic and recommendatory, reflect the Armenian diaspora's efforts to raise awareness of the true nature of what Armenians endured in 1915 and especially to induce the Turkish government to acknowledge these events as "genocide," or else suffer the reputational consequences of embracing what is being called "denialism." The resolution is the latest move to build a strong international consensus in support of the Armenian sense of grievance and pressure the Turkish government to admit the full enormity of the crimes against the Armenian people. There may also be an intention to reinforce an *appropriate* apology, should it be forthcoming, with such tangible steps as restoring stolen property and possibly even establishing a reparations fund.

The Armenian campaign also makes the wider claim that redress for a horrendous historic grievance will also act as a deterrent to similar crimes in the future. The Senate resolution, however, makes a minimal contribution to these goals. It is little more than a gesture of good will, explicitly associated with commemorating the ninety-ninth anniversary of the 1915 events. As the day of commemoration (April 24) has passed without the resolution being put on the Senate's agenda prior to its Easter recess, it becomes consigned to permanent twilight. Such an interplay of action and inaction manifests an underlying governmental ambivalence as to how the United States should formally address this issue. Why? Because the criticism of the Turkish government for the manner in which it is addressing these demands inevitably engages American foreign policy.

The Turkish foreign minister has already indicated his displeasure with such initiatives, insisting that respected historians should investigate the claim of genocide, that it is not appropriate for a third country to meddle in such matters, and that such an initiative, if formally endorsed at higher levels in Washington, will have a negative influence on resolving these persisting tensions. The Turkish narrative on 1915, which has softened during the past decade, still argues that there were atrocities and suffering for Turks as well as Armenians, including a considerable number of Turkish casualties, and that the massacres of Armenians were less expressions of ethnic hatred than of a reliance on excessive and undisciplined force to suppress an Armenian revolt against Ottoman rule at a time when Armenians were siding with invading Russians in the midst of World War I.

What Is at Stake

There are two important, intertwined concerns present: first, the whole issue of intertemporal justice—how to address events that took place one hundred years ago as fairly as possible, yet take account of the passage of time in assessing responsibility for such long-past events; second, the degree to which such an issue should be resolved by the parties rather than be addressed in the domestic politics of third countries whose governments are likely swayed by the presence or absence of aggrieved minorities.

My impression is that the current leadership in Turkey is less seriously committed to upholding the Turkish narrative than in the past, but neither is it willing to subscribe to the Armenian narrative, especially the insistence on the word *genocide*. It is not only the inflammatory nature of the word itself, but also reasonable apprehension about the "Pandora's Box" aspects of such a process, which would likely move from the word *genocide* to such delicate questions as claims for reparations and the restoration of stolen property. Undoubtedly Turkish leaders are reluctant to stir the hot embers of Turkey's nationalist political culture by acceding to the Armenian agenda. Yet with the centennial anniversary of 1915 around the corner, Turkey has its own strong incentives for seeking accommodation.

It seems important to ask what it is the Armenian campaign is seeking. Is it the belated satisfaction of having Turkey formally admit that what took place was genocide, or is it more than this? Is there embedded a further demand that Turkey honor the memory of these events by some sort of annual observance, perhaps coupled with the establishment of an Armenian Genocide Museum? Or, as signaled already, that it establish a fund and reparations procedures that will allow descendants of the victims to put forward economic claims for the harms endured? In effect, is the full range of Armenian expectations apparent at this stage? As the experience with the Holocaust suggests there is no single *event* that can permanently shut the doors of history or dry the tears of extreme remorse. At most, acknowledgment, apology, and even tangible steps initiate a *process* that will never completely end nor bring a satisfying closure to those who identify with the victims.

Parallel to the Armenian agenda is a long festering intergovernmental dispute between Turkey and the sovereign state of Armenia over control of the Nagorno-Karabakh region in the middle of Azerbaijan that has closed the border between Armenia and Turkey since 1993. The acting Armenian foreign minister, Eduard Nalbandyan, added fuel to this diplomatic fire by welcoming the Senate resolution as "an important step" toward establishing "historical truth and prevention of crimes against humanity."[21] He thus connected the international dispute over Nagorno-Karabakh to the historic

---

21. Arka News Agency, "Armenia Welcomes U.S. Senate Committee Resolution on Armenian Genocide," April 11, 2014, http://arka.am/en/news/politics/armenia_welcomes_u_s_senate_committee_resolution_on_armenian_genocide/#sthash.d3iFTz9a.dpuf.

controversy about whether the events of 1915 should be viewed as genocide, presumably to gain support from the Armenian diaspora. In an unusual way, the Armenian campaign on the question of genocide is mainly conducted under the direction of the diaspora and has been given only a secondary emphasis by Armenia itself, which has generally seemed more concerned about economic relations and the territorial dispute in Azerbaijan.

What is one to do about a course of events that occurred under distinct national and international conditions expressive of different structures and legal norms that prevailed a century earlier? I was similarly challenged recently after giving a lecture on moral responsibility in international political life. The question was posed by a Native American in the audience who angrily asked me why I had failed to advocate the restoration of the land seized in earlier centuries from the indigenous peoples who then inhabited North America, implying that my silence about such matters was an implicit endorsement of genocide. Such a reaction is understandable, but cannot be prescriptive in relation to twenty-first-century realities. Certainly it was genocidal in willing that distinct ethnic groups become extinct or endure forcible dispossession, but there was at the time no legal prohibition on such behavior and whatever moral interdiction existed was inconclusive, despite the manifest cruelty of the colonizing behavior. At this point, the clock cannot be rolled back to apply contemporary standards of justice to past wrongdoings, although ethical sensitivity and empathy are fully warranted—and present efforts to rationalize or even glorify past barbarisms are totally unacceptable.

We must begin from where we are but not end there, seeking as humane and transparent a response to these historic injustices as seems possible, given both the intervening developments and the relevant balance of forces now and then. The anticolonial movements of the last half of the twentieth century undid earlier injustices because of their capacity to mobilize effective popular resistance movements. Indigenous people do not have this capacity and are confined to what legal remedies are voluntarily conferred and to what degree documenting the past creates sufficient public sympathy to support voluntary initiatives seeking some fractional measure of moral and material rectification.

To some extent, accurate documentation is itself a form of historic redress, as was the case with the "truth and reconciliation" processes that tried, in Latin America and South Africa, to reconcile peace and justice during a transition to constitutional democracy, yet never brought anything approaching satisfaction or even closure to the victim communities. We should also learn from Nelson Mandela's willingness to overlook the structural injustices associated with economic and social apartheid in achieving the "political miracle" of a peaceful dissolution of political apartheid. Also relevant are some of the late reflections of Edward Said, who was of the opinion that despite the legally and morally unacceptable dispossession of the Palestinian people from their homes and homeland in 1948, it was now both futile and wrong to challenge any longer the existence of Israel. To resolve the conflict, in his view, required an acknowledgment of past injustices, especially the nakba, and mutual arrangements for the two peoples to live and coexist in peace under conditions of equality, security, and dignity.

Was It Genocide?

Is there a single historical truth that must be affirmed by all those of good will, and is this what the Armenian movement and Senate resolution contend? Can Turkey only express its good faith by subscribing literally to the main features of the Armenian narrative? In effect, is the litmus test of Turkish sincerity and remorse dependent upon a formal acknowledgment that what took place in 1915 was unequivocally genocide? I believe the historical truth is quite unequivocal from a factual and moral perspective: there was a systematic and deliberate effort to eliminate the Armenian minority from Turkey stemming from government orders and plans. Although this occurred in the midst of war and national upheaval, the ethnic violence was so one-sided and comprehensive as to undermine the credibility of the Turkish contention that World War I brought about an interethnic experience of shared suffering replete with atrocities for which blame cannot be exclusively attributed to Turkey or the Armenian community. This historical truth of predominant Turkish responsibility, however, is far more equivocal in relation to the further Armenian insistence that these genocidal *events* constitute the crime of genocide as embodied in the 1948 Genocide Convention, which came into force in 1951.

Criminal law is not retroactive. Even the Nuremberg judgment, which endorsed such innovations as "crimes against the peace" and "crimes against humanity," avoided any attempt to hold the Nazi leaders being prosecuted responsible for genocide, despite the magnitude of the Holocaust and the abundant documented evidence of the deliberate and planned elimination of the Jewish people. What exactly, then, is the crime of genocide? Can it be said to predate the entry into force of the Genocide Convention? If so, why was genocide ignored in the prosecution of these Nazis? The wording of Article 1 of the Genocide Convention lends an aura of ambiguity to such queries: "The contracting parties *confirm* that genocide, whether committed in time of peace or in time of war, is a crime under international law which they undertake to prevent and to punish."[22] The word *confirm* seems

---

22. Emphasis added. The full text of the Genocide Convention is available at
   www.hrweb.org/legal/genocide.html.

supportive of the view that the crime somehow preexisted the adoption of the Convention and that only the usage of the word is retroactive. Yet the concept of genocide was not conceived as a legal category until proposed in 1944 by Raphael Lemkin. I would suppose that had Lemkin persuaded the political community to adopt the Genocide Convention a decade earlier, the Nuremberg indictments would have included the crime, and possibly the decision would have given guidance as to whether the crime came into being with the treaty or antedated its ratification.

Compelling Turkey to admit a massive commission of the crime of genocide would have an array of legal implications. More flexible by far would be a process of inquiry by an international commission of independent experts, including well-respected international lawyers, which would likely conclude that the events in question were clearly genocidal in character and, if they had occurred after the Genocide Convention was adopted in 1950, would constitute genocide. The World Court, in responding to the Bosnian complaint alleging Serbian genocide, concluded that a high evidentiary bar exists even with the benefit of the Convention, but it did find that the 1995 massacre in Srebrenica was genocide. The majority decision of the highest judicial body in the UN system indirectly highlights the crucial differences between the crime of genocide and the psycho-political and sociological realities of genocidal behavior.

Finding a Solution

From the Armenian perspective, is this show of American governmental support helpful or not? I suspect that a more discreet effort would produce less defensiveness on the Turkish side and more willingness to seek a mutually satisfactory outcome. Mobilizing the U.S. Congress and French legislative bodies is somewhat similar to looking beneath the lamppost for a watch dropped in the darkness of the night. Admittedly, if the purpose is to raise awareness and mobilize support for the Armenians, such a public-relations campaign might be effective even if it stiffens Turkish resistance in the short run.

A second important concern is how to address the genocide issue given the passage of time and the interplay of preoccupations on both sides. My preference would be for both Turkish and Armenian representatives to agree that it is permissible to use the word genocide with reference to the Armenian ordeal of 1915, but with a shared understanding that doing so is without legal effect. The concept of genocide is inherently ambiguous: it simultaneously puts forward an empirical description of a set of events and a political, psychological, sociological, and ethical evaluation of those events, while also advancing the possible legal evaluation of such events as constituting a crime with a heavy burden of proof required to establish specific intent, which is a vital element of the crime.

What does not help internationally, it would seem, is posturing by the U.S. Congress. The question of whether the United States should be involved in shaping international public opinion is less significant than the substantive dispute about the events, but far from trivial. The questionable political opportunism that connects the responsiveness of Congress to a well-organized Armenian lobby in the United States does seem to make reasonable the official Turkish response that it is never helpful for a foreign government to take the antigovernment side in an unresolved controversy of this sort. It is bound to harm bilateral relations between the two countries. In effect, mutual respect for sovereignty requires governments to refrain from such meddling under almost all circumstances. One can easily imagine the furor in the United States if the Turkish parliament passed a resolution insisting that Washington finally acknowledge that Native American tribal communities were victims of genocide or that descendants of slaves are entitled to reparations. However sincere and morally plausible, in a world where legality and legitimacy are almost always matters for territorial sovereigns to resolve, the foreign source of such sentiments are deeply resented, and are more likely to produce an angry backlash than to induce an accommodating retreat.

It will probably necessitate some quiet fence-mending by the Obama presidency to maintain good Turkish-American relations, a key strategic priority. At the same time, the Turkish government should not sit still. It should do more than angrily push aside this American initiative and the related Armenian campaign, and show a more forthcoming attitude toward finding common ground to heal gaping Armenian wounds that remain open after a century. Mounting pressure is definitely raising the level of awareness, but only wisdom, empathy, and good will on both sides can overcome such an embittered past. In some respects, there is something tragic about this stand off between those who have reason to want the past to be a matter of historical reflection and those who insist that the past is forever present.

The Turkish government has reiterated its offer to establish a joint commission composed of Armenian, Turkish, and international historian to establish an authoritative narrative. Besides the likelihood that existing disagreements would be reproduced, the idea that the core concern is "historical" misses a main point: such a traumatic series of events need to be interpreted from multiple perspectives, including that of international criminal law. Establishing the factual reality, which strongly favor Armenians' empirical claims, does not resolve the question of what would qualify as an appropriate acknowledgment by the Turkish government, no does it address the lurking concern as to whether acknowledgment is sufficient, and if not, what further steps Turkey must take if it is to satisfy the demands of the Armenian campaign.

———————————————

ran

have had a long involvement with the twisting fate of Iran. After the end
f the Vietnam War in the mid-1970s, I was fearful that the next site for an
.merican military intervention would be Iran. There were as many as 45,000
.merican troops deployed in Iran, a country that played a key surveillance
le in the Cold War; Iran was a major oil producer and was viewed as a stra-
gic and ideological asset in the region. In 1953 the United States had covertly
elped overturn a democratically elected government headed by Mohammad
1ossadegh, who had aroused Washington's concern by repudiating the mon-
rchy and even more so by nationalizing the oil industry. Mossadegh was also
iisleadingly accused of exposing Iran to Soviet penetration.

This CIA operation led to the return of the Shah and a period of oppres-
ve authoritarian rule that included the torture of all those who dared ques-
on the legitimacy and practices of the regime. From an American strategic
iewpoint, the Shah was what Henry Kissinger once called that "rarest of
1ings, an unconditional ally." What this meant concretely was the Shah's
illingness to supply Israel and apartheid South Africa with oil at a time
hen other oil-producing countries in the world refused to deal with such
iscredited governments.

Against this background, a movement of opposition from below emerged
1 1978 and was in the end led by the Islamic religious leader Ayatollah
homeini, who had long been living outside of Iran as an involuntary exile.
he movement was largely nonviolent, despite being violently provoked by the
1ah's police and armed forces on several occasions. The challenge directed
: the monarchy was not subdued by the brute force of the regime, but rather
read and grew. Khomeini rejected the anguished call from partisans in the
reets—"Leaders, leaders, give us guns"—and also rejected compromises and
artial victory. The Iranian leader would settle for nothing less than com-
lete victory. Even the Shah's departure from the country in early 1979 was
isufficient. Khomeini demanded, and in due course received, a mandate to

rebuild the state from the ground up. Note the contrast with the Arab Spring upheavals in Egypt and Tunisia, which were content to rid the country of the hated ruler but otherwise sought to achieve their democratizing and economic goals through the established order associated with the old regime.

What happened in Iran after the revolutionary forces took over control of the country is complicated and controversial. What emerged was an Islamic theocracy presided over by Khomeini in the role of "supreme guide." The United States was hostile to these developments, explored military options to reverse the political outcome, and, provocatively, gave the Shah asylum so that he might receive medical treatment. When Iranian students took over the American embassy in Tehran in the fall of 1980 and held its diplomats and staff hostage for over a year, the revolution was radicalized, the opposition of the West stiffened, and moderates, even if devout Muslims, were no longer welcome in the upper echelons of government.

These tensions were further accentuated by Iran's confrontation with Israel, reversing the Shah's conciliatory approach. This phase of the conflict was further heightened in the first decade of the twenty-first century by the fiery rhetoric of the Iranian president, Mahmoud Ahmadinejad, coupled with Western concerns about Iran's nuclear program. The Iranians have claimed all along that it is an energy program, but Israel and others insist that it is aimed at giving Iran a nuclear-weapons option, which they declared to be unacceptable. Israel, the only state in the region possessing nuclear weapons, has postured belligerently during the past decade, treating evidence of a nuclear-weapons program in Iran as a war-generating red line, and has supported the imposition of harsh sanctions on Iran that exerted severe economic pressure. More recently Israel's prime minister, Benjamin Netanyahu, has challenged as insufficient President Obama's diplomatic initiative designed to ensure that Iran's nuclear program remains peaceful.

This kind of threat diplomacy has persisted, although in light of the turmoil in the region there has been a seemingly serious attempt to reach an internationally supervised arrangement that limits Iran's reprocessing capabilities in exchange for reducing the pressures exerted by sanctions and gradually normalizing relations. However, Israel's opposition and the anti-Iranian atmosphere in the U.S. Congress make it difficult to defuse the crisis and explore opportunities for normalization that might contribute to efforts to calm the situation.

The selections in this Iran chapter seek to expose this provocative behavior by the West and consider the dangerous effects of such a posture if further escalated. There is a troubling double standard that pertains to nuclear weapons and the supposed international treaty regime of nonproliferation. Israel has been permitted to acquire, possess, and develop its arsenal of nuclear weapons covertly, and is even assisted in doing so by France and the United States. Iran, in contrast, although it was actually attacked in 1980 (by neighboring Iraq, with the encouragement of Washington), has been continuously threatened with a military attack, has experienced efforts at destabilization associated with American and Israeli hostility, and has been subject to a variety of military threats and economic sanctions, is categorically prohibited from acquiring even a deterrent capability.

What is more, the West has refused even to discuss, much less advocate, the obvious means to reduce regional tensions—establishing a nuclear-weapons-free zone throughout the Middle East. There is a perverse consensus that Israel's nuclear weapons, despite its frequent wars, pose no threat, while Iran is to be stopped from acquiring any comparable capability even if it takes a war to do so. Whatever Iran chooses to do about developing a military capability, it has no prospect of overcoming its total vulnerability to threats of conventional military attack by the United States or Israel. Iran is denied any opportunity to insist on sovereign equality in relation to nuclear weapons to the effect that if it agrees to renounce the option, then others in the region should also be made to do so. The reasonableness of such a demand is underscored by the awareness that Israel possesses a huge military edge in non-nuclear capabilities and has resorted to aggressive war on several occasions to promote its national interests. Under these conditions, it would seem that Iran is entitled to either acquire a deterrent capability or be assured that its main adversary is not allowed to retain and develop nuclear weapons.

In these respects, the encirclement of Iran, reinforced by decades of punitive diplomacy, epitomizes the primacy of geopolitics in the Middle East, as differentiated from a rule-governed system of sovereign states committed to peace and stability. Such an appreciation of these security issues should not lead observers to overlook Iran's violations of human rights and repressive practices.

Confronting Iran:
Warmongering in the Middle East

November 11, 2011[1]

How many times have we heard in recent weeks either outright threats to attack Iran, mainly emanating from Israel, or the more muted posture adopted by the United States that leaves "all options" on the table, including the "military option"? What has Iran done to justify this frantic warmongering in a strategic region that is sorting out the contradictory effects of the long Arab Spring and is the contested site of the energy geopolitics that has replaced territory and minerals as the core issue of world politics?

As a matter of historical context, it is worth observing that the Western military interventions of recent years, Iraq and Libya, were both in oil-producing countries, devastating each country to achieve regime change, which remains the central tenet of the neocon/Netanyahu vision for a reconfiguration of power in the Middle East. It follows that Iran remains the only oil producer in the region that refuses to play nicely with the West and has been sanctioned to some degree ever since it achieved an anti-Western regime change back in 1979. In this setting of prewar hysteria—pouring the fuel of rumor and threat on the fire of belligerent diplomacy—I have no intention of discounting the grievances of those who bravely opposed the theocratic regime from within Iran after the fraudulent elections of June 2009 in the shape of the repressed Green Movement, but it is beside the point in the present debate.

Why talk of oil if the war momentum is explicitly preoccupied with Iran's alleged effort to obtain nuclear weapons? Let the facts speak for themselves. Where there is oil and an anti-Western government in power, recourse to the military option follows, or at least an insistence on sanctions that aim to be crippling and regime-changing. In Iraq, the smokescreen in 2003 was its stockpile of weapons of mass destruction; when that war-justifying scenario was discredited, democracy and human rights abruptly took over as the strategic rationale. Not to be overlooked, of course, was backroom Israeli pressure to destroy the Baghdad regime of Saddam Hussein, as well as the oil, involving both favorable access to the oil fields and some leverage over pricing. We all need to be reminded over and over again that Western prosperity rests on cheap oil and its future prospects crucially depend on reliable supplies at moderate prices. We need to be reminded because, as Donald Rumsfeld

---

1. http://richardfalk.wordpress.com/2011/11/11/
   criminalizing-diplomacy-fanning-the-flames-of-the-iran-war-option.

once reassured the world, "We don't seek empire."[2] Really! Concerns about oil security in the future are the real unacknowledgeable threats to the security of the West!

Such illicit interventionary diplomacy should be unmasked. For once we can look to Moscow for a benign clarification. The Russian deputy foreign minister, Gennady Gatilov, stated: "The world community will see additional sanctions against Iran as an instrument of regime change in Tehran. That approach is unacceptable to us."[3] The plausibility of this interpretation is given further credibility by Iranian exile voices calling for targeting Iran's central bank and currency, with the avowed intention of bringing such hardship to the people of Iran as to mount destabilizing pressures from below on the Tehran government. The leader of the Green Movement, Mir-Hossein Mousavi, has repeatedly spoken against international sanctions, insisting that they hurt the people of Iran and strengthen the government's hold on the population. The struggle for Iranian self-determination must be waged by the *Iranian people*, not their self-interested patrons from without. Such patrons being heeded in the Iraq case, and recently influential in the Libyan case as well, contribute to a war-making process that leaves their country in shambles. True, the West is at first ready, but not able, to pick up the pieces. The result is continuous, unresolved violent conflict, acute and widespread human insecurity, followed by eventual abandonment of the postwar reconstructive commitment. Iraq is tragically illustrative.

As has been pointed out by some opponents of this war fever, Iran has not attacked another country in two hundred years. As President Ahmadinejad recently informed Iranians in the city of Shahr-e Kord: "The Iranian nation is wise. It won't build two bombs against the twenty thousand bombs you have."[4] The former heads of Israel's Mossad, Meir Dagan and Efraim Halevy, confirm the view that Israel would not be seriously threatened even if it should turn out that Iran does come to possess a few nuclear weapons in the future. Their contention is that such a nuclear capability would only pose a threat for Iran's Sunni rivals, especially Saudi Arabia and Bahrain, as Israel would retain an overwhelming deterrent even without American

. Donald Rumsfeld, interview with Al Jazeera, quoted in "Empire Snaps Back," *Progressive*, June 2003.

. Jonathan Marcus, "Russia Rules Out New Iran Sanctions over Nuclear Report," BBC News, November 9, 2011, www.bbc.co.uk/news/world-middle-east-15659311.

. Associated Press, "Iran Will Not Retreat 'One Iota' from Its Nuclear Programme, Says Ahmadinejad," *Guardian*, November 9, 2011, www.theguardian.com/world/2011/nov/09/iran-retreat-iota-nuclear-ahmadinejad.

backing.[5] Of course, it is true that the Western alliance does not want any regional developments to destabilize its regional friends, no matter how autocratic and repressive. So much for the supposed Western embrace of the democratizing spirit of the Arab Spring! For hypocritical William Hague, the pro-Israeli foreign secretary of Great Britain, to say that Iran's nuclear program is threatening to undermine the Arab Spring by bringing about a "nuclear arms race in the Middle East"[6] is obviously to point his finger in the wrong direction. There are also murmurs in the background, perhaps to shift attention away from Israeli warmongering, to the effect that the real danger associated with Iran acquiring nuclear weapons is that Turkey and Saudi Arabia would follow suit.

If these are the serious concerns, there are other far better ways to proceed. Why is there no mention of Israel's nuclear-weapons arsenal, of the West unlawfully helping Israel to cross the nuclear threshold covertly, of Israel being one of three important states in the world that refuses to become a party to the Nonproliferation Treaty, and of Israel's refusal to discuss even the idea of a nuclear-free zone in the Middle East when Iran has announced its readiness to join one? If oil is the foremost reality of which we must not speak, then Israeli nuclearism is a close second. We understand that the Obama presidency has been reduced to silence, but why are no regional and global voices speaking on behalf of nuclear sanity? Is Israel's status as a nuclear state as untouchable a feature of a dysfunctional system of global governance as the retention of Britain and France as two of five permanent members of the UN Security Council? Such sacred cows of an entrenched world order are dooming the 99 percent as much as the demons of Wall Street!

There is a third reality of this deepening crisis: the total disregard in the public-policy debate for international law that prohibits all nondefensive uses of force, including threats to do so. This core norm of the UN Charter set forth in the language of Article 2(4) and reinforced by the International Court of Justice in the Nicaragua case in 1986[7], was built into the idea of crimes against peace that served as the basis for indicting and convicting surviving German and Japanese leaders at the Nuremberg and Tokyo trials after World War II. There is not even a lawyerlike attempt to argue the

5. Eli Clifton, "Ex-Mossad Chief: Iran Is Not an Existential Threat," *ThinkProgress*, November 4, 2011, thinkprogress.org/security/2011/11/04/361799/ex-mossad-chief-iran-isnt-an-existential-threat.

6. William Hague, "Iran's Nuclear Threat Is Escalating," *Guardian*, July 11, 2011, www.theguardian.com/commentisfree/2011/jul/11/iran-nuclear-weapons-uranium-production.

7. International Court of Justice, *Nicaragua v. United States of America*, June 27, 1986, www.icj-cij.org/docket/?sum=367&p1=3&p2=3&case=70&p3=5.

Bush's discredited doctrine of preemptive war applies to Iran; it is instead presumed that international law is totally irrelevant to the policy debate. To discuss the military option as if not circumscribed by solemn legal commitments, while building the case that Iran is subject to attack because it has violated its treaty obligations as a state pledged not to acquire nuclear weapons, is doublethink emblazoned on the sky of hard-power geopolitics. Accountability for the weak and vulnerable, discretion for the strong and mighty. This woeful message of street geopolitics is being transmitted to the peoples of the world in this crisis-building moment.

If ever there was an argument for the acquisition of nuclear weapons by Iran, the diplomacy of Israel and the West has fashioned it in a strong form. After all, Iran is being constantly threatened with attack by states far more powerful than itself; although it possesses retaliatory capacity, it is vulnerable to devastating attacks from sea, air, and land. Can we imagine a better set of conditions for acquiring nuclear weapons so as to deter an attack? If deterrence legitimates nuclear weapons for the West, why not for Iran? Would Iraq have been attacked in 2003 if it had a stockpile of nuclear weapons accompanied by delivery capacities? These questions point in two directions: the unacceptable two-tier structure of governance with respect to nuclear weaponry that the world has endured since the atomic bombs were dropped on Hiroshima and Nagasaki in 1945, and the imperative urgency of rejecting nuclear hegemony and oligarchy and moving toward a negotiated nuclear disarmament treaty. There is no morally and legally acceptable or politically viable alternative to the abolition of *all* nuclear weapons as a global policy priority of utmost urgency.

Toward a Middle East Nuclear-Weapons-Free Zone
January 28, 2012[8]

Finally, there is some argumentation in the West supportive of a nuclear-free zone (NFZ) for the Middle East. Such thinking is still treated as politically marginal and is hardly audible above the beat of the war drums. It also tends to be defensively and pragmatically phrased, as in a *New York Times* article by Shibley Telhami and Steven Kull with the full-disclosure title "Preventing Nuclear Iran, Peacefully." The article makes a prudential argument against

---

http://richardfalk.wordpress.com/2012/01/28/
nuclear-free-middle-east-desirable-necessary-and-impossible.

attacking Iran based on prospects of a damaging Iranian retaliation and the inability of an attack to destroy Iran's nuclear program at an acceptable cost. The most that could be achieved would be a short delay in Iran's acquisition of weaponry, maybe not even that. An attack seems likely to create irresistible pressure in Iran to do everything possible to obtain a nuclear option with a renewed sense of urgency.[9]

Telhami and Kull sensibly reinforce their argument by pointing to respected public-opinion surveys that show Israeli attitudes to be less war-inclined than had been generally assumed. According to a recent Israeli poll, only 43 percent of Israelis favor a military strike, while 64 percent favor establishing an NFZ in the region that includes Israel. In effect, then, establishing a NFZ that includes Israel would seem politically feasible, although not a course of action that would be entertained by the current Tel Aviv governmental political climate. We can conclude that Washington's silence with respect to such an approach confirms that the U.S. government adheres to the official Israeli line and is not particularly sensitive to the wishes of the Israeli public, even to the extent of serving America's own strong national interest in finding a peaceful solution to the conflict.

A variant of NFZ thinking was recently espoused by Prince Turki Al-Faisal, former Saudi ambassador to the United States and once the head of Saudi intelligence. He too argues that an NFZ is a better alternative than the military option, which he contends should be removed from the table. Prince Turki insists that sanctions have not altered Iran's behavior. His proposal is more complex than simply advocating an NFZ. He would favor sanctions against Iran if there is convincing evidence that it is seeking nuclear weapons, but he also supports sanctions imposed on Israel if it does not disclose openly the full extent of its nuclear weapons arsenal.[10] His approach has several additional features: extending the scope of the undertaking to all weapons of mass destruction (WMD), including biological and chemical weapons; establishing a nuclear security umbrella for the region by the five permanent members of the UN Security Council; and seeking a resolution of outstanding conflicts in the region in accordance with the Mecca Arab proposals of 2002 that call for Israeli withdrawal from Palestinian territories and the Golan Heights, a

9. Shibley Telhami and Steven Kull, "Preventing a Nuclear Iran, Peacefully," *New York Times,* January 15, 2012, www.nytimes.com/2012/01/16/opinion/preventing-a-nuclear-iran-peacefully.html.

10. Turki Al-Faisal, "Middle East Security and Non-Proliferation," speech to Manama Dialogue 2013 Fifth Plenary Session, Bahrain, December 8, 2013, video and transcript available at www.iiss.org/en/events/manama%20dialogue/archive/manama-dialogue-2013-4e92/plenary-5-fbc6/turki-al-faisal-7a7c.

well as the political and commercial normalization of relations between Israel and the Arab world.

Prince Turki warns that if such an arrangement is not soon put in place and Iran proceeds with its nuclear program, other countries in the region, including Turkey, are likely to be drawn into an expensive and destabilizing nuclear arms race. In effect, like Telhami and Kull's, Prince Turki's approach is designed to avoid worst-case scenarios, but is framed mainly in relation to the future of the region rather than confined to the Israel/Iran confrontation.

Prince Turki concretely urges establishing such a framework with or without Israeli support at a conference of parties to the Nuclear Nonproliferation Treaty (NPT) scheduled for later in the year in Finland. Israel, not a party to the NPT, has not indicated its willingness to attend the conference. As long ago as the 1995 NPT Review Conference, the Arab countries put forward a proposal to establish a WMD-free zone (WMDFZ) in the Middle East, but it has never been acted upon at any subsequent session. Israel has consistently taken the position that a complete peace in the region must precede any prohibition on the possession of nuclear weapons.

The NFZ or WMDFZ initiatives need to be seen in the setting established by the NPT regime. Israel's failure to become a party to the NPT, coupled with its covert nuclear program, resulted in its acquisition of the weaponry with the complicity of the West, as documented in Seymour Hersh's 1991 *The Samson Option*. Contrast this pattern of behavior with that of Iran, a party to the NPT that has reported to and accepted, with some friction, inspections on its territory by the Western-oriented International Atomic Energy Agency. Iran has consistently denied any ambition to acquire nuclear weapons, but has insisted on its rights under Article IV of the treaty to exercise its "inalienable right...to develop research, production and use of nuclear energy for peaceful purposes without discrimination."[11] Iran has been under constant threat of attack by Israel, has been the target for several years of Israel's dirty low-intensity war, has been the target of a congressionally funded destabilization program reinforced by U.S. diplomacy that constantly reaffirms the relevance of the military option, and operates in a political climate that excludes consideration of Israel's nuclear arsenal. What is surprising under these circumstances is that Iran has not freed itself from its NPT obligations by exercising its option to withdraw from the treaty, as it is entitled to do by Article X.

Comparing these Israeli and Iran patterns of behavior with respect to nuclear weapons, it is difficult not to conclude that Israel, not Iran, should be subjected to sanctions and pressured to participate in denuclearizing

---

. Treaty on the Non-Proliferation of Nuclear Weapons, full text available at www.un.org/en/conf/npt/2005/npttreaty.html.

negotiations. After all, Israel acquired the weaponry secretly, has not been willing to participate in the near-universal discipline of the NPT, and has engaged in aggressive wars repeatedly against its neighbors, resulting in long-term occupations. It can be argued that Israel was entitled to enhance its security by remaining outside the NPT and thus is acting within its sovereign rights. This is a coherent legalistic position, but we should all realize by now that the NPT is more a *geopolitical* than a *legal* regime and that Iran, for instance, would be immediately subject to a punitive response if it tried to withdraw from the treaty. In other words, geopolitical priorities override legal rights in the NPT setting.

The NPT is shaped by its geopolitical nature. This is best illustrated by the utter refusal of the nuclear states, above all the United States, to fulfill their obligation under Article VI "to pursue negotiations in good faith on effective measures relating to the cessation of the nuclear arms race at an early date and to nuclear disarmament, and on a treaty on general and complete disarmament under strict and effective international control." The International Court of Justice has in its 1996 Advisory Opinion on the Legality of the Threat or Use of Nuclear Weapons unanimously affirmed in its findings the legal imperative embodied in Article VI: "There exists an obligation to pursue in good faith and bring to a conclusion negotiations leading to nuclear disarmament, and on a treaty on general and complete disarmament in all its aspects under strict international control."[12] This finding has been completely ignored by the nuclear states, which had earlier made a furious failed effort to dissuade the UN General Assembly from seeking such guidance. The refusal to uphold these obligations of Article VI would certainly appear to be a material breach of the treaty that authorizes any party to regard the treaty as void. Again, the international discourse on nuclear weapons is so distorted that it is a rarity to encounter criticism of its discriminatory application, its double standards as between nuclear and nonnuclear states, and its geopolitical style of selective enforcement. In this regard it should be appreciated that the threat of military attack directed at Iran resembles the so-called Bush Doctrine of preventive war, used to justify aggression against Iraq in 2003.

In summary, it is of utmost importance to avoid a war in the Middle East arising from the unresolved dispute about Iran's nuclear program. One way to do this is to seek a NFZ or a WMDFZ for the entire region that includes the participation of Israel. What has given this approach a renewed credibility for the West is that it seems the only way to avoid a lose/lose war option and that it possesses some prudential appeal to change minds in Tehran and T

---

12. International Court of Justice, "Legality of the Threat or Use of Nuclear Weapons," advisory opinions, 1996, www.icj-cij.org/docket/index.php?p1=3&p2=4&k=e1&p3= &case=95.

Aviv, and also to engage Washington in a less destructive and self-destructive course of action. Whether this prudential appeal is sufficiently strong to overcome the iron cage of militarism that guides policy choices in Israel and the United States remains doubtful. Thinking outside the militarist box remains a forbidden activity, partly reflecting the domestic lock on the political and moral imagination of these countries by their respective military-industrial-media–think tank complexes.

I would conclude this commentary with three pessimistic assessments that casts a dark shadow over the regional future:

1. An NFZ or WMDFZ for the Middle East is necessary and desirable, but it almost certainly will not be placed on the political agenda of American-led diplomacy relating to the conflict.

2. Moves toward nuclear disarmament negotiations that have been legally mandated and would be beneficial for the world and for the nuclear states and their peoples will not be made in the current atmosphere, which blocks all serious initiatives to abolish nuclear weapons.

3. The drift toward a devastating attack on Iran will only be stopped by an urgent mobilization of antiwar forces in civil society, which seems unlikely given other preoccupations.

Kenneth Waltz's Risky "Modest Proposal"
July 6, 2012[13]

It seems surprising that the ultra-establishment journal *Foreign Affairs* would go to the extreme of publishing a lead article by the influential, recently deceased political scientist Kenneth Waltz, with the title "Why Iran Should Get the Bomb."[14] The reasoning of the article, even more than the eye-catching title, flies in the face of the antiproliferation ethos that has been the consensus among nuclear states, especially the United States. At the same time, Waltz takes pain to reaffirm his mainstream political identity. He endorses the prevailing view, without pausing to raise doubts or at least acknowledge a degree of uncertainty, that Iran is seeking nuclear weapons.

3. http://richardfalk.wordpress.com/2012/07/06/kenneth-waltz-is-not-crazy-but-he-is-dangerous-nuclear-weapons-in-the-middle-east.

4. Kenneth Waltz, "Why Iran Should Get the Bomb," *Foreign Affairs*, July/August 2012, www.foreignaffairs.com/articles/137731/kenneth-n-waltz/why-iran-should-get-the-bomb.

Waltz does suggest that Iran might be trying only to have a "breakout" capability of the sort enjoyed by Japan and several other countries: that is, the capacity to assemble a few bombs in a matter of months or less if facing a national emergency. Nowhere does Waltz allude to the recently publicized agreement among the fourteen American intelligence agencies that there is no reliable evidence that Iran has resumed its military program, reportedly abandoned in 2003. In other ways, as well, Waltz signals his general support for the American approach to Israeli security; make no mistake, he is neither a political dissenter nor a policy radical.

Waltz's Three Options

Waltz insists that aside from the breakout option, there are two other plausible scenarios worth considering: sanctions and coercive diplomacy to induce Iran "to abandon its pursuit of nuclear weapons," which he deems unlikely to overcome a genuine appetite for the bomb, or Iran defying the pressures and acquiring nuclear weapons, which he provocatively argues is the most desirable of the three options. It seems reasonable to wonder why. In essence, Waltz is arguing that experience and logic demonstrate that the relations among states become more stable and less war-prone when a balance is maintained, and that there is no reason to think that if Iran acquired nuclear weapons it would not behave in accordance with the deterrence regime that has effectively discouraged all contemplated uses of nuclear weapons since 1945. In this regard, Waltz is expressing what I regard to be a wildly exaggerated faith in the experience of a brief stretch of history and in the overall rationality and prudence of world leaders.

He does make a contextual argument that I agree with: namely, that Israel alone possessing a regional nuclear monopoly is more dangerous and undesirable than Iran becoming a second nuclear state in the region. Israel if deterred by Iran's nuclear weapons, would be more likely to contribute to peace and security in region than if allowed to maintain its regional nuclear monopoly. If a standoff were to occur, it seems likely that it would reduce the risks of threat and use in the Middle East, although—as with any regime of deterrence—an indeterminate risk would remain. But to say that A (Iran gets the bomb) is better than B (breakout capability but no bomb) and C (sanctions and diplomacy persuade Iran to forego the bomb) is to forget about D. D—which we will get to in a moment—is far better than A, B, and C in relation to sustainable stability, but also because it implicitly acknowledges that the very idea of basing security upon a threat to annihilate hundreds of thousands, if not more, of innocent persons is a moral abomination that has already implicated the nuclear states in a security policy that would be genocidal, if not omnicidal, and certainly criminal.

This antinuclear posture was substantially endorsed by a slim majority of International Court of Justice judges in a groundbreaking 1996 advisory opinion.[15] The Court's strong findings as to international law were, not surprisingly, treated as irrelevant by the nuclear states, most explicitly by the United States. In effect, the view in Washington seemed to be that policies governing nuclear weapons were too important to be determined by lawyers.

The Case for Option D

What, then, is Option D? Significantly, Waltz does not even mention it. He has undoubtedly thought of it, but he must think it is so inconsistent with the hard-power realities of global diplomacy as to seem foolish and irrelevant even to discuss. Option D would involve the negotiation and implementation of a nuclear-weapons-free zone throughout the Middle East, reinforced by nonaggression commitments, normalization of economic and political relations, and, ideally, a just and sustainable Palestine/Israel peace treaty. Needless to say, D is not in the Netanyahu playbook. Possibly no Israeli leader would be willing to give up the nuclear arsenal that Israel has been developing over the last four decades. It seems fair to conjecture that this is also not in Waltz's playbook; if put forward, it would put him at odds with the realist camp and his piece would likely have been rejected by the ideologically vigilant editors of *Foreign Affairs*.

Waltz's preference for A, an Iranian bomb, is an extension of his longstanding advocacy of proliferation as desirable and his confidence in the logic of deterrence (that is, the rationality of not using the bomb because of a fear of nuclear retaliation) to an absurd degree, well beyond even the extreme rationality upon which the most influential war thinkers rely. In this sense, Waltz is sensibly equating the Middle East with the rest of the world, refusing to engage in the widespread practice of ethnoreligious profiling: Israel's bomb is tolerable, maybe even beneficial, because Israel is a rational state aligned with the West, while Iran's bomb would be a world-order disaster because Iran is irrational and governed by Islamic zealots who have declared their implacable hostility to Israel. If such distinctions are to be made, which is doubtful, it is Israel that has been threatening war and pushing for coercive diplomacy, while Iran has so far peacefully tolerated a variety of severe provocations and acts of war, such as the assassinations of several of its nuclear scientists, the infection of its enrichment centrifuges with the Stuxnet computer virus, and verified violent covert acts designed to destabilize the regime in Tehran. Had such incidents been reversed and the Israel nuclear arsenal been the target of

---

5. International Court of Justice, "Legality of the Threat or Use of Nuclear Weapons," advisory opinions, 1996, www.icj-cij.org/docket/index.php?p1=3&p2=4&k=e1&p3=4&case=95.

disruptive acts by Iran, it is 100 percent likely that Israel would have immediately gone to war against Iran, quite likely setting the entire region on fire.

Objections to Option A

My basic objection to Waltz's position is a disagreement with two of his guid-
ing assumptions. First, that other countries would not follow Iran across the
nuclear threshold, an assessment he bases largely on their failure to acquire
nuclear weapons in response to Israel's acquisition. Surely Saudi Arabia and
Turkey would not, for reasons of status and security, want to remain non-
nuclear states in a neighborhood in which both Israel and Iran had the bomb.
Such an expansion of the regional nuclear club would become more prone to
accident, miscalculation, and the sort of social and political pathology that
makes nuclear weaponry generally unfit for human use, whatever the region
or occasion. In this respect, the more governments that possess the bomb, the
more likely it seems that one of these "irrational" scenarios will become history, with catastrophic consequences.

Second, Waltz does not single out nuclear weapons for condemnation on
ethical or prudential grounds. In my view, seeking the bomb and then using
it against helpless Japanese cities at the end of World War II was certainly one
of the worst instances of Promethean excess in human history, angering the
gods and exhibiting a species death wish. Leaders have acknowledged this
moral truth from time to time. Barack Obama did so in a widely heralded
2009 Prague speech in which he envisioned a world without nuclear weapons
as a feasible and desirable future goal. Yet Obama the politician seems unable
and unwilling to take the heat that following through on such a bold vision
was certain to entail. In the end, antinuclearism, for leaders, seems mainly
an exercise in *rhetoric*, apparently finding attentive ears among the Nobel
Prize committee, but without any *behavioral* reality. From time to time the
public mounts a populist challenge to nuclear-weapons policies but, again,
nothing happens. Any government or political organization that acquires the
bomb embraces one or another nuclearist fallacy to the effect that it is better
to have the bomb than not to have it. In this regard, they tend to view it as the
ultimate hedge against an external attack, presupposing the absurd hubris of
thinking that an enemy will always act rationally.

It is also the case that the secrecy surrounding nuclear-weapons policy,
especially doctrines governing their use, injects an absolutist virus into the
vital organs of a democratic body politic. There is no participation by the
people or even their elected representatives in relation to such an ultimate
political decision, vesting in a single person and perhaps his most intimate
advisors a demonic capability to inflict apocalyptic damage. We now know
that even beyond the devastation and radiation, the smoke released by the

use of as few as fifty nuclear bombs seems likely to generate so much smoke as to block sunlight from the earth for as long as a decade, dooming much of the world's agriculture and inducing a "nuclear famine." Such tragic consequences would not be confined to the belligerent societies but would be an ordeal for the entire planet.

It is for these reasons that I would call Kenneth Waltz dangerous, not crazy. Indeed, his kind of instrumental rationality is dominant in many influential places around the world and helps explain the development and retention of nuclear weapons, despite the risks and the immorality of the undertaking. If human society is ever to be again relatively safe, secure, and morally coherent, a first step is to renounce nuclear weapons unconditionally and proceed with urgency to negotiate an agreed, phased, monitored, and verified international treaty to ensure the total elimination of this weaponry from the face of the earth. It is not only that deterrence depends on perfect rationality over time and across space, it is also that deterrence by the threat it relies upon to deter thereby commits a continuing crime against humanity of unprecedented magnitude and clarity!

All of the options Waltz considers are appraised within a doctrinal framework of the effectiveness and acceptability of nuclear deterrence. There is no Option E, the determined effort to rid the world altogether of such weaponry. To do so indirectly subverts the implied major premise of the war system to the effect that history is made by the side that has the greater hard-power capability to inflict pain and destruction and is prepared to act when provoked. From such an angle, it becomes clearer why the irrationality of developing, retaining, and even deploying the weapons has never overcome the acute rationality associated with their threatened use in certain situations. A political leader of a sovereign state holding standard realist views is almost certain never to voluntarily relinquish the most powerful weapon ever conceived.

Was It Wrong to Support the Iranian Revolution?
October 9, 2012[16]

I have often reflected upon my own experience of the Iranian Revolution. In the aftermath of the Vietnam War I believed that the United States would face its next major geopolitical challenge in Iran: partly because of the CIA's role in overthrowing Mohammad Mossadegh's elected constitutional

16. http://richardfalk.wordpress.com/2012/10/09/was-it-wrong-to-support-the-iranian-revolution-in-1978-because-it-turned-out-badly.

government to restore the repressive Shah (Mohammad Reza Pahlavi) to power in 1953; partly because there were 45,000 American troops deployed in Iran, along with a network of strategic assets associated with Cold War anti-Soviet priorities; partly because a generation of young Iranians, many of whom had studied abroad, had experienced torture and abuse at the hands of the SAVAK, Tehran's feared intelligence service; partly because of the intense antiregime opposition of an alienated middle class angered by the Shah's reliance on international capital in implementing the "White Revolution"; and partly because the Shah pursued a regionally unpopular pro-Israel and pro-apartheid South Africa policy. Against this background, and on the basis of my decade-long involvement in opposing the American role in Vietnam, I helped form and chaired a small, unfunded committee devoted to promoting human rights and favoring nonintervention in Iran. I was greatly encouraged to do this by several of my students who were either Iranian or political activists focused on Iran.

In this period, while I was on the Princeton faculty, the committee organized several events on the internal situation in Iran, including critiques of the American role that was dramatized by Jimmy Carter's 1978 New Year's Eve toast to the Shah while a guest at the palace as "an island of stability," insensitive to the anti-Shah hostility building up in the country. Such absurdly inappropriate sentiments by the most decent of recent American presidents were undoubtedly sincere, but bore witness to what is seen and unseen by the best of American leaders when the world is understood according to the protocols of geopolitics. It was Henry Kissinger who more realistically praised the Shah in his memoirs, calling him "that rarest of leaders, an unconditional ally."[17] It was this sense of Iran's subordination to the United States that increased hostility toward the Pahlavi regime across the broad spectrum of Iranian opinion and explained what was not then understood: why even those sectors of the Iranian establishment who had benefited most from the Shah's regime did not fight for its survival but ran away and hid as quickly as they could.

Although I was critical of the established order in Iran, the timing and nature of the Iranian upheaval in 1978 came as a complete surprise to me. It also surprised the American ambassador in Iran, William Sullivan, who told me during a meeting in Tehran at the height of the domestic turmoil that the embassy had worked out twenty-six scenarios of possible destabilization in Iran and not one had accorded any role to Islamist resistance. He added in our meeting that as late as August 1978 a CIA analysis had concluded that Iran "is not revolutionary or even in a pre-revolutionary situation." In fact, seeing the world through a blinkered Cold War optic led the

17. Henry Kissinger, *White House Years* (New York: Simon & Schuster, 1979), 1261.

U.S. government to continue funding Islamist groups because of their presumed anticommunist identity—the first major experience of "blowback," to be disastrously repeated in Afghanistan. The unrest in Iran started with a relatively minor incident in early 1978 (although some observers point to demonstrations a year earlier), which gradually deepened until it became a revolutionary process engulfing the entire country. My small committee in the United States tried to interpret these unexpected developments, inviting informed speakers, sponsoring meetings, and beginning to appreciate the unlikely role being played by Ayatollah Khomeini as an inspirational figure. I was invited to visit Iran to witness the unfolding revolutionary process by Mehdi Bazargan, a moderate and respected early leader in the anti-Shah movement, who was appointed prime minister of an interim government by Khomeini on February 4, 1979. In explaining the appointment, Khomeini foreshadowed an authoritarian turn in the revolutionary process. His chilling words were not sufficiently noticed at the time:

> Through the guardianship [*velayat*] that I have from the holy lawgiver [the Prophet], I hereby pronounce Bazargan as the Ruler, and since I have appointed him he must be obeyed. The nation must obey him. This is not an ordinary government. It is a government based on the sharia. Opposing the government means opposing the sharia of Islam.... Revolt against God's government is a revolt against God. Revolt against God is blasphemy.[18]

In January 1979 I went to Iran for two weeks in a three-person delegation. My companions were Ramsey Clark, a former American attorney general who had turned strongly against American foreign policy during the last stages of the Vietnam War, and Philip Luce, a longtime antiwar activist associated with religious NGOs who had gained worldwide attention a decade earlier when he showed a visiting congressional delegation the infamous, inhuman "tiger cages" the Saigon government used to imprison its enemies in South Vietnam. The three of us embarked on this mission generally sympathetic with the anti-Shah movement, but uncertain about its real character and likely political trajectory. I had met previously with some of those who would emerge prominently, including Abolhassan Banisadr, who was living as a private citizen in Paris and dreamed of becoming the first president of a post-Shah Iran, an idealistic man who combined a devotion to Islam with a liberal democratic agenda and an Muslim approach to economic policy that he had personally developed. His dream was fulfilled, but not at all in the manner that he hoped. He did become the first president of the Islamic Republic of Iran, but his eminence was short-lived as the radicalization of the

---

18. Quoted in Baqer Moin, *Khomeini: Life of the Ayatollah* (New York: Macmillan, 1999), 204.

political climate under Khomeini led to his impeachment after less than two years. Banisadr was forced to flee the country, returning to Paris a fugitive of the revolution he had so recently championed. Of course, such a pattern was not novel. Past revolutions had frequently devoured their most dedicated adherents.

I had also become a close friend of Mansour Farhang, a progressive Iranian-American professor of international relations and a highly intelligent advocate of the revolutionary developments in Iran as they unfolded in 1978. Farhang was appointed as ambassador to the UN by the new government, but soon resigned his post and denounced the regime he had worked to install as a new species of "religious fascism." There were others, also, who inclined me in this period of struggle against the Pahlavi dynasty to view the revolutionary developments in Iran favorably, but who later became its bitter opponents.

My visit took place at a climactic moment in the Iranian Revolution. The Shah left the country on January 17, 1979, while we were in Iran, to the disbelief of ordinary Iranians, who thought the initial reports were at best a false rumor and at worst a trick to entrap the opposition. When the public began to believe that the unbelievable had actually happened, there were spontaneous celebratory outpourings everywhere we were. On that very evening we had a somewhat surreal meeting with the recently designated prime minister, Shapour Bakhtiar. Bakhtiar was a longtime liberal critic of the monarchy living outside the country, whom the Shah had appointed a few weeks earlier as a desperate concession aimed at calming the rising revolutionary tide. It was a futile gesture, one Khomeini dismissed with the greatest contempt, showing his refusal to consider what at the time struck many of his supporters as a prudent compromise. Bakhtiar lasted less than two months, left the country, and was assassinated in his home in the outskirts of Paris a decade or so later.

While in Iran we had the opportunity to have long meetings with a range of religious figures, including Ayatollah Mahmoud Taleghani and Ayatollah Mohammad Kazem Shariatmaderi, both of whom impressed us deeply with their combination of principled politics and empathy with the long suffering of the Iranian people. After leaving Iran, we stopped in Paris and spent several hours with Ayatollah Khomeini on his last day in France before his triumphal return to Iran. At that point, Khomeini was viewed as the "icon" of the revolution but not as its future political leader. Indeed, Khomeini had told us that he looked forward to "resuming his religious life" in Qom when he returned to Iran, and that he had entered the political arena most reluctantly because the Shah's rule had caused "a river of blood" to flow between the people and the state. There were many intriguing facets of our meeting with the "dark genius" of the Iranian Revolution, which I will leave for another post. My impression of Khomeini was of a highly intelligent, uncompromising rong-willed, and severe individual, himself somewhat unnerved by the ıexpected happenings in a country he had not entered for almost twenty ears. Khomeini insisted on portraying what had happened in Iran as an slamic Revolution"; he corrected us if we made any reference to an "Iranian evolution." In this respect he was obviously disenchanted with nationalism well as royalism (he spoke of the Saudi dynasty as deserving the same fate the Pahlavis), evidently envisioning the revival of the Islamic caliphate and s accompanying borderless *umma*.

I returned from Iran with a sense of excitement about what I had wit-essed and experienced, feeling that the country might be giving the world needed new progressive political model that combined compassion for the ople as a whole with a shared spiritual identity. There was no doubt that, at e time, Khomeini and Islamic identity had mobilized the Iranian masses in manner that was far more intense and effective than had ever been achieved various forms of leftist agitation and ideology. Some of those we met in an were cautious about what to expect, saying the revolution had unfolded oo fast" for a smooth transition to constitutional governance. Others oke about counterrevolutionary tendencies or voiced conspiratorial views the effect that the overthrow of the Shah had been engineered by British telligence, that Ayatollah Khomeini was a British agent, or that it was an merican response to the Shah's successful push for higher oil prices within PEC. We were guests in the home of an anti-Shah mathematician in Tehran, dedicated democrat who told us that his recent reading of Khomeini's pub-hed lectures on Islamic government had made him extremely fearful about hat would happen in post-Shah Iran. Also, some Iranian women we met ere worried about threats to the freedoms they enjoyed under the Shah and ıhappy about the new dress code of the revolution, which was already mak-g the *chador* virtually mandatory. Some of those we spoke who had sup-orted the revolution insisted that once a new political order was established ere would be a feminist outcry to the effect that "we're next!" Other secular omen told us that they enjoyed wearing the *chador* because it gave them a elcome relief from spending time on cosmetics and the various ways that odern Western fashion treated women as "objects" designed to awaken otic desires among men.

Despite encountering these reservations about the Iranian future, I turned from Iran deeply impressed by having touched "the live tissue of volution." There was an extraordinary feeling of societal unity and soli-rity that seemed to embrace the whole population, at that moment sur-ounting divisions of class and ethnicity and even leading those with ligious identifications to bond with liberal secular elements. It was a oment of historic mobilization. Although the future was unknowable, the release of positive energy that we experienced was remarkable. It included walking in a peaceful and joyous demonstration of several million in Tehran to celebrate the departure of the Shah and the victory of the revolution. Such an outpouring of love and happiness lent credibility to our hopes that Iran would go forward as a liberated society to produce a humane and distinctive form of governance.

It was not long afterward that what had seemed so promising degenerated into a process that was deeply disturbing: a new disposition toward severely abusing opponents and the emergence of a new, religiously grounded autocracy that seemed as unscrupulous as its predecessor. Khomeini surfaced as the supreme leader of this harsh regime without ever being elected. To be sure, there were violent counterrevolutionary forces at work in Iran, and there were suspicions that the United States was maneuvering behind the scenes to repeat its 1953 coup. There is no doubt that the United States encouraged Saddam Hussein to attack Iran in 1980, hoping at least to detach the oil province of Khuzestan from the country and possibly even to topple the Khomeini government. However these developments are interpreted, there seemed little likelihood that the values underlying the courageous campaign against the Shah would ever again achieve the spirit of unity and liberation that we found in Iran during our visit in early 1979.

I wrote and spoke publicly about my impressions of the revolution before it encountered these reactionary troubles. Ever since, I have been sharply criticized for my early show of support for Ayatollah Khomeini; my subsequent misgivings, even active opposition, were ignored. This pattern is not unusual and I might try to give my side of the story at some later point, but now I wish to concentrate on another part of the experience and talk about the relation between my positive perceptions in phase one and my disillusionment in phase two. I want to raise the question as to whether my enthusiasm in phase one was itself a misguided indulgence in utopian longing that necessarily ends in a reign of terror. Such is the essential thesis of Crane Brinton's influential *Anatomy of Revolution*. This view is partially also endorsed by Hannah Arendt's *On Revolution,* which expresses admiration for the American Revolution because it did not attempt to achieve a social transformation beneficial to the poor and demonization of the French Revolution because it did insist upon achieving a just society, which led in her view to a bloody struggle with the threatened privileged classes and to revolutionary terror.

Such a question was posed for me with stark vividness when I read recently a brilliantly provocative essay by Slavoj Žižek entitled "Radical Intellectual or, Why Heidegger Took the Right Step (Albeit in the Wrong Direction) in 1933," especially the short section "Michel Foucault and the Iranian Event published in his breathtaking book *In Defense of Lost Causes.* Žižek's bas support for greeting such historically charismatic events with approval is based on the idea that faith in liberating the moral potential of human society is the only alternative to complicity in the exploitation and demeaning of the multitudes and passivity in the face of pervasive structural injustice. Žižek makes an important distinction between Heidegger's temporary embrace of Nazism and Foucault's of the Iranian Revolution, although he takes note of the similarities, especially the attractive quality of the transcendent moment of collective unity and its associated visionary embrace of a just future for the entire people. He seeks to distinguish the appropriateness of the enthusiasm and longing from the actual deformity of the events.

In this assessment, Žižek sides with the outlook of the French philosopher Alain Badiou and the Irish playwright Samuel Beckett: "Better a disaster of fidelity to the Event than a non-being of indifference toward the Event... one can go on and fail better, while indifference drowns us deeper and deeper in the morass of imbecilic Being."[19] Of course, it is a radical claim to insist that deformed societal structures face us with such a stark choice between revolution and complicity via indifference. Such a view rejects reformism and liberal perspectives because of their acceptance of the structures in place and rejection of more radical challenges on behalf of justice.

Rethinking, after more than thirty years, my own sequence of enthusiasm, disillusionment, and opposition, I am assisted by Žižek's disquisition, although I would not pose the issues of choice so starkly. What seems to me important is to side with the revolutionary impulse. I am not sure that our historical experience gives us any confidence that revolutionaries are learning to "fail better," although they are definitely learning to "fail differently"— for instance, compare the Arab Spring with the Iranian Revolution or Mao's Cultural Revolution with the Soviet experience with Stalinism.

Was it a mistake of perception, a radical form of wishful thinking, to underestimate or fail to apprehend earlier the negative potential of the Iranian Revolution when I visited the country in late 1978, and again in early 1980 in the aftermath of the hostage crisis? Or was it correct to give voice to the positive potential that seemed to surface so compellingly during those moments of collective excitement and unity, as well in most of those with whom I spoke during the 1979 visit? Are Žižek and Badiou correct to separate the revolutionary vision so sharply from its actual dismal human results, or is this an incriminating instance of the irresponsibility of radical thought with an infantile appreciation of revolutionary ideals that ignores the wisdom of serious conservative warnings about the demonic outcomes of every effort to wreck existing institutions and challenge class relations abruptly?

---

9. Slavoj Žižek, *In Defense of Lost Causes* (London: Verso, 2009), 7.

Are we as a species destined to see our dreams of a just and sustainable future always shattered by the deforming effects of struggles for and against new arrangements of governing authority and class relations? Are we condemned, in other words, to banish our dreams from the domain of responsible politics and confine our efforts to marginal reformist initiatives?

Posing such questions is easier than resolving them. I am inclined to think that my response to what took place in Iran was authentic at its various phases, reflecting my best understanding of the unfolding circumstances and adjustments to my evaluations phase by phase. I prefer such a view, even in retrospect, to indifference to the Shah's oppressive regime—while realizing that drastic change, especially in a country endowed with abundant oil reserves, is almost certain to be a rocky road. Should I have been more immediately suspicious of Ayatollah Khomeini and the Islamic dimensions of the revolution? Probably, but it was not clear at the time, because the leading religious figures in Iran were articulating a vision of a just future for Iran even if the future made it clear that their preference was for some kind of theocracy. It should also be pointed out that some religious leaders did seem to envision a humane sequel to the Shah's Iran that would be inclusive, humane, and sensitive to the human rights of all Iranians, but their voices did not prevail.

I continue to believe that despite the dangers of visionary politics, it is the only hope we have as a species of creating a sustainable and just future for humanity. In ending, I should be clear that I have consistently supported reformist efforts in Iran over the years since the ouster of Banisadr and others, including the presidency of Mohammad Khatami (1997–2005) and the more recent Green Revolution. As with the days of the Shah, Iran urgently requires an emancipatory politics that liberates from *within* and regenerates the hopes of the Iranian people. What Iran does not need is an Israeli-American military strike or destabilization moves funded and promoted from *without*. Intervention by way of military attack or even in the form of strong economic sanctions (as at present) stabilizes the regime in Tehran and imposes added hardships on the Iranian people. As I have argued in the past, the best and only acceptable way to address the questions of nuclear weapons in the Middle East is through establishing a nuclear-weapons-free zone that includes Israel. To avoid even discussing such an option illuminates the strategic submission of American foreign policy to Israeli governmental priorities, even in cases such as this where the Israeli public is split and the response to an attack, if it happens, is likely to inflict severe harm on Israel and risk transforming the entire region into a war zone.

———————

Getting the Law and Politics Right in Iran

March 23, 2013[20]

In an important article in the *New York Times*, James Risen summarized the consensus of the intelligence community as concluding that Iran had abandoned its program to develop nuclear weapons in 2003 and that no persuasive evidence exists that it has departed from this decision.[21] It might have been expected that such news, based on the best evidence produced by spending billions to get the most reliable possible assessments of such sensitive security issues, would produce a huge sigh of relief in Washington. On the contrary, it has been totally ignored, including by the highest officers in the government. The president has not even bothered to acknowledge this electrifying conclusion that should have put the brakes on what appears to be a slide toward a disastrous regional war. We must ask why such a prudent and positive course of action has not been adopted, or at least explored, given that the American debate proceeds on the basis of the exact opposite assumption—that Iran's quest for nuclear weapons is a virtual certainty. This contrary finding is quite startling. The Republican presidential candidates and even President Obama make it seem as if Iran is, without doubt, hell-bent on having nuclear weapons as soon as possible. With such a misleading approach, the only question that seems worth asking is whether to rely on diplomacy backed by harsh sanctions to achieve the desired goal or whether only an early attack can stop Iran from crossing the nuclear threshold.

It seems perverse that this public debate should be framed in such a belligerent and seemingly wrongheaded manner. After all, the United States was stampeded into a disastrous war against Iraq nine years ago on the basis of deceptive reports about its supposed stockpile of weapons of mass destruction, trumped-up allegations by exiles, and media hype. I would have assumed that these bad memories would make Washington very cautious about drifting toward war with Iran, a far more dangerous enemy than Saddam Hussein's Iraq. It would seem that at present the politicians distrust reassuring intelligence reports while being perversely willing to go along with the intelligence community when it counsels war as a "slam dunk."

Reinforcing this skepticism about Iran's nuclear intentions is a realistic assessment of the risk posed in the unlikely event that the intelligence

---

20. http://richardfalk.wordpress.com/2012/03/23/
why-not-get-the-law-and-politics-right-in-iran.

21. James Risen, "U.S. Faces a Tricky Task in Assessment of Data on Iran," *New York Times*, March 17, 2012, www.nytimes.com/2012/03/18/world/middleeast/iran-intelligence-crisis-showed-difficulty-of-assessing-nuclear-data.html.

community's consensus is wrong and that Iran succeeds in acquiring nuclear weapons after all. As former heads of the Mossad and others have pointed out, the existential threat to Israel even then would still be extremely low. It would be obvious that Iran's few bombs could never be used against Israel or elsewhere without producing an annihilating response. There is no evidence that Iran has any disposition to commit national suicide.

There is a further troubling aspect of how this issue is being addressed. Even the officials Risen interviewed presume that if the evidence existed that Iran possesses a nuclear-weapons program, a military attack would be a permissible option. Such a presumption is based on the irrelevance of international law to a national decision to attack a sovereign state and on a tacit endorsement of "aggressive war," seemingly forgetting that such recourse to war was criminalized back in 1945 and is widely treated as the principal conclusion of the Nuremberg judgment.

This dubious thinking has gone unchallenged in the media, in government pronouncements, and even in diplomatic posturing. We need to recall that at the end of World War II, when the UN was established, states agreed in the UN Charter to give up their military option except in clear instances of self-defense. To some extent this prohibition has been eroded over the years, but in the setting of Iran policy it has been all but abandoned without even the pressure of extenuating circumstances.

Of course it would be unfortunate if Iran acquired nuclear weapons, given the instability of the region and the general dangers associated with their spread. But no international-law argument or precedent is available to justify attacking a sovereign state because it goes nuclear. After all, Israel became a stealth nuclear-weapons state decades ago without a whimper of opposition from the West, and the same goes for India, Pakistan, and even North Korea.

There are better policy options worth exploring that uphold international law and have a good chance of leading to regional stability. The most obvious option is containment, which worked for decades against an expansionist Soviet Union with a gigantic arsenal of nuclear weapons. A second option would be to establish a nuclear-weapons-free zone for the Middle East, a idea that has been around for years and enjoys the endorsement of most governments in the region, including Iran. Israel might seem to have the most to lose by a nuclear-free zone because it alone in the region currently possesses nuclear weapons, but it would benefit immensely from the reduction in regional tensions and probable economic and diplomatic side benefits, particularly if accompanied by a more constructive approach to resolving the conflict with the Palestinian people. The most ambitious option, given political credibility by President Obama in his Prague speech of 2009 expressing a commitment to a world without nuclear weapons, would be to table proposal for complete nuclear disarmament on a step-by-step basis. Each of these approaches seems far preferable to what is now planned. They are prudent, accord with common sense, and show respect for international law and a passion for the peaceful resolution of conflict, and at minimum deserve to be widely discussed and appraised.

As it is, there is no legal foundation in the Nonproliferation Treaty or elsewhere for the present reliance on threat diplomacy in dealing with Iran. These threats violate Article 2(4) of the UN Charter, which wisely prohibits not only uses of force but also *threats* to use force. Iran diplomacy presents an odd case, as political realpolitik and international law clearly point away from the military option, yet the winds of war are blowing ever harder. Perhaps even at this eleventh hour our political leaders can awake to realize anew that respect for international law provides the only practical foundation for a rational, prudent, and sustainable foreign policy in the twenty-first century.

7

Iraq

In many respects the tragedies experienced by Iraq during the last several decades reflect the interplay of authoritarian rule and geopolitical rivalry of a global and regional scope. During the Cold War, Iraq was a contested zone between Moscow and Washington. After the Iranian Revolution in 1979, Iraq became valuable as a strategic influence and was encouraged by the United States to attack Iran. When the calculations of those who encouraged the attack went wrong, then the idea gained support that it was beneficial to allow these two states, both deemed problematic in relation to the Western political agenda, to fight it out with neither winners nor losers. Moscow shared this view, so the bodies piled up.

After the Iran-Iraq War finally came to an end in 1989, with Baghdad's resources depleted, Saddam Hussein looked south toward oil-rich Kuwait as a means to restore Iraq's regional stature. With a still-contested set of diplomatic assurances from the United States, Iraq quickly conquered Kuwait in 1990, annexing it as a province. Such aggression against a sovereign state brought about a regional and geopolitical response led by the United States, which proposed a "new world order" that would finally fulfill the role envisioned by the drafters of the UN Charter to protect the victims of aggression and punish the aggressors. After a near-unanimous Security Council imposed a period of sanctions on Iraq, it mandated force and the First Gulf War commenced in early 1991. It was an exhilarating victory for the United States, accomplishing surrender with minimal casualties and little cost. As President George H. W. Bush was proud to claim, the inhibitions on American uses of force arising from the outcome of the Vietnam War had finally been overcome.

In these posts, this shadow cast by the Vietnam War seems to me as relevant as ever. I differ dramatically from the prevailing view among American policy planners and their colleagues in Tel Aviv. To me the primary lesson of

Vietnam is that military intervention based on superior weaponry is almost always morally and legally wrong. I admit that the UN mandate to restore Kuwait's sovereignty had wide backing at the time and that it was given formal legal backing. Yet the operational reality of the war and its punitive aftermath was one in which the civilian population of Iraq was made to suffer disproportionately. In effect, the UN was converted into an instrument of American-led regional politics, exercising no supervisory role in carrying out the campaign and seemingly not treating the war option as a last resort after all diplomatic remedies had been tried and failed.

In this sense, the First Gulf War created a false confidence in warfare as a means to sustain Western control over recalcitrant political forces in regions where vital economic and political interests were at stake. As I have argued, the combination of oil and Israel, along with the consolidation of Europe within the framework of the European Union, made the Middle East the pivot of global politics in the post–Cold War world.

When the neoconservative George W. Bush assumed control of American foreign policy in 2000, his White House held from the outset the belief that the earlier war had not seized the opportunity of military victory to push for a political victory in the form of regime change, followed by reconstructing the Iraqi state. When 9/11 came, this gave the neoconservatives the pretext they needed, combined with a contrived threat of nuclear weaponry, to launch the Iraq War. Unlike in 1991, the UN Security Council, despite an all-out political effort, refused to give its backing and the United States went ahead in March 2003 with its invasion and occupation of the country. In doing so, it defied both international law and massive civil-society opposition. Unlike the recovery of Kuwaiti sovereignty and regime change in Iraq, the challenge of reconstructing the Iraqi state along lines designed in Washington ended in political failure of the first degree.

In the three posts that make up this chapter I try to analyze this failure centering on several kinds of confusion. First of all, there is a false analogy to the generally effective state-reconstructing occupations of Germany and Japan after World War II. Second is the misleading notion that a battlefield victory and military occupation were necessary preconditions for political reconstruction of the Iraqi state, especially when the displaced regime was headed by a hated dictator. Third is the apparent lack of cultural sensitivity. Saddam Hussein may have been hated by the Shi'a majority but was seen as having benefited the Sunni minority and having kept the society as a whole, despite its deep ethnic and religious cleavages and hierarchies, under conditions of tolerable order compared to what followed.

I felt that the Iraqi undertaking would be tragic for the Iraqi people and would mainly illustrate that the most important lessons of the Vietnam experience had not been learned and earlier mistakes were being repeated in new forms. As in Vietnam, the United States spent billions to disguise its defeat by financing a "surge" that was supposed to neutralize the resistance, mainly by way of bribing local ethnic leaders. But lo and behold, what has emerged is a divided polity, with Kurds semisovereign in the north, ISIS holding considerable territory in Sunni northeast regions, and the Baghdad government exercising its corrupted authority mainly in the Shi'a south. The emergence of ISIS is in one sense the second coming of a political configuration headed by Sunni extremists, this time with religious mobilizing claims. In another sense, it is a sociopathic reaction to the American occupation's stress on de-Baathification, centered on Paul Bremer's purge of the officer corps of the armed forces, elements of which are now evidently leading the ISIS military operations shocking the world with their grisly atrocities. As has become clear, the preoccupation with the threat to Western interests posed by ISIS is causing a realignment of priorities, with a new willingness to view even the Assad regime in Damascus as a partial ally.

Above all, Iraq as the centerpiece of this post–Cold War period confirms the central conclusion of this entire book: that "democracy" and Washington's policy agenda in the region are irreconcilable. The best that the U.S. government can hope for is the sort of regime that has emerged in Egypt after the 2013 military coup or the kind of dynastic absolutism of such Gulf monarchies as Saudi Arabia, Bahrain, and the United Arab Emirates. Tunisia, politically blessed by the absence of oil, has so far mostly been allowed to go its own way, unlike such oil-rich countries as Iran, Libya, and above all Iraq. Against this background, these posts should be read as reflections on the failure of intervention and the devastation wrought by a hostile occupation.

Occupying Iraq and Higher Education: The Ghent Charter

January 4, 2011[1]

For Americans, the long occupation of Iraq is measured almost entirely by the American casualty count and the cost to taxpayers, now estimated to be over $3 trillion, an amount large enough to make major inroads on global poverty and preventable disease. The loss and disruption of Iraqi lives, the devastation of the country, and the long suffering inflicted on the people of Iraq do not enter into these calculations. Much attention is given to whether the outcome can be called a success or was somehow beneficial for the people of Iraq, without any notice of the enormous human price paid by a people that was never consulted, in typical imperial behavior. Iraq is the poster child of postcolonial colonialism, which disregards the ethos of self-determination in pursuit of geopolitical goals such as oil, regional hegemony, Israeli priorities, and what is grandiosely called "grand strategy."

For Iraqis, the occupation followed a frightening "shock and awe" onslaught in 2003 that had been preceded by twelve years of punitive sanctions that took hundreds of thousands of civilian lives, which in turn followed the Gulf War, which deliberately devastated the infrastructure of the country to a degree that a respected UN report described the country as bombed "back to the stone age"—a phenomenon Madeleine Albright notoriously described at the time on prime-time TV as "worth it" when Lesley Stahl stated that sanctions had killed half a million children.[2]

During this period Iraq shifted from being the country with the most impressive development statistics in the region to becoming a failed state in every sense: increasing poverty, loss of skilled personnel in all sectors, declining literacy, declining life expectancy, staggering unemployment, destruction of cultural life, pervasive civic violence, lethal religious conflict, and all forms of acute insecurity.

True, Saddam Hussein governed Iraq oppressively, especially victimizing the Kurdish minority and the Shi'a majority, but there was a high degree of social order, material progress, and economic stability. True, Iraq was

---

1. http://richardfalk.wordpress.com/2011/01/04/244.
2. Madeleine Albright, interview with Lesley Stahl, *60 Minutes*, CBS, May 12, 1996, www.youtube.com/watch?v=FbIX1CP9qr4. The UN report, along with other assessments of the war damage, are discussed in Colin Rowat, "UN Agency Reports on the Humanitarian Situation in Iraq," Campaign Against Sanctions on Iraq, University of Cambridge, November 25, 2001, www.casi.org.uk/briefing/000707versailles.pdf.

disruptive presence in the region, attacking Iran (with U.S. encouragement) in 1980 and then invading and annexing Kuwait in 1990. Yet nothing can vindicate the American-led response based on war, punitive sanctions, and prolonged occupation. By now it should be evident that the forcible destruction of the Hussein regime caused a far worse humanitarian catastrophe than did the abuses, however dreadful, associated with its governance. Military intervention has been uniformly shown to be a darkly dysfunctional corrective for abusive governance, especially in the postcolonial era. The tragedy inflicted on the people of Iraq is a direct result of American crimes of aggression, war crimes, and crimes against humanity. If there is a lesson in all this, it is that imperial grand strategy, as it is playing out in the Middle East and Central Asia, is intrinsically criminal, and its cruel impositions can only be defeated by campaigns of global solidarity. Neither states nor the United Nations possess the political will or capabilities to oppose effectively these extensions of colonial behavior in the postcolonial era. The realization of human rights is essentially a societal challenge; unless abuse reaches the level of genocide or ethnic cleansing, violations should never serve as a pretext for military intervention, even if disguised as "humanitarian intervention."

By now, there are no excuses left to ignore the horrors that accompany foreign military occupation. The prolonged experiences of Iraq, Palestine, and Afghanistan provide a consistent confirmation that benevolent claims of the occupier are disguises for exploitation, corruption, oppression, and violence against innocent civilians.

The shocking portrait of what occupation has meant for academicians and students is depicted by the Ghent Charter (reproduced in the Appendix), which has been endorsed by prominent educators in Europe and elsewhere, including the rector of the University of Ghent. The Brussels Tribunal has played a leading part in exposing these realities afflicting Iraqi universities. It is important that all of us, especially those paying taxes in the United States to finance this occupation, understand that our silence is complicity. Those of us associated with teaching and research in American universities especially bear an additional responsibility to exhibit even now our solidarity with those who have suffered and are suffering in Iraqi academic communities. We know that many faculty members have been murdered since 2003 (more than five hundred confirmed cases), particularly those who spoke out and acted against the occupation, and many more have fled the country permanently. The departure of university personnel is part of a wider exodus of middle-class Iraqis—estimated at over two million—depriving the country of the sort of social fabric essential to avoiding predatory forms of foreign economic exploitation. We who devote our lives to higher education realize the importance of educated and dedicated young people to the well-being of a country. If Iraq's future is to be restored to some semblance of decency, its institutions of higher learning will need to become safe and hospitable for students and faculty.

In the meantime, read the Ghent Charter and weep!

The Iraq War: 10 Years Later

March 17, 2013[3]

After a decade of combat, casualties, massive displacement, persisting violence, enhanced sectarian tension and violence between Shi'a and Sunnis, periodic suicide bombings, and autocratic governance, a negative assessment of the Iraq War seems nearly universal. Not only the regionally destabilizing outcome (including the blowback effect of perversely adding weight to Iran's overall diplomatic influence), but the reputational costs in the Middle East associated with an imprudent, destructive, and failed military intervention make the Iraq War the worst American foreign-policy disaster since its defeat in Vietnam, undertaken with an even less persuasive legal, moral, and political rationale. The ongoing blowback from the "shock and awe" launch scenario represents a huge and, it is to be hoped, irreversible setback for the American global domination project in the era of hypertechno-geopolitics.

Most geopolitical accounting assessments do not bother to consider the damage to the United Nations and international law arising from an aggressive use of force in flagrant violation of the UN Charter, embarked upon in the face of the Security Council's refusal to provide a legitimating authorization for the use of force despite great pressure mounted by the United States. The UN further harmed its own image when it failed to reinforce its refusal by offering some kind of support to Iraq as the target of this contemplated aggression. This failure was compounded by its post-attack role in lending full support to the unlawful American-led occupation, including its state building mission. In other words, not only was the Iraq War a disaster from the perspective of American and British foreign policy and the peace and stability of the Middle East region, it was also a severe setback for the authority of international law, the independence of the UN, and the quality of world order.

In the aftermath of the Vietnam War, the United States was supposedly burdened by what policymakers derisively called "Vietnam Syndrome." This was Washington shorthand for psychological inhibitions about engagement

---

3. http://richardfalk.wordpress.com/2013/03/17/the-iraq-war-10-years-later.

in military interventions in the non-Western world due to negative attitudes toward such imperial undertakings among the American public and in the government, especially among the military, who were widely blamed for the Vietnam disaster. Many American militarists at the time complained that the Vietnam Syndrome was a combined result of an antiwar plot engineered by the liberal media and a response to an unpopular draft that required many middle-class Americans to fight in a distant war that lacked both popular support and a convincing strategic or legal rationale and seemed to be on the wrong side of history, which, as the French found out in their own Indochina War, favors anticolonial wars of liberation. The flag-draped coffins of dead young Americans were shown on TV, leading defense hawks to contend somewhat ridiculously that "the war was lost in American living rooms." The government made adjustments that took these rationalizations seriously: the draft was abolished, an all-volunteer professional military was complemented by large-scale private security firms, and technological innovations and doctrinal adjustments were designed to minimize American war casualties. Efforts were also intensified to assure media support for subsequent military operations by "embedding" journalists in combat units and more carefully monitoring news reporting.

President George H. W. Bush told the world in 1991, immediately after the Gulf War, that "we've finally kicked the Vietnam Syndrome once and for all."[4] In effect, President Bush was saying to the grand strategists in the White House and Pentagon that American military power was again available to do the work of empire around the world. What the Gulf War showed was that on a conventional battlefield, in a desert war, American military superiority would be decisive in producing a quick victory with minimal costs in American lives and bringing about a surge of political popularity at home. This new militarist enthusiasm created the political base for recourse to the NATO war in 1999 to wrest Kosovo from Serb control. To avoid casualties, air attacks were conducted from high altitudes. The war took more time than expected, but was interpreted as validating war planners' claim that the United States could now fight and win "zero-casualty wars." There were no NATO combat deaths in the Kosovo War, which produced a "victory" by ending Serbian control over Kosovo as well as demonstrating that NATO could still be used and useful even after the disappearance of the Soviet threat.

More sophisticated American war planners understood that not all challenges to U.S. interests around the world could be met with air power in the absence of ground combat. Increasingly, political violence involving geopolitical priorities took the form of transnational violence (as in the

---

George H. W. Bush, Remarks to the American Legislative Exchange Council, March 1, 1991, www.presidency.ucsb.edu/ws/?pid=19351.

234 Chaos and Counterrevolution

9/11 attacks) or was situated within the boundaries of territorial states and involved Western military intervention designed to crush societal forces of national resistance. The George W. Bush neocon presidency badly confused its new self-assurance about the conduct of international battlefield warfare, where military superiority dictates the political outcome, and its old nemesis from Vietnam War days, counterinsurgency warfare (also known as low-intensity or asymmetric warfare), in which military superiority controls the battlefield but not the endgame of conflict, which depends on winning the allegiance of the territorial population.

General David Petraeus rose through the ranks of the American military by repackaging counterinsurgency warfare in a post-Vietnam format, relying upon an approach developed by noted guerrilla-war expert David Galula, who contended that in the Vietnam War the fatal mistake was supposing that such a war would be determined 80 percent by combat battles in the jungles and paddy fields, with the remaining 20 percent devoted to capturing the "hearts and minds" of the indigenous population. Galula argued that counterinsurgency wars could only be won if this formula was inverted. This meant that 80 percent of future U.S. military interventions should be devoted to nonmilitary aspects of societal well-being: restoring electricity, providing police protection for normal activity, building and staffing schools, improving sanitation and garbage removal, and providing health care and jobs.

Afghanistan and then Iraq became the testing grounds for applying these nation-building lessons, only to reveal in the course of their lengthy, destructive, and expensive failures that the militarists and their civilian counterparts had learned the wrong lessons. These conflicts were wars of national resistance, a continuation of the anticolonial struggles against West-centric domination; regardless of whether the killing was complemented by sophisticated social and economic programs, it still involved pronounced and deadly challenge by foreign interests to the national independence and rights of self-determination that entailed killing Iraqi women and children and violating their most basic rights through the unavoidably harsh mechanics of foreign occupation. It also proved impossible to disentangle the planned 80 percent from the 20 percent, as the Iraqi people's hostility to their supposed American liberators demonstrated over and over again, especially as many Iraqis on the side of the occupiers proved to be corrupt and brutal, sparking popular suspicion and intensifying internal polarization. The truly "fatal mistake" is the failure to recognize that when the American military and its allies attack and occupy a non-Western country, especially in the Islamic world, when they start dividing, killing, and policing its inhabitants, popular resistance will be mobilized and hatred toward the foreign "liberators" will spread. This is precisely what happened in Iraq, and the suicide bombings to this day suggest that the ugly patterns of violence have not stopped even with the end of America's direct combat role.

The United States was guilty of a fundamental misunderstanding of the Iraq War, displayed to the world on May 1, 2003, when George W. Bush theatrically declared a wildly premature victory from the deck of an American aircraft carrier USS *Abraham Lincoln*, with the notorious banner proclaiming "mission accomplished" plainly visible behind the podium as the sun sank over the Pacific Ocean. Bush reveled in this misunderstanding, assuming that the attack phase of the war was the whole war, forgetting about the more difficult and protracted occupation phase. The real Iraq War was about to begin—that is, the violent internal struggle for the political future of the country, made more difficult and protracted by the military presence of the United States and its allies. This counterinsurgency sequel to occupation would not be decided on the kind of battlefield where arrayed military capabilities confront one another, but rather through a war of attrition waged by hit-and-run domestic Iraqi forces abetted by foreign volunteers, opposed to the tactics of Washington and to the overall aura of illegitimacy attached to American military operations in a Third World setting. This war has a shadowy beginning and a still-uncertain ending and has become, like Vietnam and Afghanistan, a quagmire for intervening powers. There are increasing reasons to believe that the governance of current Iraqi leader Nouri al-Maliki resembles the authoritarian style of Saddam Hussein more than the supposed constitutional liberal regime that the United States pretends to leave behind, and that the country is headed for continuing struggle, possibly even a disastrous civil war fought along sectarian lines. In many respects, including the deepening of the Sunni/Shi'a divide, the country and its people are worse off than before the Iraq War (though by so concluding, I am not doubting the cruelty, criminality, and discriminatory character of the Hussein regime).

The Iraq War was a war of aggression from its inception, an unprovoked use of armed force against a sovereign state in a situation other than self-defense. The Nuremberg and Tokyo war-crimes tribunals convened after World War II declared such aggressive warfare to be a "crime against peace" and prosecuted and punished surviving political and military leaders of Germany and Japan as war criminals. We can ask why have George W. Bush and Tony Blair not been investigated, indicted, and prosecuted for their roles in planning and prosecuting the Iraq War. As folk singer Bob Dylan instructed us long ago, the answer is "blowin' in the wind"—or, in more straightforward language, such impunity is one more crude display of geopolitics. Bush's and Blair's countries were not defeated and occupied, their governments never surrendered and discredited, so such strategic failures (or successes) are exempted from legal scrutiny. These are the double standards that make international criminal justice a reflection of power politics more than of evenhanded global justice.

Global civil society, with its own limited resources, had challenged both the onset of the Iraq War and its actual unfolding. On and around February 15, 2003, what the *Guinness Book of Records* called "the largest antiwar rally in history" took the form of about three thousand demonstrations in eight hundred cities located in more than sixty countries and, according to the BBC, involved an estimated six to ten million people. Although such a global show of opposition to recourse to war was unprecedented, it failed to halt the war. It did, however, have the lasting effect of undermining the American claims of justification for the attack and occupation of Iraq. It also led to an unprecedented effort by groups around the world to pass judgment on the war by holding sessions in which peace activists and international law experts alleged its criminality and called for war-crimes prosecutions of Bush and Blair. As many as twenty such events were held in various parts of the world, with a culminating Iraq War Tribunal convened in June 2005 that included testimony from more than fifty experts, including several from Iraq, and a jury of conscience headed by author and activist Arundhati Roy.

There is also the question of the complicity of countries that supported the war with troop deployments, such as Japan, which dispatched a thousand members of its self-defense units to Iraq in July 2003 to help with noncombat dimensions of the occupation, a clear breach of international law and morality inconsistent with Article 9 of the Japanese Constitution. This was coupled with Tokyo's diplomatic support for the war from start to finish. Should such a record of involvement have any adverse consequences? It would seem that Japan might at least review the appropriateness of its complicit participation in a war of aggression and how that diminishes the credibility of its claim to uphold the responsibilities of membership in the United Nations. At least it provides the people of Japan with a moment for national soul-searching to think about what kind of world order will in the future best achieve peace, stability, and human dignity.

Are there lessons to be drawn from the Iraq War? I believe there are. The overwhelming lesson is that, in this historical period, intervention by the West in the non-West, especially when not authorized by the UN Security Council, can rarely succeed in attaining their stated goals. More broadly, counterinsurgency warfare involving a core encounter between Western invading and occupying forces and a national resistance movement will not be decided on the basis of hard-power military superiority but by the dynamics of self-determination associated with the party that has the more credible nationalist credentials, including the will to persi in the struggle for as long as it takes and the capacity to capture the high moral ground in the ongoing legitimacy struggle for domestic and international public support. It is only when we witness the dismantling of many of America's more than seven hundred acknowledged foreign military bases around the world and the end of its military interventions globally that we can hope that the correct lessons of the Iraq War are finally being learned. Until then there will be further attempts by the U.S. government to correct the tactical mistakes that it claims caused past failures in Iraq (and Afghanistan). New interventions will undoubtedly be proposed in coming years, probably leading to costly new failures and further controversies as to why such wars were fought and lost. American leaders will remain unlikely to acknowledge that the most basic mistake is militarism itself and the accompanying arrogance of occupation, at least until this establishment consensus is challenged by a robust antimilitarist grassroots political movement not currently visible.

ISIS, Militarism, and the Violent Political Imagination
September 18, 2014[5]

The beheading of American and British journalists who were being held hostage by ISIS creates a truly horrifying spectacle and quite understandably mobilizes political will to destroy a political actor that so shocks and frightens the Western sensibility, which is far from free from responsibility for such lurid incidents. Never in modern times has there been a clearer example of violence begetting violence.

We need to ask: to what end? Political leaders in the West are remarkably silent and dishonest about what it is that they wish to achieve in this region beset since 2011 by a quite terrifying outbreak of political extremism, whether from above, as in Syria, Egypt, and Israel, or from below, as with ISIS and the al-Nusra Front.

It is difficult to recall that at the start of 2011, just three years ago, progressive voices around the world were inspired by the Arab Spring upheavals that burst upon the political scene unexpectedly, especially in Egypt and Tunisia. These extraordinary events appeared to repudiate the prevailing patterns of authoritarian, exploitative, and corrupt collaboration between

http://richardfalk.wordpress.com/2014/09/18/
isis-militarism-and-the-violent-imagination/

oppressive domestic elites, neoliberal economic forces, and the regional imperial juggernaut that kept this humanly disastrous reality stable for so long. Yet even during that time of optimism about the Arab future, a closer scrutiny of what was happening disclosed many reasons to be worried. It is helpful to look to this recent past to have some comprehension of the perplexing present.

A Revolutionary Spirit without Revolutionary Action

The goals of these upheavals were far too ambitious to be realized by such limited challenges to the established order. The Arab Spring movements were essentially confined to getting rid of a hated ruler. Associating single individuals such as Mubarak, Ben Ali, or al-Assad with the grievances of an exploited and oppressed people overlooks the degree to which class interests and entrenched bureaucracies constituted structures. The popular forces bravely challenging the status quo lacked leadership, a program, and even a clear agenda, and naively expected the remnants of the old regime to disappear or go along with the anguished call of mass discontent that sought bread, freedom, and dignity as the effect of removing the hated leader.

This innocence of exaggerated expectations made a remarkable achievement more vulnerable to reversal than was generally understood at the time, when the immediate results seemed so stunning. What particularly impressed thoughtful commentators was the "new subjectivity" of the Arab masses. It had long been presumed that these Arab publics were reconciled to their fate and would remain passive victims. They rose up with such force and resolve, surprising the world, and themselves, with courageous display of self-empowerment and political creativity. It was also impressive that these upheavals, each distinct, shared a vision of an inclusive democracy with respect for all classes, religious and ethnic identities, genders, and political persuasions.

The reluctance to challenge the old order more fundamentally and punitively became coupled with a paradoxical and perverse situation of dependence on the old regime to manage in good faith the transition to the promised new dawn of constitutional democracy and freely elected political leaders. There seemed to be no understanding that the old elites had interests that had been generally served by the previously established order and would inevitably be threatened by the longings of the people, including moves toward greater social and economic equity threatening the prior acceptance of predatory arrangements with neoliberal globalization.

Preconditions for Transformative Political Ambitions

There seemed little awareness in these movements of Lenin's insistence that a successful transformative politics necessarily depends on substantially destroying the prior state structures (or, as it was put during the French Revolution, "you can't make an omelet without breaking eggs")—that is, rebuilding the new transformed state from the ground up and getting rid of the old bureaucracy. This generalization is especially true if the old order was managed by indigenous leadership and not imposed from without, as in the colonial era. Hannah Arendt argued in her book *On Revolution* that only if the overthrow of the former regime does not have a radical social agenda, as was the case with American Revolution, does the possibility of a smooth and peaceful transition exist. Excluding the prospects for improved material conditions, including jobs for youth, was a political impossibility in the Arab world, where conditions of mass misery partially explained the role of oppressive structures and the assignment of security forces to prevent workers from organizing effectively.

Revealingly, in contrast to the activists in Tahrir Square, Ayatollah Khomeini in Iran encouraged a kind of Islamic Leninism, rejecting all pleas to reach compromises with the Shah's regime in exchange for social peace and shared political power. From the perspective of late 2014, we take note of contrasting realities: Iran's Islamic Republic is celebrating its thirty-fifth anniversary without a serious threat to its governance, while the so-called Egyptian Revolution barely lasted two years before the old regime was fully restored in a more extreme form under the bloody military leadership of General el-Sisi.

Underestimating Political Islam

There were additional factors at work in Egypt and the region. Perhaps most significantly, those who sought to liberalize governance structures without shaking their foundations greatly underestimated the electoral strength of political Islam, especially the Muslim Brotherhood. Although the ideals of the Tahrir movement affirmed inclusionary democracy, the assumption of many who initially championed a new political order was that the MB would participate as a minority presence that would not displace the old urban ruling class or threaten its privileges. When this turned out to be wrong, it immediately shifted the political balance in such a way as to promote counterrevolution. As Europe discovered after 1848, nothing is worse for progressive politics than for revolutionary ambitions to exceed revolutionary means.

This situation was further stressed by the rich and influential Gulf oil dynasties, which felt deeply threatened by the Arab upheavals and cared for more about their own stability than they did about promoting Sunni politics in the region. These governments were disturbed by the fall of Mubarak and hoped for a political reversal in Egypt, welcoming the counterrevolution with an avalanche of funding, without blinking when this new military leadership proceeded to commit major atrocities against members of the MB and to criminalize the organization. It should not be ignored that this counterrevolutionary violence also served the strategic interests of Israel and the United States, restoring stability, marginalizing Muslim and democratizing forces, and avoiding the emergence of governments much more inclined to support Palestinian aspirations and to challenge neoliberal links with global capitalism. Into this mix must also be added the political ineptness of the MB, neither appreciating the limits of its popular support nor recognizing that its political hegemony would never be accepted by either the remnants of the old regime nor by secular liberals, who wanted Mubarak overthrown but not the system. In this sense, it appears in retrospect that it was a great mistake for the MB to withdraw its earlier pledge to refrain from seeking to dominate the parliamentary elections or compete for the presidency.

Not Forgetting Iraq or Syria

If we consider other developments in the region, there is another disturbing "truth": the region at this stage seems better off being governed in an authoritarian manner than by either the George W. Bush sort of "democracy promotion" or the political responses to the kind of popular uprisings that erupted in Syria, Egypt, Yemen, Bahrain, and elsewhere but turned out to be unsustainable. The least bad outcomes, as of now, appear to be those countries where the old authoritarian regimes prevailed without much struggle (e.g., Morocco) and made a few gestures of reform, averting both civil strife and a more brutal turn in authoritarian rule. The alternatives to authoritarianism in the region now seem far worse: terrible civil warfare (as in Syria) or chaos without respite (as in Libya). Given the mess that unfolded in Iraq during a decade of American occupation, what Washington policymaker would not at this point secretly consider the second coming of Saddam Hussein in Iraq as a gift from the gods?

Syria, as well, sent the wrong signal throughout the region. First, there was a popular challenge to the Assad regime that occasioned a bloody counterinsurgency campaign. Then outside forces—Turkey, the United States, Gulf countries—teamed up as the "Friends of Syria Group" to help the insurgency prevail, badly underestimating the military capabilities and political support of the Damascus government, which enabled it to withstand these efforts. Instead of regime change there began an ongoing civil war that has taken upwards of 200,000 lives, causing millions to flee the country as refugees and millions more to become internally displaced. Neighboring countries were destabilized, the unresolved Syrian struggle gave rise to various forms of Islamic extremism within Syria and in the region, and al-Assad's atrocities gave license to others in the region (such as el-Sisi) to commit crimes against humanity with the prospect of impunity.

What lessons can we learn? Above all, be careful what you wish for. Above all else, the last several decades should teach the West that the days of staging successful colonial interventions at acceptable costs are long past and that pre-mising postcolonial interventionist diplomacy on a moral crusade of human rights, democracy, and counterterrorism fools almost no one, except some of the people in the metropole, and wins few real friends in the target societies other than cynical opportunists or desperate insurgents. If intervention is followed by military occupation, many of those who were initially willing to accept any and all outside help to get rid of the hated leader quickly get disillusioned and turn on their earlier benefactor, a process dubbed "blowback."[6] If the intervention is not followed by an occupation, the results are not much better. Piles of bodies and debris are left behind, but the new reality is likely to be, as in Libya, ungovernable chaos, with armed militias substituting for the rule of law. Washington tends to call such situations "failed states," as if it had nothing to do with the collapse of governance.

America's and NATO's Unlearned Lessons

America and NATO should have learned the limits of military superiority and the problematics of occupation from their failures in Afghanistan and Iraq. Military superiority and shock-and-awe tactics can generally overwhelm a Third World government and quickly destroy its military capability, but that is only the initial, easy phase of an effort to control the political future of a targeted country. Notoriously, George W. Bush didn't understand this when he infamously announced "mission accomplished" to the world immediately after Iraqi *military* resistance crumbled and Saddam Hussein was driven from power. Phase two of the Iraq undertaking involved occupation and state-building neoliberal style, and the emergence of formidable *political* resistance. The early glow of victory soon fades away, and a variety of troubles start to overwhelm the intervening side. A movement of national resistance takes shape and adopts insurgent tactics against the foreign invader that take away many of the benefits of military superiority that earlier achieved an easy battlefield victory.

Resistance consists of various acts of violent disruption that gradually turn a hostile and foreign occupation into a long nightmare. The high-tech

---

See Chalmers Johnson, *Blowback: The Costs and Consequences of American Empire* (New York: Metropolitan, 2004).

weaponry of the occupier remains an effective killing machine, but it increasingly kills the wrong people, alienates far more, and seems helpless to establish minimal order, much less deliver on the promise of democracy, economic prosperity, and human rights for all. The occupier's prime objective becomes crafting a graceful exit that disguises its abandonment of the original enterprise—or, if that fails, leaving in a humiliating manner, unable to disguise the defeat. It should have been evident from the outset in Iraq that the effort to embed democracy was in tension with the strategic goal of integrating the country in accord with Western ideas of security and political economy. Turning over security to an indigenous, partisan army trained to safeguard a government put in place by a military intervention is truly a "mission impossible."

Strategic Failure

What was the real outcome of both of these major military interventions that cost many lives, generated mass refugee and internally displaced populations and expended trillions of dollars? In Afghanistan the results were a mixture of chaos, the destabilization of Pakistan, and the reemergence of the Taliban as a formidable political force. In Iraq the ironic outcome, after a decade of occupation, was a strategic victory for Iran and its pro-Shi'a foreign policy along with sectarian strife and widespread chaos, culminating during the past year with the emergence of ISIS. ISIS had the audacity to proclaim itself the Islamic State and to found a new caliphate without regard to international borders.

In both societies these results are exactly the opposite of the goals set by the intervening side. What were their real motivations? There are, I believe three overlapping answers: for oil, for arms sales and the political economy of militarism, and to ensure the desired strategic hegemony of the American-Israeli partnership throughout the Middle East.

These failures result from a basic disconnect. Securing the neoliberal priority of assuring access to Middle Eastern oil at stable prices, bolstered by maximum Western private-sector investment, depends upon maintaining good relations with stable governments and receptive societies. Stable political structures, given the American commitment to Israel together with capitalist predatory behavior, produces a hostile cleavage between state and society throughout the region, making political order fully dependent on effective authoritarian governance. Under these conditions it is evident that any claimed commitment to human rights and democracy hypocritical and at best peripheral. Such claims serve as misleading rationalizations for intervention in a postcolonial era in which naked imperial justifications are no longer credible. It puts the West in the position

inevitably collaborating with national elites that suppress the most fundamental human right of their own peoples—that of national self-determination, highlighted as Article I of both the International Covenant on Civil
and Political Rights and the International Covenant on Economic, Social,
and Cultural Rights.

Remembering Vietnam

Relying on military intervention to achieve the goals of foreign policy is not
a new recipe for political failure, and such an approach should have been discarded long ago for *realist* reasons. A repudiation of interventionary diplomacy should have been the crucial lesson from the Vietnam War. America
won all the big battles, controlled every combat zone, and yet lost the war. A
Vietnamese military commander's response, made to an American official
who insisted that despite the *political* outcome of the war, the United States
was never defeated *militarily* by Vietnam, is worth pondering: "That may be
so, but it is also irrelevant."[7]

Understanding why it is irrelevant is the great unlearned lesson. It should
by now be clear even to the most dimwitted realpolitik analyst that every colonial war since World War II was won by the militarily inferior side. Perhaps
the most dramatic instance of people power triumphing over imperial power
occurred in India's defeat of the mighty British Empire without firing a shot.
In Indochina and Algeria, French colonialism finally gave way to national
movements with far worse weaponry. National resilience, in the end, proves
stronger than foreign military and police control.

The real untold story of this string of losses sustained by the West is the
empowerment of people, eventually accorded moral and legal respect by a
global diplomatic process that now seems a false gesture of imperial disem-
powerment. The moral claims of and legal right to self-determination were
formally acknowledged and accepted, but the geopolitics of power and wealth
went on as before and continued at great costs to seek by force of arms what
could not otherwise be justly acquired.

The 2014 Israeli military operation against the helpless people of Gaza is
an extreme illustration of this dynamic. No people in the Middle East have
endured as much cruelty and suffering as have the Palestinians during their
long national movement for independence and sovereignty. Likewise, no state
has been as determined as Israel to rely on its vastly superior military capabilities to maintain control, expand, and ruthlessly suppress opposition. Yet,
after nearly seventy years of dispossession, occupation, militarist subjugation,
and Western backing of all of these, the Palestinians are far from defeated.

Quoted in J.M. Taw and R. C. Leicht, *The New World Order and Army Doctrine*
(Santa Monica, CA: Rand, 1992), 12.

In the recent one-sided 2014 Protective Edge campaign, more than 2,100 Palestinians were killed, 75 percent of whom were civilians, as compared to Israel's seventy dead, of whom sixty-five were members of the IDF. This suggests that "state terrorism" is far deadlier for the civilian population than is the violence of enemy resisters. But consider the political dynamics: Israel's reason for staging this horror show seemed to be mainly to convince the collaborationist leadership in Ramallah to stop cooperating with Hamas and to weaken Hamas's organizational structure and political support decisively. Military dominance produced great devastation combined with a political defeat: Hamas gained in popularity not only in Gaza, but even more so in the West Bank, where new polls show that in any forthcoming election Hamas would easily win over the Palestinian Authority—which was unlikely before Israel launched its latest deadly attack to once more "mow the lawn" in Gaza.

The next concern, following from what has been argued, is: why should such a clear pattern of repeated failures not lead to policy adjustments? The political elites of the world are hard-wired to think within an anachronistic realist box in which military power is the controlling force of history. Such thinking is also part of the political culture of the United States, where security is correlated with hard power, no matter the facts. When horrific crimes are committed in movie theaters and schools, where innocent persons are willfully slaughtered by a deranged heavily armed individual, the militarized mentality of the citizenry leads not to demands for the prohibition of assault weapons in private hands but, perversely, to a surge in private arms sales.

The ISIS Challenge Revisited

This brings us back to ISIS and what might be done to improve the situation rather than worsen it. Barack Obama has presided over shaping the regional response. He was confronted by a multifaceted dilemma. He was elected president twice partly to end American engagement in overseas wars, especially in the Middle East, yet here he was once more rallying the region and Europe for yet another war against an adversary that posed no discernable threat to the American people. To overcome this awkward fact, it was necessary to dramatize the barbarism of ISIS tactics, pointing to the American victims of ISIS atrocities, and at the same time promise there would be no American casualties. Barbarous as these atrocious acts are, beheadings are unfortunately not new to the region and are regularly used by the Saudi government in punishing convicted criminals. True, these incidents involve American and British nationals who were innocent of wrongdoing, but the emphasis was not so much placed on their innocence as on the horrifying technique used to carry out the executions.

Here is the core problem: America's leadership in the region depends on actively protecting the authoritarian status quo, especially in the Gulf, and so doing nothing about ISIS is not an option. What Obama is proposing to do repeats the old formula of failure: air strikes; training, arming, and advising friendly forces (Iraqi Kurds, moderate Syrians, Iraqi military units); disrupting ISIS's overseas recruiting and funding. Obama's program is a pale version of post-Vietnam counterinsurgency doctrine in which risks of American casualties must be minimized while air power, including drones, private contractors, and native ground forces with their own political agendas are relied upon to carry out the dirty work. Yet, as in earlier encounters, the likely result is to induce chaos and alienation arising from public resentment of accidental targeting of innocent civilians and a standoff that causes great suffering to the society, including producing many refugees and internally displaced persons. Its prescriptions are almost certain to make any situation worse than just leaving it alone.

Of course, there are far preferable options, but to adopt these requires looking below the surface. It would have to start with admitting that the American occupation of Iraq was the proximate cause of the emergence of ISIS, especially due to the purge of Baathist elements in the government and armed forces and the encouragement of Shi'a sectarianism. Abandoning sectarian maneuvers is one way to avoid some of the worst recent mistakes.

Another productive path presupposes an American diplomatic outlook oriented around wider ethical and world-order concerns. Such an adjustment would require loosening ties to Israel and following a rational line of geostrategic self-interest in the Middle East. Such a course of action, hardly ever mentioned because it seems too unrealistic, would involve taking three steps: bringing Iran into the effort to find a political solution for the Syrian civil war; proposing a nuclear-free zone throughout the Middle East; and exerting pressure on Israel to uphold Palestinian rights under international law. This is a distinctly *political* approach that contrasts with the *militarism* that has produced destructive turbulence in the region in the period ever since the partial stabilities of the Cold War era collapsed along with the Berlin Wall in 1989.

Militarist geopolitics seems destined to lead to yet another Western catastrophe in the tormented Middle East. There is no political will visible anywhere on the horizons of world politics that might pose a humane challenge to such disaster-prone policymaking. So the murderous cycle of violence repeats itself yet again, the alien militarism of this Western-led coalition confronting the indigenous violence of ISIS, which the mistakes of the West helped nurture. Dispiriting repetition occurs instead of uplifting innovation, and the wheels of violence turn with accelerating velocity.

Appendix

The Ghent Charter in Defense of Iraqi Academia

The UN High Commissioner for Refugees, António Guterres, has noted that Iraq is the world's best-known conflict but the least well-known humanitarian crisis. The humanitarian community has only belatedly begun to acknowledge the extent of the greatest conflict induced displacement in the history of the Middle East. According to UNHCR figures, there are now 2.7 million internally displaced Iraqis and 2.2 million refugees, mostly in neighboring states. One in six Iraqis is displaced. Over eight million Iraqis are in need of humanitarian assistance. A 2006 study published in the prestigious medical journal the *Lancet* estimated 654,965 excess deaths in the four years following the U.S.-led invasion of 2003. The prestigious British polling agency ORB estimated 1.2 million deaths in September 2007. The October 2010 estimate of Just Foreign Policy stands at +1.4 million excess deaths.

A little known aspect of the tragedy is the systematic liquidation of Iraq's academics. Under the current occupation, Iraq's intellectual and technical class has been subject to a systematic and ongoing campaign of intimidation, abduction, extortion, random killings and targeted assassinations. Running parallel with the destruction of Iraq's educational infrastructure, this repression led to the mass forced displacement of the bulk of Iraq's educated middle class — the main engine of progress and development in modern states. The absence of this middle class has resulted in the breakdown of public services, affecting all sectors and layers of Iraqi society. The number of killings of Iraqi academics has continued to rise. By the end of 2006, the UK's *Independent* reported that over 470 academics had been killed, while the *Guardian* stated that the figure stood at 500 from Baghdad and Basra universities alone. By October 2010 there were 449 cases recorded on the Brussels Tribunal database. Even amid the horrifying levels of violence following the invasion in 2003, the killings of academics have stood out for their highly selective character. In the vast majority of cases it appears that the victims have been specifically singled out, either as the immediate target of professional assassins or as the object of so-called kidnappings, which resulted in their deaths.

The International Medical Corps reports that populations of teachers in Baghdad have fallen by 80%. Medical personnel also has left in disproportionate numbers. Roughly 40% of Iraq's middle class is believed to have fled by the end of 2006, the U.N. said. Most are fleeing systematic persecution and have no desire to return. The director of the United Nations University International Leadership Institute published a report on 27 April 2005 detailing that since the start of the war of 2003 some 84% of Iraq's higher education institutions have been burnt, looted or destroyed. Between March 2003 and October 2008, 31,598 violent attacks against educational institutions were reported in Iraq, according to the Iraqi Ministry of Education (MoE). Since 2007 bombings at Al-Mustansiriya University in Baghdad have killed or maimed more than 335 students and staff members, according to the UNESCO report *Education Under Attack 2010*. A 12-foot-high blast wall has been built around the campus. To this date, there has been no systematic investigation of this phenomenon by the occupation authorities. Not a single arrest has been reported in regard to this ongoing terrorization of the intellectuals.

The Iraqi education system, once the showcase of the Middle East, has virtually collapsed, following 13 years of international sanctions and 7 years of war and occupation. One in five Iraqis between the ages of 10 and 49 cannot read or write a simple statement related to daily life. While Iraq boasted a record low illiteracy rate for the Middle East in the 1980s, illiteracy jumped to at least 20% in 2010 and is among the highest in the region. Illiteracy rates among women in some communities are as high as 40–50%. Corruption is rampant. The Iraqi Interior Ministry has admitted that more than 9000 civil servants, including high ranking staff in the prime minister's office, have provided purchased fake university degrees. Meanwhile, money assigned to the education sector has been diverted to "security."

Taking into consideration these facts, the undersigned:

1. Request that an independent international investigation be launched immediately to probe these extrajudicial killings. This investigation should also examine the issue of responsibility to clearly identify who is accountable for this state of affairs. We appeal to the special rapporteur on summary executions at HCHR in Geneva.

2. Appeal to organizations that work to enforce or defend international humanitarian law to put these crimes on the agenda.

3. Call upon academics and students to help end the silence that surrounds ongoing crimes against Iraqi academics and the destruction of Iraqi's educational infrastructure, and to support

Iraqi academics' and students' right and aspiration to live in an independent, democratic Iraq, free of foreign occupation and hegemony.

4. Ask that European governments grant asylum to Iraqi scholars and not deport them in contravention of UNHCR guidelines for the handling of Iraqi asylum applications.

5. Insist that the Iraqi academic community in exile be given the opportunity to return voluntarily to their jobs, by providing guarantees for their security so they can do their work without fear or government interference.

6. Call upon academics worldwide to forge links between their universities and Iraqi educators, both in exile and in Iraq. This can take the form of Internet exchanges, direct faculty and student exchanges, joint research projects, and general support, direct (research grants, material assistance) and indirect (public campaigns to highlight the plight of Iraqi academics and students). We call to support efforts to set up and grant scholarships to Iraqi exiled lecturers. Education authorities in the Middle East and elsewhere should provide opportunities for Iraqi academics to gain experience in institutions of higher education abroad and offer generous scholarships to Iraqi students at undergraduate and graduate levels.

7. Urge that all measures be taken to ensure that no educator/academic is dismissed from, or denied the right to return to, jobs on the basis of gender, race or sectarian affiliation. Students of all backgrounds should similarly be guaranteed the right to pursue secondary and higher education without discrimination.[1]

---

www.ipetition.com/petition/ghentcharter

Acknowledgments

This book was composed in tandem with my recently published *Palestine: The Legitimacy of Hope*. Both were derived from my blog posts from the last several years. During this period I served as UN Special Rapporteur for Occupied Palestine on behalf of the Human Rights Council. Because Israel refused to cooperate with the mandate, expelling me in December 2008 when I sought entry on an official UN mission and never relenting, I needed to shift my fact-finding efforts to neighboring countries, especially Egypt, Jordan, and to a lesser extent Lebanon. This put me in frequent touch with the unfolding of events in the Arab world during this tumultuous time and with many friends and colleagues who were deeply immersed in these events.

I benefitted greatly from conversations with Egyptian friends, learning particularly from Emad Shahin and Philip Rizk. In a more scholarly mode, I greatly appreciated the writing of Esam Al-Amin, especially his *The Arab Awakening Unveiled*, and Farhad Khosrokhavar, particularly his *The New Arab Revolution that Shook the World*. I learned also during several meetings in Lebanon while on an academic visit to lecture at the American University in Beirut (AUB) and the Institute for Palestine Studies.

My second main point of contact was a result of my long association with Turkey, where I spend several months each year, with additional trips to take part in various events. I have been fortunate to count as friends several leading members of the Justice and Development Party, which has been governing the country since 2002, as well as an array of leading academic specialists. In recent years I have acted as Senior Advisor to the POMEAS Project, associated with the Istanbul Policy Center of Sabancı University, which has focused on the struggle for democracy in the region.

A third, less intense experience of the region has resulted from several trips to Morocco in my role as a member of the Scientific Committee of the Moulay Hicham Foundation, which holds annual meetings on substantive issues of concern to the region under the chairmanship of Olivier Roy. I have benefited from the high quality of discussion at these gatherings, held in Marbella, Spain, during the last two years, as well as enjoyed the convivial atmosphere greatly facilitated by the charm and efficiency of the principal coordinator, Catherine Cornet. My experience of Morocco has been long enriched by the knowledge and wisdom of my dear, longtime friends Miriam Lowi and Abdellah Hammoudi.

Finally, I would mention my periodic attendance at the Rhodes Forum on Global Dialogue, which brings together an array of political and academic personalities from around the world. These experiences on the island of Rhodes have benefited greatly from the intellectual leadership of Fred Dallmayr, long a friend and a model for lucid, creative, and progressive thinking dedicated to a humane future for all peoples and appreciative of their diversities of ethnicity, religion, culture, and history.

As with my Palestine book, I have been the beneficiary of the dedicated and energetic team at Just World Books, which combines high standards of professionalism with an idealistic engagement in the struggle for global justice. Such a dual identity is not common in current-day publishing, and that it happens here is a tribute to the leadership and guidance Helena Cobban provides not only to her staff but to authors like me, as well. It has been my great pleasure to again be a beneficiary of Helena's dedicated enthusiasm about producing and distributing books that she believes in.

Again, also, I thank Sarah Grey for gifting this manuscript with her exceptional editorial skills. Without her contributions there would certainly be less coherence and more repetition. As I said in relation to my earlier book any author who has Sarah as an editor should consider himself blessed, both by her professional excellence and her warm spirits.

The book is gratefully dedicated to Moulay Hicham and his wife Malika who have been steadfast and warm friends ever since Princeton days twenty five years ago. Moulay Hicham has facilitated my work in recent years. It has been a great joy for me to witness his development and many accomplishments over the years.

I have shared this intellectual journey with Hilal Elver, my wife for twenty years. Her Turkish background and our shared and varied experience of the country has been more enriching than anything that has transpired in my adult life. This exposure to Turkish life has given rise to great admiration and affection for the Turkish people and their extraordinary cultural heritage.

It hardly needs to be said that the situation in the Middle East remains in flux, and that the one certainty is the uncertainty of the unfolding future As the Arab Spring caught many of us by surprise, so have the viciousness and chaos of its aftermath. The peoples of the region have suffered terribly from these recent excesses, and I can only hope that the future will bring relief and rekindle the hopeful prospects that seemed so promising in early 2011.